"His name will endure through the ages, and so also will his work."

Frederick Engels

KARL MARX

HIS LIFE AND WORK

DOCUMENTS
AND
PHOTOGRAPHS

London & Wellingborough

First English edition published in Great Britain by
Collet's (Publishers) Limited

Denington Estate
Wellingborough
Northants, NN8 2QT

Contributors:
    N. N. IVANOV (general editor)
    T. D. BELYAKOVA
    Y. P. KRASAVINA

Introduction by
    D. I. ANTONYUK and N. N. IVANOV

Translated by VIC SCHNEIERSON

Designed by VICTOR CHISTYAKOV

ISBN   0569-09095-4

Printed in the USSR

CONTENTS

INTRODUCTION

A hundred years have passed since the day when, parting with his friend forever, Frederick Engels said: "His name will endure through the ages, and so also will his work!"

Marx's life was an exploit. His genius of thinker, his unexampled courage and unbending willpower, his faith in the victory of the working class, enabled him to endure all trials, to make staggering theoretical discoveries, and to work out the theory of scientific communism, a powerful tool of cognising and transforming the world. And alongside Marx's name stands that of Frederick Engels.

Lenin described their scientific analysis, which proved that capitalism would inevitably collapse and that communism would replace it, as a great service. They had shown proletarians of different countries, he wrote, "their role, their task, their mission, namely, to be the first to rise in the revolutionary struggle against capital and to rally around themselves in this struggle *all* working and exploited people".

Marx's theoretical legacy, the history of his life and work, are cherished by the working class and all other working people as a rich source of experience and knowledge—an exploit in the name of humanity's radiant future.

* * *

This album is a documentary chronicle of the life and work of Karl Marx. It is made up mostly of documents and photographs from the repositories of the Karl Marx and Frederick Engels Museum in Moscow, the Central Party Archives and the Library of the CPSU Central Committee's Institute of Marxism-Leninism. Photographs of Marx and Engels, of their many associates, of the members of Marx's family, facsimiles of manuscripts and first editions of Marx's and Engels's major works, and a most valuable collection of engravings—all these priceless items make up the fabric of this album. They produce a graphic picture of Marx's life and times. The material is essentially presented in chronological order, showing the milestones in Marx's life and work.

The chapter *1818-1841* contains a graphic account of Marx's childhood and youth, of his school and university years.

The chapter opens with a mid-19th century engraving of Trier (Trèves) in Prussia's Rhine Province, where Marx was born and raised. There are photographs of the house in which he was born on May 5, 1818, and of the Trier Gymnasium, which he attended from age 12 to 17. Photographs of Marx's favourite teachers, Johann Hugo von Wyttenbach and Johann Steininger, who influenced his development and vision of the world, are also given.

The 17-year-old Marx's inner world is well reflected in his school-leaving composition. For him man's vocation was to serve people, labouring for the good of humanity. These humanitarian ideas had, indeed, guided Marx throughout his life. He dedicated to them all his strength, his many gifts, and his inexhaustible energy.

Finishing the gymnasium in 1835, Marx studied jurisprudence first in Bonn University and, later, in the University of Berlin. In an engraving of that time Marx is portrayed amidst other students belonging to the Trier Association (Landsmannschaft) at Bonn University. A drawing by artist Grinstein depicts Marx as student, his strong-willed, energetic visage, wavy black hair, and searching eyes.

Of interest, too, among the material related to Marx's university period, is the facsimile of the only extant letter that Marx wrote to his father. "During my first term I spent many a sleepless night," he writes in it about his inner searchings, "fought many a battle, and endured much internal and external excitement." Quite early in his life, Marx became aware of the importance and need for critically assimilating the accumulation of humanity's knowledge. He strove to know more, to analyse, understand, and find the truth.

Much of his time as student he spent learning philosophy and history. "It became clear to me," he observed in his letter, "that there could be no headway without philosophy." And, indeed, he made a thorough study of Kant, Fichte and Hegel, those classics of German idealist philosophy of the end of the 18th and early 19th

centuries, and also of the works of Feuerbach, their eminent materialist contemporary. This was for Marx an excellent school of theoretical thinking, which played an enormous part in the subsequent evolution of his world outlook.

In his student years in Berlin, Marx associated with members of a circle of followers of the Hegelian philosophy, the Young Hegelians, who utilised Hegel's philosophy to attack religion and the political system in Germany. No more than 20 at the time, Marx was the most authoritative among them.

The chapter also deals with Marx's doctoral dissertation, the *Difference Between the Democritean and Epicurean Philosophy of Nature*. Facsimiles are given of the certificate Marx received on finishing Berlin University, and of his Doctor of Philosophy diploma.

The doctoral dissertation was an important phase in Marx's ideological development and a vivid sample of his profoundly original thinking. The 23-year-old Marx set forth his atheistic outlook, and emphasised that philosophy should look upon reality in an active manner.

The chapter *1842-1844* contains some unique material.

Marx set out on his lifelong political struggle as an associate of the *Rheinische Zeitung*, a Cologne newspaper, in 1842. Here he developed his skills of political fighter, his critical mind and organising talent, and his journalistic gifts as well as fearlessness. The chapter contains facsimiles of Marx's articles in the *Rheinische Zeitung*, where he exposed the ruling classes and defended the politically and socially downtrodden masses. In the musty atmosphere of royal Prussia, Marx's revolutionary journalism had the effect of a thunderclap. To quote Lenin, the *Rheinische Zeitung* articles were evidence of "Marx's transition from idealism to materialism and from revolutionary democracy to communism".

In the summer of 1843, Marx married Jenny von Westphalen, a childhood friend. They spent the summer and autumn in Kreuznach. The album contains a fine portrait of Jenny as a young girl, which Marx's grandson, Edgar Longuet, presented as a gift to the Institute of Marxism-Leninism in Moscow. Jenny had good looks, a good brain, a sense of dedication, and the loving heart of wife and mother—all of which made her a fond companion and her husband's faithful helper.

For Marx, the stay in Kreuznach was a time of intensive study. He produced an uncompleted manuscript, which was not published until long after his death. It first appeared in the Soviet Union under the title of *Contribution to the Critique of Hegel's Philosophy of Law* in 1927.

Much of the chapter is devoted to young Frederick Engels, portrayed as a versatile gifted young man with a profoundly philosophical mentality, absolute absence of fear, and the single-mindedness of a revolutionary.

The reprisals against the *Rheinische Zeitung*, and thereupon its suppression in 1842, did not dampen Marx's militant spirit. He resumed his revolutionary, journalistic and scientific endeavours in Paris. Documents and photographs present a graphic account of that period of Marx's life in exile.

Of special interest here is the evidence that, while studying French revolutionary history, he associated with workers and was active in the revolutionary clubs of the French capital. He spoke with deep respect of the working man, of the workers' thirst for knowledge, their lofty aspirations and courage. "The brotherhood of man is no mere phrase with them, but a fact of life," Marx said, "and the nobility of man shines upon us from their work-hardened bodies." Marx made a close study of the various currents of utopian socialism and communism that existed in those days.

His study of the workers' movements of his day led Marx to espouse the cause of the proletariat, to which he remained faithful until his death. For him, the proletariat, that most viciously exploited class bereft of property, was the main revolutionary force called upon to destroy capitalist oppression and build a new society. Marx's definition of the proletariat's historic mission as builder of socialist society was, in Lenin's words, the chief element in Marxism.

Marx's final acceptance of materialism, his passage from revolutionary democracy to communism, was highlighted by his articles in the *Deutsch-Französische Jahrbücher*, which he published jointly with Arnold Ruge, the Young Hegelian, in Paris in 1844. Here he emphasised the necessary connection between theory and practice. "Theory," he wrote, "becomes a material force as soon as it has gripped the masses."

The chapter *1844-1848* describes how Marx and Engels worked out the theoretical principles of the scientific world outlook, and their efforts to establish a proletarian party.

A reproduction of the title page of Marx's and Engels's first joint book, *The Holy Family*, which was published in Frankfort on the Main in February 1845, is given early in the chapter. As Engels put it, Marx and he had set out to create a study of real people as they developed in history.

Expelled from France in February 1845 for his revolutionary activity, Marx moved to Brussels. Illustrations depicting the Belgian capital and landmarks in the history of the working-class movement reproduce the environment in which Marx carried on his work.

Of interest here is the facsimile of a page from Marx's notebook with the famous *Theses on Feuerbach*, and pages from the manuscript of Marx's and Engels's joint work, *The German Ideology*, which presents their materialist view of history in an integral form for the first time. It was never published in their lifetime, and was first put out by the Institute of Marx-Engels-Lenin in Moscow in 1932.

Pages from Marx's most important manuscripts are reproduced generously throughout this album. They show different stages in his theoretical search. Passages copied out of the works of various authors are given, and preliminary versions written for the purpose of what Marx called self-clarification. Some of them represent complete works constituting an integrated whole both in content and literary virtue.

Marx was no armchair scholar, as some bourgeois historians would have us believe. He saw the purpose of his life in fusing the new revolutionary theory, that of scientific socialism, with the working-class movement, so as to make that theory a material force, an instrument for the world's revolutionary transformation. At 29, Marx became organiser and leader of the Communist League (1847-52), the first international organisation of the proletariat. His loyalty to the communist cause, his consideration for the needs and interests of the working people, and his gifts of political organiser earned him the deep respect of the workers, of all those who took part in the revolutionary movement.

The chapter depicts the struggle that Marx and Engels fought against "true socialism", against Weitling's sectarianism, against Proudhonism and various other petty-bourgeois theories, thus paving the way for the emergence of a proletarian political organisation. The immense role played by Marx and Engels in the founding of the Communist League is depicted.

A page from the rough version of the second section of the *Manifesto of the Communist Party*, the only one that is extant, is a valuable relic. The first two lines are in the hand of Marx's wife, providing added evidence of the big part she played as her husband's faithful helper and secretary. Of interest, too, is the facsimile of the initial outline plan for the third section made by Marx in December 1847-January 1848 on the back of the cover of one of his notebooks. The chapter contains reproductions of the first editions of the *Manifesto* in German (1848), English, French, Italian, and other languages. Among these is the Russian edition, translated by Georgi Plekhanov and put out in Geneva in 1882 with a preface by Marx and Engels where they wrote that "Russia forms the vanguard of revolutionary action in Europe".

"This little booklet," Lenin wrote, "is worth whole volumes: to this day its spirit inspires and guides the entire organised and fighting proletariat of the civilised world." The *Manifesto of the Communist Party* has, indeed, spread across the world and is still as relevant and vital as it was when first written.

The chapter *1848-1849* contains a wealth of highly varied illustrations. Along with documentary facsimiles, it contains engravings produced by witnesses of the events of those years. They give the reader a taste of the atmosphere that prevailed during the revolutions of 1848 and 1849 that swept across Europe from Paris to Budapest, and from Berlin to Palermo. One lithograph shows rebels destroying the royal throne in the Tuileries

on February 24, 1848. Others portray episodes from the revolutions in Germany, Austria, Italy and Hungary. One of them, by an unknown artist of the mid-19th century, reproduces a revolutionary episode that occurred in Berlin on March 18, 1848: crowds of people surrounding the royal palace are being attacked by the troops; streets are clad in barricades.

Of interest to the present-day reader are rare lithographs, entitled "People demonstrating in Pest in March 1848", "Italian national flag being raised in Venice on March 17, 1848", and "Chartists demonstrate in London on April 10, 1848".

During the revolutions of 1848 and 1849, Marx and Engels were at the centre of the revolutionary events. "Marx," wrote Engels of his friend, "was before all else a revolutionist... Fighting was his element. And he fought with a passion, a tenacity and a success such as few could rival." The revolutionary articles that Marx and Engels wrote during that period, their speeches at public meetings and other gatherings, like their work in various democratic and workers' societies, are a model of how to combine theory and practice, how to probe deeply into the events.

A central place in the chapter is the portrayal of Marx as editor of the *Neue Rheinische Zeitung*. Reproduced are issues with Marx's articles showing the essence of the political conflicts and summing up the experience of the revolutionary masses, and dealing with the national liberation movements of Czechs, Hungarians, Poles, and Italians. Marx resolutely attacked the reactionary policies of the German bourgeoisie, which was making concessions to the king and the feudal lords, and turning its back on the revolution and the people's revolutionary gains. Of special interest here is the German workers' platform in that bourgeois democratic revolution, *Demands of the Communist Party in Germany*, drawn up by Marx and Engels.

Marx's remarkably powerful article, entitled "The June Revolution", a pearl of revolutionary journalism, is vividly illustrated in this album. The article has immortalised the heroism of the proletariat as it embarked on struggle against the capitalist system, and, indeed, showed its revolutionary mission and certain final victory.

The chapter deals with Marx's activity at the critical period of the revolution in Germany. He appealed for resistance to reactionaries, who were on the offensive, by all possible means: refusing to pay taxes, organising an armed militia to repulse the enemy, and forming committees of public safety. The chapter ends with a reproduction of the last issue of the *Neue Rheinische Zeitung* printed in red ink on May 19, 1849.

Bourgeois historians have chosen to describe the brief period between March 1848 and November 1849 as the mad year that had, they claimed, upset the natural course of events. As the chapter shows, the period saw a tremendous surge of Marx's creativity, and was the first test of the principles of his revolutionary theory.

The chapter *1849-1863* covers a period that followed the defeat of the European revolutions of 1848 and 1849. This low ebb of the revolutionary movement, the years when reaction was triumphant, were the hardest in Marx's life. He and his family were compelled to move to England. Soon, Frederick Engels, too, moved there. For the two friends their banishment became lifelong.

Official England received Marx inimically. For a long time, he could not have his articles published in the press. He was unable to earn a livelihood.

The chapter shows Marx's varied activity during that period, rallying proletarian revolutionaries and summing up the experience of the recent revolutions. The chapter also deals with Marx's scientific and journalistic pursuits and the impact they made on public opinion. It reproduces an issue of the *Neue Rheinische Zeitung. Politisch-ökonomische Revue*. Most of the contributions (articles, surveys and reviews) to it were by Marx and Engels. The journal contains a series of Marx's articles, which were eventually published under separate cover in 1895, after Marx's death, as *The Class Struggles in France, 1848 to 1850*, giving a materialist view of that period of French history and propounding crucial points for the workers' revolutionary tactics.

In those years of reaction, Marx and Engels continued to groom proletarian revolutionaries. Marx's home in London was, indeed, a sort of revolutionary headquarters. It was visited by associates, and prominent members of the labour movement in various countries. "His power of 'drawing out' people, of making them feel that he was interested in what interested them was mar-

vellous," Eleanor Marx-Aveling wrote in her recollections of her father.

The album contains photographs of Marx's and Engels's closest comrades, among them Wilhelm Wolff, Friedrich Lessner, Edgar von Westphalen (Jenny's younger brother), Georg Eccarius, Ludwig Kugelmann, Wilhelm Liebknecht, August Bebel, Paul Lafargue, and many others.

At the height of the reaction, the Prussian police struck out at members of the Communist League. It faked evidence to portray the Communist League as a secret terrorist organisation in a bid to discredit the revolutionary and democratic movement. Marx and Engels did their utmost to frustrate the designs of the police. Marx exposed the foul police manoeuvres and the judiciary in a pamphlet entitled, *Revelations Concerning the Communist Trial in Cologne* (1853). Of interest is an engraving by an unknown artist portraying the tribunal in session. Among the defendants are eminent members of the Communist League: Roland Daniels, Friedrich Lessner, who was Marx's close friend and associate, Hermann Becker, a democratic journalist active in the Communist League, and Communist League members Peter Nothjung and Abraham Jacobi. Despite the ludicrous nature of the charges, the bourgeois court dealt out vicious penalties.

Marx took all the trials of the revolutionary and liberation movement very close to heart, no matter how far from London they occurred. His articles of 1850 to 1860 deal with various aspects of the workers' movement in Britain, Germany and France, the liberation struggle of the Italians and Poles, the struggle against slavery in the United States, the Indian Mutiny in 1857-59, and the Taiping rebellion in China that shook the foundations of the Celestial Empire. His attention was also attracted to events in Afghanistan, Algeria, and Persia. Marx described the liberation struggles of the peoples of Latin America against Spanish rule as an example of victorious insurrection against colonialists.

During the painful years of reaction, the friendship and collaboration between Marx and Engels grew still closer. For twenty long years, Engels had had to reside in Manchester, several hundred kilometres distant from Marx and his family, who resided in London. He was employed in a firm of which his father was part owner, and was thus able to afford Marx continual financial help. Throughout that period Marx and Engels communicated mainly by correspondence. "If one were to attempt to define in a single word the focus, so to speak, of the whole correspondence," wrote Lenin, who had carefully studied the correspondence of Marx and Engels, "the central point at which the whole body of ideas expressed and discussed converges—that word would be *dialectics.*" Indeed, Lenin drew up a précis covering a considerable part of the correspondence between Marx and Engels.

Much space in this chapter is devoted to Marx's family. Having contributed all his funds to revolutionary propaganda in the *Neue Rheinische Zeitung*, Marx had lived on the edge of poverty for many years. He and his family went without many essentials. But even the direst straits could not make Marx depart from the road he had charted for himself. "I laugh at the so-called practical men and their wisdom," Marx wrote. "If one wanted to be an ox, one could, of course, turn one's back on the sufferings of humanity and look after one's own hide." Faith in his own theory and the certainty that the workers would one day win, supported him in the blackest hours of his life. Marx's all-conquering optimism endured slanderous attacks in the press, governmental reprisals, and the intrigues of his political enemies. In her recollections of her father, Eleanor Marx remembered him as a vivacious and jolly man with an ebullient sense of humour and vitality, whose sincere laughter was contagious and irrepressible. She referred to him as the most friendly, kind and responsive of comrades.

Marx was a loving father. He liked the company of his children, and often spent his hours of rest with them. They saw him as a playmate, and listened to his yarns with rapt attention. For the swarthy colour of his skin and black hair his wife and children called him the Moor.

For Marx London was an observation post in studying capitalist society. He devoted himself mainly to studying political economy in preparation for writing the future *Capital*. Wilhelm Liebknecht recalled: "Study! Study! That was the categoric injunction that we heard often enough from him and that he gave us by his example and the continual work of his mighty brain."

Marx spent nearly all his days from nine in the morning to seven in the evening in the British Museum, the richest book repository of that time, poring through a variety of books and taking notes. His own library contained nearly a thousand volumes, which is added evidence of how much work Marx did with literary sources. Of that library, Engels wrote: "The whole of these books constitute a library so unique, and so complete at the same time, for the history and the study of Modern Socialism and all the sciences on which it is dependent..." Some of Marx's books contain copious notes and marks in their owner's hand. Marx had hundreds of books in Russian, including the works of Nikolai Chernyshevsky, Nikolai Dobrolyubov, Alexander Herzen, Georgi Plekhanov, Maxim Kovalevsky, Nikolai Flerovsky (Bervi), Pyotr Lavrov, and Alexander Engelhardt.

The album contains all the extant photographs of Karl Marx, and quite a few of Frederick Engels.

The earliest photograph of Marx dates to 1861. It portrays Marx at 43, a known revolutionary whose works have a wide readership among Socialists and advanced workers in many countries.

A photograph of Marx in Hanover dates to 1867. He had come to that city to visit a friend, Ludwig Kugelmann, after completing the first volume of *Capital*, the manuscript of which he had turned in to Hamburg publisher Otto Karl Meissner.

Three years before, a photograph had been taken of Marx and his daughters Jenny, Laura and Eleanor, together with Engels. It is the only one portraying the two friends together. Unknown for 84 years, it was first published in 1948 when Edgar Longuet, Marx's grandson, gave it as a gift to the Institute of Marxism-Leninism in Moscow.

Of interest, too, are photographs of Marx taken in 1875. Of one of them, Engels wrote: "It is the last and the best picture, in which the Moor appears in all his cheerful Olympic calm, certain of victory." Engels ordered 1,200 copies of that photograph for Socialists in different lands, whereupon it was reproduced many times in the press. On one of the photographs Marx made the inscription: "Greetings and fraternity, Karl Marx, June 27, 1880." A copy of that photograph had been in Lenin's possession.

In February 1882, the year before he died, Marx was photographed for the last time in his life. His aging visage bore signs of the many decades of privation and intense labour, but his calm and searching eyes were, as before, imbued with vitality, confidence, and youthful energy.

The chapter *"Capital"* is devoted to Marx's economic research, to the work he had done on his scientific economic theory.

Lenin described *Capital* as Marx's chief and fundamental study setting forth scientific socialism. Marx himself considered it the work of his life. Indeed, it summed up four decades of titanic labour that culminated in truly great discoveries. In *Capital* the Marxist doctrine is presented in its most lucid terms and is given profound economic, social, political and historical backing.

Marx subjected capitalist society to an incisive analysis by the method of dialectical and historical materialism. He probed deep into the mechanism of capitalist society and discovered the laws that made it function, and demonstrated the transient nature of capitalism. Engels commented: "As long as there have been capitalists and workers on earth no book has appeared which is of as much importance for the workers..."

Between these covers is reproduced Marx's letter to Maurice La Châtre, the publisher of the first volume of *Capital* in French, in which Marx accepted his proposal to publish *Capital* in instalments. The closing words in that letter sound like a motto for pioneers in science: "There is no royal road to science, and only those who do not dread the fatiguing climb of its steep paths have a chance of gaining its radiant summits." To be sure, these words refer first of all to Marx himself. Wilhelm Liebknecht put it thus: "A revolutionary in science and a revolutionary *through* science, he scaled the highest peak of science in order to come down to the people and to make science a common asset of the people."

The chapter illustrates the first editions of Volume I of *Capital* in German, Russian, French, and English.

The Russian edition of 1872 was the first translation of Marx's main work into a foreign language. It was put out in 3,000 copies, exceeding its first German edition thrice over.

The police in different countries started files on the book and its author soon after the appearance of the first volume. In one of his letters, Marx described a curious order issued by the tsarist censors saying *Capital* need not be prosecuted because "only a few will

read it in Russia, and still fewer will understand it". The tsarist authorities would soon rue that decision: all the 3,000 copies of the first Russian edition found a readership. Whereupon *Capital* was blacklisted by the tsarist secret police.

The ideas set forth in *Capital* became widespread in Russia, and Marx soon noted that the book was "more read and appreciated [in Russia] than anywhere else".

After the appearance of Volume I of *Capital*, Marx continued work on volumes II and III until the end of his life. The wish to sum up the latest developments, coupled with Marx's striking scientific honesty, made him rewrite and revise many sections of the two volumes over and over. "I should under no circumstances have published the second volume before the present English industrial crisis had reached its climax," Marx wrote to Nikolai Danielson in a letter dated April 10, 1879. "It is therefore necessary to watch the present course of things until their maturity before you can 'consume' them 'productively', I mean '*theoretically*'."

Before writing on the ground rent for the third volume of *Capital*, Marx made a special study of agrarian relations in Russia. Russia, Engels wrote, "was to play the same role in the part dealing with ground-rent that England played in Book I in connection with industrial wage-labour".

Nowadays, an especially big interest is aroused by Marx's thoughts contained in *Capital* concerning crucial aspects of the economy in socialist society. It stresses the special significance of regulating working time and distributing social labour between various production groups. Highly important, too, is the idea that the true wealth of society, and its further growth, depend on the productivity of labour and "the more or less copious conditions of production under which it is performed".

The chapter depicts Engels's enormous contribution to preparing volumes II and III of *Capital* for the printer. This Engels considered his life's work. In April 1883 he wrote: "Marx has left behind a fat manuscript for the second part of *Capital* which I've got to read right through (and in what a handwriting!) before I can say how printable it is... In any case, the *main thing* is *available*." Not only did Engels have to read Marx's illegible handwriting, but also decipher the text and rewrite the manuscripts. Engels compounded the manuscripts, made countless editorial corrections, and wrote many explicative passages. Noting the great part Engels had played in preparing the manuscripts of volumes II and III of *Capital* for the printer, Lenin said those two volumes had been the labour of two people—Marx and Engels.

Lenin studied *Capital* thoroughly himself, and encouraged its study by others. In his works, Marx's ideas were taken further. Lenin brought Marx's economic theory abreast of the new times, and elaborated on the doctrine of imperialism being the last stage of capitalism.

The album's chapter on the *First International* is an account of how the International Working Men's Association was founded, and what it did. We are shown Marx's role as founder and leader of that first international proletarian mass organisation.

Orest Vereisky's picture, "Founding of the First International", portrays the meeting in St. Martin's Hall in London on September 28, 1864. Among the leaders of the workers' movement of different countries gathered on the presiding platform, we see Marx. At that time, as Engels put it, Marx was the only man who "was clear about what had to be done and what had to be founded, and this was the man who back in 1848 had flung the call to the world: workingmen of all lands, unite!"

Marx was the heart and soul, and leader, of the International. And his work in the International was the crowning achievement of his revolutionary activity. It was he who worked out all the programmatic documents of the International, and it was he who defined its tasks and tactics.

The chapter traces Marx's consistent efforts to assert the principles of scientific socialism in the international proletarian organisation, and to educate the working class in the spirit of socialist ideals. In the main documents of the International and in dozens of resolutions, addresses and articles, Marx helped workers to understand that conquest of political power and repatterning society on socialist lines was the proletariat's historic mission. The working class could radically change its condition only if it took the path of revolutionary struggle, he used to say.

The chapter shows that Marx was continuously battling against ideological currents hostile to the interests of the workers. As

Lenin wrote, "In uniting the labour movement of various countries, striving to channel into joint activity the various forms of non-proletarian, pre-Marxist socialism (Mazzini, Proudhon, Bakunin, liberal trade-unionism in Britain, Lassallean vacillations to the right in Germany, etc.), and in combating the theories of all these sects and schools, Marx hammered out a uniform tactic for the proletarian struggle of the working class in the various countries."

An important part was played by the address of the International's governing body to workers' societies, calling on them to join the IWA. It was issued in London in the summer of 1865. The membership of the International grew rapidly. It was joined by a number of large English trade unions, and sections of the IWA sprang up in scores of towns in different countries. Posters put out by the General Council certifying affiliation with the International were displayed on the premises of workers' societies.

The IWA cards of membership belonging to Frederick Engels and Hermann Jung, which are extant, are reproduced between these covers, and we see Marx's signature on them among those of members of the General Council. Alongside is a facsimile of the special stamps put out by the General Council to keep track of membership dues.

Pages of the Minute Book recording attendance at General Council meetings show that Marx was never absent when members of that body gathered in the modest-sized hall of the two-storeyed house on Greek Street, a quiet London thoroughfare, and later in the house in High Holborn Street. "During the time of the International," Friedrich Lessner recalls, "he never missed a meeting of the General Council."

A worldwide economic crisis erupted in 1866. Strikes proliferated in Britain, France, Switzerland, Belgium, Germany, and other European countries. The engravings that are published in this album, by artists who had witnessed the events, are graphic evidence of the intensity of the struggle. The International aided the strikers effectively, and substantially increased its influence on the international working class. It became known all over the world. Its prestige grew steeply. The chapter contains a facsimile of an address issued by the International's General Council, entitled "A Warning". It was written by Marx to counter the attempts of British industrialists to use German and Danish workers as strikebreakers.

Some of the material illustrates the help Marx and the International gave Socialists of different countries in working out their programmes and tactics. It tells of Marx's and the International's contribution to the political enlightenment of the working class in various countries, and the struggle against Proudhonist and Bakuninist influences.

In 1867 the Irish national liberation movement reached a peak of intensity. Examining the struggle of the Irish people, Marx arrived at the conclusion that the workers' struggle in the metropolitan country should back up the Irish national liberation movement. Documents of the International exposed the English bourgeoisie's policy of fanning national and religious antagonisms between English and Irish workers. This deliberate division of the proletariat, Marx noted, was the instrument whereby the bourgeoisie retained its grip on power. Marx occupied himself organising meetings in defence of the Irish people, and drawing up resolutions for the International's General Council demanding that Ireland should be granted independence.

The support of the Irish liberation movement by Marx and the International stimulated the political awareness of the English workers. As Lenin noted, the International's tactics on the Irish question was a remarkable model of how the proletariat of the oppressor nations should behave vis-à-vis national movements.

The chapter contains material concerning the congresses and conferences of the International, reflecting Marx's efforts to spread and consolidate socialist principles in the organisation. The Third Congress of the International, held in Brussels, called for socialisation of railways, arable land, minerals, mines and quarries. It showed the consequences of using machinery in capitalist factories. "On the one side," says a draft resolution of the Congress drawn up by Marx, "machinery has proved a most powerful instrument of despotism and extortion in the hands of the capitalist class;... on the other side the development of machinery creates the material conditions necessary for the superseding of the wages-system by a truly social system of production."

The resolutions of the Brussels Congress were evidence of the further spread of Marxism, the growing number of its followers, and the ideological defeat of its opponents—the Proudhonists and liberal trade unionists.

Much attention is devoted in the chapter to Marx's elaboration of the principles of proletarian internationalism and the workers' education in the internationalist spirit.

The chapter also refers to the activity of the Russian section of the International, and presents photographs of its members. The leader of the Russian section was Nikolai Utin, who was active in the populist Land and Freedom organisation. A tsarist court had sentenced him to death *in absentia* for his revolutionary activity. Among members of the section was the unforgettable Russian woman-revolutionary Elizaveta Dmitrieva-Tomanovskaya, Anna Korvin-Krukovskaya, V. I. Bartenev, and others.

Declaring its resolve to join the International, the Russian section requested Marx to represent it on the General Council. In his reply, Marx accepted with pleasure. He devoted considerable attention to the Russian section, briefed its members regularly on the work of the General Council, sent them various important assignments, and so on.

"The economic oppression of the Russian people," the programme of the Russian section said, "is entirely the same as the oppression of the entire European and American proletariat... Wherever the situation is the same, the means of eliminating it and replacing it with a new system of social and individual relationships should also be the same." These provisions reflect the influence of the Inaugural Address of the International, which was written by Marx.

The chapter on the *Paris Commune* contains a great variety of material: decrees, notices and posters, photographs, engravings, facsimiles of the revolutionary press, and so forth. This material illustrates the glorious 72-day history of the Commune.

One of the engravings depicts the solemn moment when the Paris Commune was proclaimed on March 28, 1871. Socialist Ranvier reads the declaration on elections to the Commune before a crowd of workers, artisans, and National Guardsmen. Beside it is a reproduction of the Declaration of the Paris Commune dated March 29, 1871, a priceless relic that announced the inauguration of the world's first workers' government.

There are photographs of those times showing the guns of the National Guard which the troops of Thiers had tried to capture so as to disarm the people of Paris, portraying Communards on the barricades, and so on.

Marx and Engels saw the Paris Commune as a spiritual offspring of the International, and devoted all their energy and experience to aiding the Communards who, as they put it, were "storming heaven". Lenin described Marx as a participant in the Paris revolution, to which he devoted his characteristic ardour and passion.

The documents and illustrations in the chapter deal with the conclusions drawn in one of Marx's fundamental works, *The Civil War in France*, written on the heels of the Paris revolution.

Referring to Marx's analysis, Lenin wrote: "There is no trace of utopianism in Marx, in the sense that he made up or invented a 'new' society. No, he studied the *birth* of the new society *out of* the old, and the forms of transition from the latter to the former, as a natural-historical process."

Although the Paris Commune did not live for long, Marx managed to spot in it formative but already sufficiently distinct features of the proletarian dictatorship as a new historical type of state.

The chapter contains photographs of leaders and active participants in the Paris Commune. Such intrepid revolutionaries as Edouard Vaillant, who had been active in the International and was member of the Paris Commune's executive commission, Charles Delescluze, the Commune's military delegate and publicist who laid down his life on the barricades in Paris, Louise Michel, the Red Maid of the Commune, Walery Wróblewski and Jaroslaw Dombrowski, the Polish revolutionary democrats and heroes of the Commune, and many others, whose memory is inscribed in the history of the liberation struggle. A stirring part in the Paris Commune was played by Russian revolutionaries—Elizaveta Dmitrieva-Tomanovskaya, Anna Korvin-Krukovskaya, Anna Pustovoitova, Pyotr Lavrov, and others.

Cartoons of Paris Commune times reproduced in this album are valuable and interesting. Most of them were published in large numbers on separate sheets. They are mostly by Pilotell, Moloch, Said, and Daumier. Commune cartoonists made fun of the Versailles clique, and small wonder, for as Marx wrote, everything about them was a caricature.

Despite the mudslinging of the bourgeois press, Marx and Engels saw to it that the ideas of the Paris Commune should spread among workers in different countries. In letters to his associates, Marx defined the proletarian class essence of the Commune. "The present rising in Paris," he wrote to his friend Ludwig Kugelmann, "even if it be crushed by the wolves, swine, and vile curs of the old society—is the most glorious deed of our Party since the June insurrection in Paris."

The chapter shows the epic struggle of the Paris Communards against the reactionaries in Versailles. There is an engraving of a street battle in one of the workers' quarters of Paris, where the Communards resisted bitterly. Among those defending the barricades were women and children. Another engraving shows the final battle at Père Lachaise Cemetery, where some 200 Communards put up a last-ditch stand against the Versailles troops.

A painting by Pichio, a member of the Paris Commune, portrays the brutal killing of the last handful of the Commune's heroic defenders beside a wall in the Père Lachaise Cemetery.

"Working men's Paris, with its Commune," Marx wrote at the time when the Commune lay in shambles and there seemed no end to the reprisals of reaction, "will be for ever celebrated as the glorious harbinger of a new society. Its martyrs are enshrined in the great heart of the working class. Its exterminators history has already nailed to that eternal pillory from which all the prayers of their priests will not avail to redeem them."

And these words came true. The Paris Commune elevated the workers' movement to a new level. Marx absorbed this experience to elaborate on his doctrine of class struggle, revolution, and dictatorship of the proletariat. The heroic stand of the Communards is admired by all people aspiring to progress and communism. The immortal revolutionary traditions of the Paris Commune helped to unite all segments of the international working-class and communist movement, and to promote proletarian internationalism.

The chapter about the Paris Commune closes with an account of the London Conference and the Hague Congress of the First International, both of which, acting on the experience of the Paris Commune, adopted a resolution on political action of the working class and founding independent national working-class parties.

The chapter *1873-1883* covers the last ten years of Marx's life, abounding in tense theoretical and practical revolutionary activity.

The chapter opens with material about the continuing work on volumes II and III of *Capital*. It is a time when Marx is engrossed in studying new phenomena in the capitalist economy. He refers in his notes to the emergence in the United States of large stock companies, and to the rise of financial and industrial magnates such as Vanderbilt and Rockefeller. In Europe, too, he observes, *"industrial production and large-scale commerce have become increasingly dependent on the banks, on the big capitalists"*. These conclusions drew upon the first signs of the impending era of imperialism and of proletarian revolutions.

While working on the second and third volumes of *Capital*, Marx increasingly studied economic and social developments in Russia and the United States. He examined statistical handbooks and other publications on landed property provided by his Russian friends. His study of Russia covered a lot of ground. From agrarian relations he went on to examine Russia's economic development on the whole, its history, the condition of the peasant masses, and Russian literature. In fact, Russia occupied a conspicuous place in Marx's research of the last ten years of his life. A list of books Marx drew up under the head, "Russian on My Bookshelf" (1881), contains nearly 120 titles. Lenin wrote: "Marx and Engels, who both knew Russian and read Russian books, took a lively interest in the country, followed the Russian revolutionary movement with sympathy and maintained contact with Russian revolutionaries."

Marx attached great importance to the endeavours of Nikolai Chernyshevsky. He had a high opinion of him as publicist, scholar, and revolutionary democrat. Chernyshevsky's exposures of the tsarist authoritarian regime, his unshakeable faith in the coming socialist order, and profound knowledge of Russia, were highly commended by Marx and Engels.

It had been Marx's intention to write a biography of Chernyshevsky, but illness prevented him from carrying out his plan.

The chapter contains material about V. V. Bervi's book, *The Condition of the Working Class in Russia*, which he wrote under the pen-name of N. Flerovsky, and which Marx had studied closely. Indeed, Marx described Bervi as an impartial observer and industrious worker.

During the last period of his life, while devoting his main attention to political economy, Marx also studied chemistry, agrochemistry, biology, geology, mineralogy, and physiology. For years, too, he studied mathematics, engaging in research. In the early 1880s, in fact, he produced two original manuscripts, entitled, "On the Concept of the Derived Function" and "On the Differential".

World history, too, engaged Marx's attention. He perused dozens of historical books and, among others, Schlosser's nine-volume *Universal History*, taking notes and copying passages referring to the period from the 1st to the 17th century.

Thousands of people lacking ideological seasoning and experience in class struggle joined the working-class movement in the latter half of the 19th century. In the circumstances, it was especially necessary to see to the purity of Marxism. In a number of distinctly polemical works, Marx defended and elaborated on the principles of his revolutionary doctrine, attacking Bakuninism and Lassalleanism. A special place here goes to the *Critique of the Gotha Programme*, which became a programme document of scientific communism.

In the last few years of his life, just as during the period of the First International, Marx was the focus to which led the threads from various leaders of the European and American socialist and working-class movement, and from the newly-founded socialist parties of some European countries. Socialists turned to him, as did various other participants in the liberation movement, for help and advice. "The rest of my life," Marx said, "will be devoted, like my efforts in the past, to the triumph of the social ideas which one day, be sure of it, will bring about the universal rule of the proletariat."

* * *

The 20th century has seen the embodiment in practice of scientific communism, for it is a century of the revolutionary transformation of society on the basis of the Marxist doctrine, which was elaborated upon in Leninism, the doctrine of Lenin.

Marxism-Leninism is a genuinely scientific theory of the development of society. "It expresses the vital interests of the working people, and the ideals of social justice," said Mikhail Gorbachev at the 27th Congress of the CPSU. "It derives its vitality from its everlasting youthfulness, its constant capacity for development and creative generalisation of the new facts and phenomena, and from its experience of revolutionary struggle and social reconstruction."

The Great October Socialist Revolution, the main event of the 20th century, was Marxism-Leninism's greatest triumph, for it ushered in the new era of transition from capitalism to socialism. The proletariat of Russia, which carried out the socialist revolution, was led by the Bolshevik Party with Lenin at its head. Thanks to the October Revolution, the ideas of Marxism-Leninism became a great material force of worldwide significance.

Under the leadership of Lenin's Communist Party, the Soviet people carried out radical revolutionary transformations in all areas of material, social, political, and intellectual life. They built a socialist society, and carried into effect Marx's prediction of a society of social justice in which the economy, politics, ideology and culture are the expression of truly humanitarian ideals, governed by the principle, "All in the name of man, all for the good of man". The rich theoretical and practical experience of the CPSU accumulated when building socialist society, has become part of the international revolutionary scientific theory, and represents a new stage in its development and implementation.

The emergence of the socialist world system and the successes scored by the socialist countries are vital evidence that the theory and practice of scientific communism, which is exercising ever

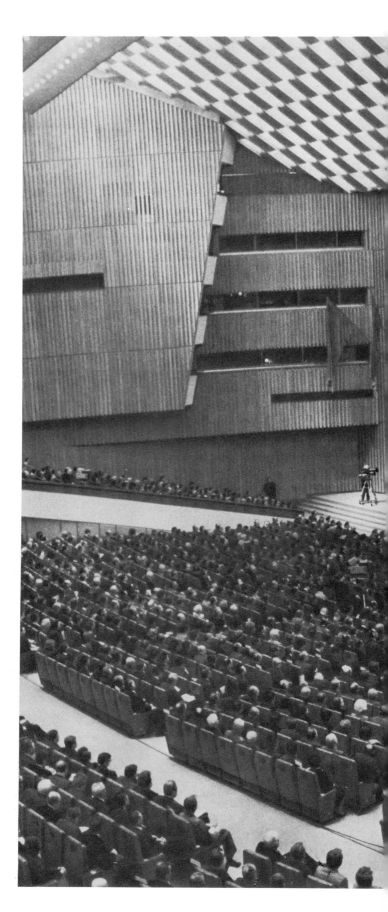

greater influence across the world, is workable and effective. The growing prestige and power of the countries of the socialist community—this is evidence of the great vitality of the ideas of Marx-Engels-Lenin.

The communist parties in capitalist countries, acting on the principles of Marxism-Leninism and proletarian internationalism, apply them imaginatively to the specific conditions in their countries.

History has proved that only Marxism-Leninism as theory and socialism as social practice can provide the answers to questions that arise ever more sharply in all parts of the world. And the deeper the great historical process of the revolutionary renewal of the world goes, the greater is the significance of Marxism-Leninism.

* * *

Associates and staff of the Institute of Marxism-Leninism of the CC CPSU, and those of the Karl Marx and Frederick Engels Museum participated in preparing this publication. Use was made of the English 50-volume edition of the works of Marx and Engels, the scientific biographies of Karl Marx and Frederick Engels, and the works of Soviet and foreign Marxist historians.

KARL MARX

HIS LIFE AND WORK

1818-1841

If we have chosen the position in life in which we can most of all work for mankind, no burdens can bow us down...

Karl Marx

1. Trier in the 1830s

Karl Marx was born on May 5, 1818 in Trier, Rhine Province, Prussia.

"SINCE 1815 RHENISH PRUSSIA HAS BEEN CONSIDERED ONE OF THE MOST PROGRESSIVE PROVINCES IN GERMANY, AND RIGHTLY SO...

"IT IS THE ONLY PART OF GERMANY WHOSE SOCIAL DEVELOPMENT HAS ALMOST REACHED THE LEVEL OF MODERN BOURGEOIS SOCIETY: DEVELOPED INDUSTRY, EXTENSIVE TRADE, ACCUMULATION OF CAPITAL AND FREE OWNERSHIP OF LAND; THE PREDOMINANCE IN THE TOWNS OF A STRONG BOURGEOISIE AND A NUMEROUS PROLETARIAT AND IN THE COUNTRYSIDE OF A MULTITUDE OF DEBT-RIDDEN ALLOTMENT PEASANTS..."

FREDERICK ENGELS

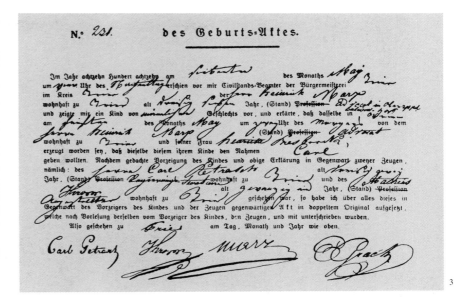

2. The house in Trier where Marx was born

3. The birth certificate of Karl Marx

"In the year eighteen hundred and eighteen, on the *seventh day* of the month of *May*, at *four* o'clock in the *afternoon*, there appeared before me ... *Herr Heinrich Marx*, domiciled in *Trier*, aged *thirty-seven*, by profession *barrister of the Higher Court of Appeal*, who showed me a *male* child and stated that the said child had been born in *Trier*, on the *fifth day* of the month of *May* at *two* o'clock in the *morning*, to *Herr Heinrich Marx, barrister* by profession, domiciled in *Trier*, and his wife *Henriette Presborck*, and that they wished to give the name *Carl* to this their child..."

Heinrich Marx (1777-1838), *Marx's father*, councillor of justice in Trier, was a widely read man of no mean accomplishments, a connoisseur of classical literature and a serious student of philosophy. His progressive philosophical views, however, went along with moderately liberal political convictions. Karl was a loving son who deeply respected his father.

Henriette Marx, née Presborck (1787-1863), *Marx's mother*, dedicated herself to caring for the family and raising her nine children.

4. A view of the living room in an early 19th-century Trier home (reproduced by the Museum of German History in the German Democratic Republic)

5. The Porta Nigra, one of the important Roman remains in Trier

6. *The gymnasium in Trier which Marx attended from October 1830 to September 1835*

7. *The favourite books of schoolboy Marx*

Among the teachers at the Trier Gymnasium, schoolboy Marx was especially fond of the headmaster, Johann Hugo Wyttenbach, who taught history and philosophy, and Johann Steininger, the maths and physics teacher. Their progressive views influenced the development of Marx's outlook.

8. *Johann Hugo Wyttenbach (1767-1848)*

9. *Johann Steininger (1794-1874)*

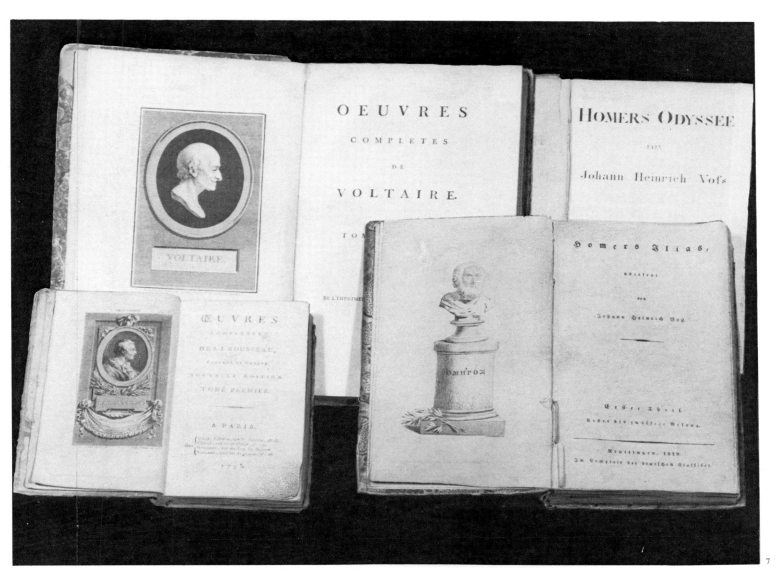

7

8

9

The years Marx attended school witnessed a number of revolutionary events in various West European countries.

The July revolution occurred in France in 1830, followed by a revolution in Belgium in September of that year, and uprisings in Poland in 1830 and 1831.

The proletariat burst into the arena of political struggle in the 1830s, with weavers rebelling in 1831 and 1834 in Lyons, a major textile centre in France. In the latter half of the 1830s Chartism, a revolutionary workers' mass movement, came into being in England.

11

10. *The July 1830 revolution in France. "To arms, Citizens!" was the general cry. "Form your own battalions!"*

11. *The revolution in Belgium. September 1830*

12. *Suppression of the Lyons weavers' uprising, 1834*

12

13

13. *The Chartist uprising in Newport,
South Wales, England, in November
1839*

14

A mass demonstration for a united Germany and political freedoms was held on May 27, 1832, beside the ruins of Hambach Castle in the Palatinate.

14. *The Hambach festivities of May 27, 1832*

15. *"The National Festivities of the Germans in Hambach", 1832*
The cover of a pamphlet

The pamphlet contained speeches made at the Hambach festivities. In 1833, during a police search in the Trier Gymnasium, a copy of the pamphlet was found in the possession of one of the boys. It was confiscated.

Das Nationalfest

der

Deutschen

zu

Hambach.

Unter Mitwirkung eines Redaktions-Ausschusses

beschrieben

von

J. G. A. Wirth.

Erstes Heft.

Neustadt a/H. 1832.
In Commission bei Philipp Christmann

Preis 30 kr. zur Gründung eines Fonds für deutsche politische National-Journalistik.

15

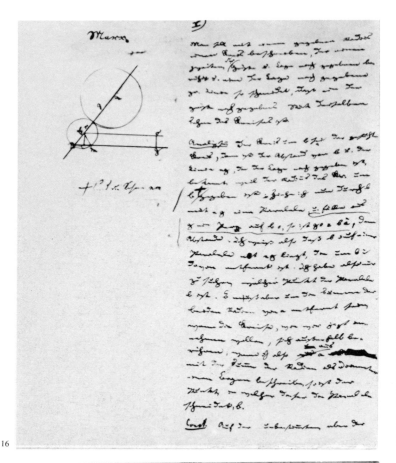

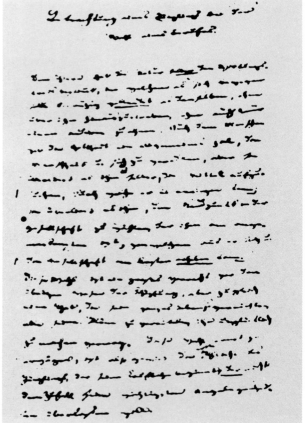

16

17

16. *A page of Marx's examination paper in mathematics*

17. *Karl Marx,* "Reflections of a Young Man on the Choice of a Profession". *First page of the school-leaving composition written in August 1835*
Facsimile

18

"WE CANNOT ALWAYS ATTAIN THE POSITION TO WHICH WE BELIEVE WE ARE CALLED; OUR RELATIONS IN SOCIETY HAVE TO SOME EXTENT ALREADY BEGUN TO BE ESTABLISHED BEFORE WE ARE IN A POSITION TO DETERMINE THEM... THE CHIEF GUIDE WHICH MUST DIRECT US IN THE CHOICE OF A PROFESSION IS THE WELFARE OF MANKIND...

"IF HE WORKS ONLY FOR HIMSELF, HE MAY PERHAPS BECOME A FAMOUS MAN OF LEARNING, A GREAT SAGE, AN EXCELLENT POET, BUT HE CAN NEVER BE A PERFECT, TRULY GREAT MAN...

19

"IF WE HAVE CHOSEN THE POSITION IN LIFE IN WHICH WE CAN MOST OF ALL WORK FOR MANKIND, NO BURDENS CAN BOW US DOWN, BECAUSE THEY ARE SACRIFICES FOR THE BENEFIT OF ALL; THEN WE SHALL EXPERIENCE NO PETTY, LIMITED, SELFISH JOY, BUT OUR HAPPINESS WILL BELONG TO MILLIONS..."

19. A view of Bonn in the 1840s

20. Bonn University. Marx attended the Department of Law from October 15, 1835 to August 22, 1836

18. The Certificate of Maturity issued to Karl Marx on his leaving the Trier Gymnasium on September 24, 1835
Sheet One

"...FROM *TRIER*, 17 YEARS OF AGE, OF *EVANGELICAL* FAITH, SON OF *BARRISTER-AT-LAW, HERR JUSTIZRAT MARX* IN *TRIER*, WAS *FIVE* YEARS AT THE GYMNASIUM IN TRIER...
"I. MORAL BEHAVIOUR TOWARDS SUPERIORS AND FELLOW PUPILS *WAS GOOD.*
"II. APTITUDES AND DILIGENCE. *HE HAS GOOD APTITUDES...*"

20

21

22

23

21. *Members of the Trier Students' Association (Lands-*
mannschaft) at Bonn University, 1836. Karl Marx is
fourth from right

22. *Karl Marx the student*

23. *Certificate issued to Marx at Bonn University when*
he transferred to Berlin University. August 22, 1836
First and last sheets

24

25

27

28

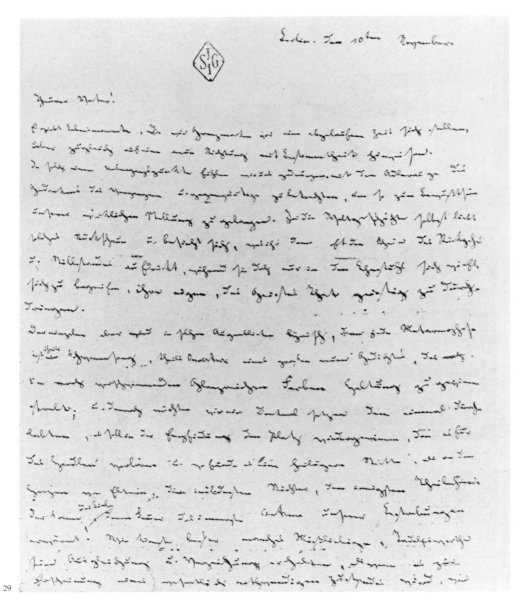

29

30. Stralow, a suburb of Berlin where Marx took a holiday in the spring of 1837

31. The house in Stralow where Marx spent his holidays

32. A memorial to Marx's stay in Stralow, unveiled in 1967

On coming to Stralow, Marx had, as he put it, "got to know Hegel from beginning to end, together with most of his disciples". Marx did not accept Hegel's conservative political ideas, but eagerly espoused his dialectical method of cognition.

"THEREIN LAY THE TRUE SIGNIFICANCE AND THE REVOLUTIONARY CHARACTER OF THE HEGELIAN PHILOSOPHY ... THAT IT ONCE FOR ALL DEALT THE DEATH BLOW TO THE FINALITY OF ALL PRODUCTS OF HUMAN THOUGHT AND ACTION."

FREDERICK ENGELS

29. Marx's letter to his father in Trier, November 10, 1837

A fragment

"DEAR FATHER,

"THERE ARE MOMENTS IN ONE'S LIFE WHICH ARE LIKE FRONTIER POSTS MARKING THE COMPLETION OF A PERIOD BUT AT THE SAME TIME CLEARLY INDICATING A NEW DIRECTION...

"AFTER MY ARRIVAL IN BERLIN, I BROKE OFF ALL HITHERTO EXISTING CONNECTIONS, MADE VISITS RARELY AND UNWILLINGLY, AND TRIED TO IMMERSE MYSELF IN SCIENCE AND ART...

"POETRY, HOWEVER, COULD BE AND HAD TO BE ONLY AN ACCOMPANIMENT; I HAD TO STUDY LAW AND ABOVE ALL FELT THE URGE TO WRESTLE WITH PHILOSOPHY... I DID GAIN A GENERAL VIEW OF THE MATERIAL AND A LIKING FOR IT... IT BECAME CLEAR TO ME THAT THERE COULD BE NO HEADWAY WITHOUT PHILOSOPHY...

"BUSY WITH THESE VARIOUS OCCUPATIONS, DURING MY FIRST TERM I SPENT MANY A SLEEPLESS NIGHT, FOUGHT MANY A BATTLE, AND ENDURED MUCH INTERNAL AND EXTERNAL EXCITEMENT...

"FROM THE IDEALISM WHICH, BY THE WAY, I HAD COMPARED AND NOURISHED WITH THE IDEALISM OF KANT AND FICHTE, I ARRIVED AT THE POINT OF SEEKING THE IDEA IN REALITY

31

33

Great classical German philosophers.

33. Immanuel Kant (1724-1804)

34. Johann Gottlieb Fichte (1762-1814)

35. Georg Wilhelm Friedrich Hegel (1770-1831)

A split occurred among the disciples of Hegel after he died in 1831. The left wing of the Hegelian school who called themselves Left or Young Hegelians—Strauss, the brothers Bruno and Edgar Bauer, Feuerbach, and others, drew radical conclusions from Hegel's philosophy, and sharply attacked all religious and philosophical dogmas. From criticising religion they went on to criticising politics.

Marx made close friends with members of the Doctors' Club, a Berlin circle of Young Hegelians, and soon became one of the club's moving spirits.

36. Bruno Bauer (1809-1882)

37. David Friedrich Strauss, The Life of Jesus, *Vol. I, Tübingen, 1835-36*

The title page

38. David Friedrich Strauss (1808-1874)

35

Streitschriften

zur Vertheidigung meiner Schrift

über das

Leben Jesu

und zur Charakteristik

der gegenwärtigen Theologie.

Von

Dr. David Friedrich Strauß.

ERSTES HEFT:

Herr Dr. Steudel oder die Selbsttäuschungen des ver-
ständigen Supranaturalismus unserer Tage.

Tübingen,
bei C. F. Osiander.
1837.

37
38

39. Letter of Young Hegelian Moses Hess to writer Berthold Auerbach, September 2, 1841

A fragment

"BE READY TO MEET THE GREATEST AND PERHAPS THE *ONLY* LIVING *REAL PHILOSOPHER*... DR. MARX, AS MY IDOL IS CALLED, IS STILL A VERY YOUNG MAN (HE CAN BE NO MORE THAN 24), WHO WILL DEAL THE FINAL BLOW AT MEDIEVAL RELIGION AND POLITICS; HE COMBINES THE MOST PROFOUND PHILOSOPHICAL EARNESTNESS WITH THE KEENEST WIT; IMAGINE TO YOURSELF ROUSSEAU, VOLTAIRE, HOLBACH, LESSING, HEINE AND HEGEL COMBINED INTO ONE PERSONALITY; AND I MEAN *COMBINED*, NOT MECHANICALLY MIXED—AND THIS WILL GIVE YOU AN IDEA OF DR. MARX."

40. An allegory on criticism of religion by Left Hegelians David Strauss, Bruno Bauer and Ludwig Feuerbach; Bruno Bauer is shown riding an ostrich (Strauss in German) and chasing a lion, eagle, bull and angel, which symbolise religion, into a river aflame (Feuerbach in German)

39

40

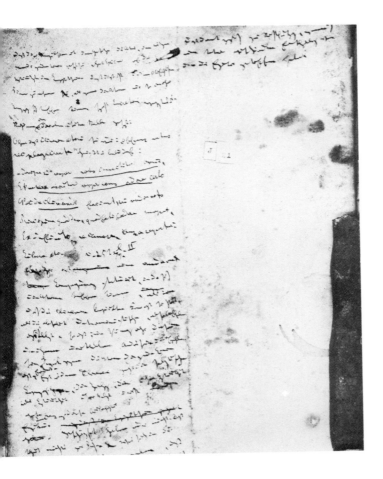

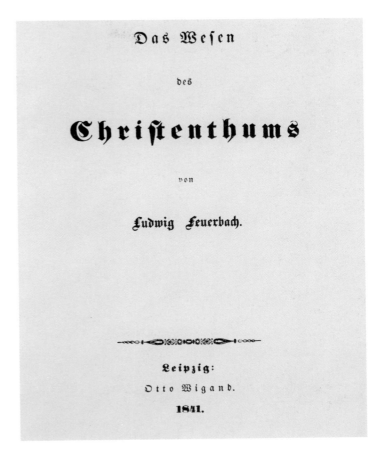

Das Wesen

des

Christenthums

von

Ludwig Feuerbach.

Leipzig:
Otto Wigand.
1841.

43

44

41. Books which Marx read while working on his dissertation in 1839-41

42. A facsimile of a page from Marx's notebook with comments on Epicurean, Stoic, and Skeptic philosophy made in Berlin when working on his dissertation in 1839

43. Ludwig Feuerbach, The Essence of Christianity, *Leipzig, 1841*

The title page

In 1841 Marx read Ludwig Feuerbach's *Essence of Christianity.*

"...CAME FEUERBACH'S *ESSENCE OF CHRIST-IANITY*... WITHOUT CIRCUMLOCUTIONS IT PLACED MATERIALISM ON THE THRONE... ONE MUST HIMSELF HAVE EXPERIENCED THE LIBERATING EFFECT OF THIS BOOK TO GET AN IDEA OF IT. ENTHUSIASM WAS GENERAL; WE ALL BECAME AT ONCE FEUERBACHIANS."

FREDERICK ENGELS

44. Ludwig Feuerbach (1804-1872)—eminent German materialist philosopher of the pre-Marxian period

45. Certificate issued to Marx on March 30, 1841, on finishing Berlin University

Sheet one

46. Difference Between the Democritean and Epicurean Philosophy of Nature

Marx's doctoral dissertation

A fragment

47. Jena University

48. Diploma conferring on Marx the academic degree of Doctor of Philosophy issued at Jena University on April 15, 1841

Now Marx, vested with the doctoral degree, and Bruno Bauer were planning to teach philosophy at Bonn University, but the Prussian Government's stepped up repressions prevented this.

QUOD

FELIX FAUSTUMQUE ESSE IUBEAT

SUMMUM NUMEN

AUCTORITATE

HUIC LITTERARUM UNIVERSITATI

AB

FERDINANDO I

IMPERATORE ROMANO GERMANICO

ANNO MDLVII CONCESSA

CLEMENTISSIMIS AUSPICIIS

SERENISSIMORUM

MAGNI DUCIS ET DUCUM SAXONIAE

NUTRITORUM ACADEMIAE IENENSIS

MUNIFICENTISSIMORUM

RECTORE ACADEMIAE MAGNIFICENTISSIMO

AUGUSTO ET POTENTISSIMO PRINCIPE AC DOMINO

CAROLO FRIDERICO

MAGNO DUCE SAXONIAE VIMARIENSIUM ATQUE ISENACENSIUM PRINCIPE LANDGRAVIO THURINGIAE
MARCHIONE MISNIAE PRINCIPALI DIGNITATE COMITE HENNEBERGAE
DYNASTA BLANKENHAYNII NEOSTADII AC TAUTENBURGI

PRORECTORE ACADEMIAE MAGNIFICO

VIRO PERILLUSTRI ATQUE AMPLISSIMO

ERNESTO REINHOLDO

PHILOSOPHIAE DOCTORE ARTIUMQUE LIBERALIUM MAGISTRO
MAGNI DUCIS SAXONIAE VIMARIENSIS ET ISENACENSIS A CONSILIIS AULAE INTIMIS PHILOSOPHIAE PROFESSORE PUBLICO ORDINARIO

DECANO ORDINIS PHILOSOPHORUM ET BRABEUTA

MAXIME SPECTABILI

VIRO PERILLUSTRI ATQUE EXCELLENTISSIMO

CAROLO FRIDERICO BACHMANNO

PHILOSOPHIAE DOCTORE

SERENISSIMI DUCIS SAX. ALTENBURGENSIS A CONSILIIS AULAE INTIMIS MORALIUM ET POLITICES PROFESSORE PUBLICO ORDINARIO INSTITUTORUM
MAGNI DUCALIUM MINERALOGICORUM DIRECTORE INSTITUTI HISTORICI PARISIENSIS SOCIETATUM CAESAREAE PETROPOLITANAE MINERALOGICAE
REGIAE DRESDENSIS MINERALOGICAE POLYTECHNICAE PARISIENSIS ARTIUM ET SCIENTIARUM PUBLICAE APUD TRAIECTINOS ARTIUM ET LITTERARUM
GANDAVIENSIS SCIENTIARUM ET ARTIUM ANTVERPIENSIS MEDICORUM ET PHYSICORUM BRUXELLENSIS DOCTRINARUM DE RERUM NATURA
PHILADELPHIENSIS IN AMERICA SEPTENTRIONALI ET LATINAE IENENSIS ALIARUMQUE SOCIO

ORDO PHILOSOPHORUM

VIRO PRAENOBILISSIMO ATQUE DOCTISSIMO

CAROLO HENRICO MARX

TREVIRENSI

DOCTORIS PHILOSOPHIAE HONORES

DIGNITATEM IURA ET PRIVILEGIA

INGENII DOCTRINAE ET VIRTUTIS SPECTATAE INSIGNIA ET ORNAMENTA

DETULIT

DELATA

PUBLICO HOC DIPLOMATE

CUI IMPRESSUM EST SIGNUM ORDINIS PHILOSOPHORUM

PROMULGAVIT

IENAE DIE XV M. APRILIS A. MDCCCXLI

TYPIS BRANII

1842-1844

The chief thing in the doctrine of Marx is that it brings out the historic role of the proletariat as the builder of socialist society.

Marx first advanced it in 1844.

V. I. Lenin

1. Karl Marx the student

2

2. A view of Cologne in the mid-19th century

3. Cologne of the 1840s

Karl Marx stayed in Cologne, one of the biggest cities of Germany and the hub of Rhenish economic life, from October 1842 to May 1843.

In Prussia, the early 1840s witnessed a surge of feudal reaction. New instructions of the Prussian Government (1841) afforded more scope to the reactionary censors. Political journalism became the battlefield between forces of reaction and progress. Marx joined the fray with enthusiasm.

4. Karl Marx, Comments on the Latest Prussian Censorship Instruction

From the symposium Anekdota zur neuesten Philosophie und Publicistik, *Vol. I, 1843*

Marx wrote this article, the first in his long journalistic career, in 1842. His criticism of censorship was here laced with resolute condemnation of the vicious nature of the feudal absolutistic regime. The article was not published

3

Abonnements-Preis: vierteljährlich In Köln 1 Thlr. 12½ Sgr. Auswärts 1 Thlr. 12½ Sgr.

Rheinische Zeitung

für

Politik, Handel und Gewerbe.

Insertions-Gebühren: Die enggedruckte Petitzeile 1 Sgr. Briefe werden frankirt erbeten.

Nro 289 — Köln, Sonntag den 16. Oktober — 1842

Uebersicht des Inhalts.

Amtliche Nachrichten.

Deutschland. Köln, 15. Okt. Der Communismus und die Augsb. Allgem. Zeitung. — Barmen, 13. Okt. Erläuterungen. — Berlin, 10. Okt. Nähere Bestimmung zu der Verordnung vom 18. Febr. d. J. — 12. Okt. Die sichere Unterbringung der Mündelgelder. — Von der Spree, 12. Okt. Die Befugnisse des ständischen Central-Ausschusses. — Posen, 8. Okt. — Mainz, 14. Okt. Die deutsche Industrie-Ausstellung. — Frankfurt a. M., 14. Okt. Theilnahmlosigkeit der Bürger bei der Wahl zur gesetzgebenden Versammlung. — Unbilligkeiten der Thurn und Taxischen Postverwaltung. — Aus Baiern, 11. Okt. Die politischen Gefangenen und ihre Amnestie. — München, 10. Okt. Schelling verläßt den baierischen Dienst. — Leipzig, 12. Okt. — Wien, 8. Okt. Ernennung des Erzbischofs von Carlowitz.

Schweiz. Vom Genfersee, 8. Oktober. Differenzen der Schweiz mit Frankreich und Baden.

Belgien. Brüssel, 14. Oktober. Untergang der österreichischen Fregatte Bellona.

Frankreich. Paris, 13. Oktober. Der „National" über England und Belgien. — Das „Journal des Debats" gegen Rußlands Maßregeln in Betreff der katholischen Kirche. — Ueber die Besteuerung der Staats-Renten.

Großbritannien und Irland. London, 11. Okt. Nähere Aufschlüsse über Ludwig Napoleon's Expedition.

Handels- und Börsennachrichten.

Beiblatt. Hannover und der Zollverein. — Eine Selbstschau von Heinrich Zschokke. — Die Einschüchterung und Bestechung bei den Parlamentswahlen in England.

Amtliche Nachrichten.

Chronik des Tages.

Berlin, 12. Okt. Se. Majestät der König haben Allergnädigst geruht: dem Kammerherrn Freiherrn von Stillfried zu Lomnitz bei Görlitz die Annahme des von den regierenden Fürsten zu Hohenzollern-Hechingen und Siegmaringen Durchlauchten ihm verliehenen Ehrenkreuzes 2ter Klasse des Fürstlich Hohenzollernschen Hausordens zu gestatten.

Den Fabrikanten Julius Wirth und Karl Voos zu Peresfotten bei Solingen ist unter dem 9. Oktober 1842 ein Patent „auf eine Walzvorrichtung für Tafelmesser, Klingen, Hobeleisen und Bruchbandfedern, in der durch eine Zeichnung und Beschreibung nachgewiesenen Zusammensetzung," auf sechs Jahre, von jenem Tage an gerechnet, und für den Umfang der Monarchie ertheilt worden.

Deutschland.

*** **Köln**, 15. Oktober. Die Nro. 284 der Augsburger Zeitung ist so ungeschickt, in der Rheinischen Zeitung eine Preußische Communistin zu entdecken, zwar keine wirkliche Communistin, aber doch immer eine Person, die mit dem Communismus phantastisch kokettirt und platonisch liebäugelt.

Ob diese unartige Phantasterei der Augsburgerin uneigennützig, ob diese müßige Gaukelei ihrer aufgeregten Einbildungskraft mit Spekulationen und diplomatischen Geschäften zusammenhängt, mag der Leser entscheiden, — nachdem wir das angebliche corpus delicti vorgeführt haben.

Die Rheinische Zeitung, erzählt man, habe einen communistischen Aufsatz über die Berliner Familienhäuser in ihr Feuilleton aufgenommen und mit folgender Bemerkung begleitet: Diese Mittheilungen „dürften für die Geschichte dieser wichtigen Zeitfrage nicht ohne Interesse sein"; folgt daher nach der Augsburger Logik, daß die Rheinische Zeitung „dergleichen ungewaschenes Zeug empfehlend aufgetischt." Also wenn ich z. B. sage: „folgende Mittheilungen des Mephistopheles über den innern Haushalt der Augsburger Zeitung dürften nicht ohne Interesse für die Geschichte dieser wichtig thuenden Dame sein", so empfehle ich die schmutzigen „Zeuge", aus denen die Augsburgerin ihre bunte Garderobe zusammenschneidet? Oder sollten wir den Communismus schon deshalb für keine wichtige Zeitfrage halten, weil er keine courfähige Zeitfrage ist, weil er schmutzige Wäsche trägt und nicht nach Rosenwasser duftet?

Allein mit Recht grollt die Augsburgerin unserm Mißverstand. Die Wichtigkeit des Communismus besteht nicht darin, daß er eine Zeitfrage von höchstem Ernst für Frankreich und England bildet. Der Communismus besitzt die europäische Wichtigkeit von der Augsburger Zeitung zu einer Phrase benutzt worden zu sein. Einer ihrer Pariser Korrespondenten, ein Convertit, der die Geschichte behandelt, wie ein Conditor die Botanik, hat jüngst einmal den Einfall gehabt: die Monarchie müsse die socialistisch-communistischen Ideen in ihrer Weise sich anzueignen suchen. Versteht Ihr nun den Unmuth der Augsburgerin, die uns nie verzeihen wird, daß wir den Communismus in seiner ungewaschenen Nacktheit dem Publikum bloßgestellt; versteht Ihr die verbissene Ironie, die uns zuruft: so empfehlt Ihr den Communismus, der schon einmal die glückliche Eleganz besaß, eine Phrase der Augsburger Zeitung zu bilden!

Der zweite Vorwurf, der die Rheinische Zeitung trifft, ist der Schluß eines Referats aus Straßburg über die bei dem dortigen Kongreß gehaltenen communistischen Reden, denn die beiden Stiefschwestern hatten sich in die Beute so getheilt, daß der Rheinländerin die Verhandlungen und der Baierin die Mahlzeiten der Straßburger Gelehrten zufielen. Die inkriminirte Stelle lautet wörtlich also:

> Es ist heute mit dem Mittelstande so wie mit dem Adel im Jahre 1789; damals nahm der Mittelstand die Privilegien des Adels in Anspruch und erhielt sie, heute verlangt der Stand, der Nichts besitzt, Theil zu nehmen am Reichthume der Mittelklassen, die jetzt am Ruder sind. Der Mittelstand hat sich nun heute gegen eine Ueberrumpelung besser vorgesehen als der Adel im Jahre 89 und es steht zu erwarten, daß das Problem auf friedlichem Wege wird gelöst werden.

Daß Sieyes Prophezeihung eingetroffen und daß der tiers état Alles geworden ist und Alles sein will, Bülow-Cummerow, das ehemal. Berl. politische Wochenblatt, Dr. Kosegarten, sämmtliche feudalistische Schriftsteller bekennen es mit wehmüthigster Entrüstung. Daß der Stand, der heute nichts besitzt, am Reichthum der Mittelklassen Theil zu nehmen verlangt, das ist ein Faktum, welches ohne das Straßburger Reden und trotz dem Augsburger Schweigen in Manchester, Paris und Lyon auf den Straßen Jedem sichtbar umherläuft. Glaubt etwa die Augsburgerin ihr Unwillen und ihr Schweigen widerlegten die Thatsachen der Zeit? Die Augsburgerin ist impertinent im Fliehen. Sie reißt aus vor verfänglichen Zeiterscheinungen und glaubt, der Staub, den sie beim Ausreißen hinter sich aufwirbelt, so wie die ängstlichen Schmähworte, welche sie auf der Flucht zwischen den Zähnen hinmurmelt, blendeten und verwirrten die unbequeme Zeiterscheinung wie den bequemen Leser.

Oder grollt die Augsburgerin der Erwartung unseres Korrespondenten, die unläugbare Collision werde sich „auf friedlichem Wege" lösen? Oder wirft sie uns vor, daß wir nicht sofort ein probates Rezept verschrieben und einen sonnenklaren Bericht über die unmaßgebliche Lösung des Problems dem überraschten Leser in die Tasche spielten? Wir besitzen nicht die Kunst mit einer Phrase Probleme zu bändigen, an deren Bezwingung zwei Völker arbeiten.

Aber liebste, beste Augsburgerin, Sie geben uns bei Gelegenheit des Communismus zu verstehen, daß Deutschland jetzt arm ist an unabhängigen Existenzen, daß 9/10 der gebildeteren Jugend den Staat anbetteln um Brod für ihre Zukunft, daß unsere Ströme vernachläßigt, daß die Schifffahrt darniederliegt, daß unsern ehemals blühenden Handelsstädte der alte Flor fehlt, daß die freien Institutionen erst auf langsamen Wege in Preußen erstrebt werden, daß der Ueberfluß unserer Bevölkerung hülflos umherirrt, um in fremden Nationalitäten als Deutsche unterzugehen und für alle diese Probleme kein einziges Rezept, kein Versuch „klarer über die Mittel zur Ausführung" der großen That zu werden, die uns von all' diesen Sünden erlösen soll! Oder erwarten Sie keine friedliche Lösung? Fast scheint ein anderer Artikel derselben Nummer, von Karlsruhe datirt, dahin zu deuten, wo selbst in Bezug auf den Zollverein die verfängliche Frage an Preußen gerichtet wird: „Glaubt man, eine solche Krisis würde vorüber gehen wie eine Rauferei um das Tabakrauchen im Thiergarten?" Der Grund, den Sie für Ihren Unglauben debütiren, ist ein communistischer. „Nun lasse man eine Krisis über die Industrie losbrechen, lasse Millionen an Kapitals verloren gehen, Tausende von Arbeitern brodlos werden." Wie ungelegen kam unsere „friedliche Erwartung," da Sie einmal beschlossen hatten, eine blutige Krisis losbrechen zu lassen, weshalb wohl in Ihrem Artikel Großbritannien auf den demagogischen Arzt Dr. M'Douall, der nach Amerika ausgewandert, weil „mit diesem königschen Geschlecht doch nichts anzufangen sei", nach Ihrer eigenen Logik empfehlend nachgewiesen wird.

Eh' wir uns von Ihnen trennen, möchten wir Sie noch vorübergehend auf Ihre eigene Weisheit aufmerksam machen, da es bei Ihrer Methode der Phrasen nicht wohl zu umgehen ist, harmloser Weise hie und da einen Gedanken, zwar nicht zu haben, aber ebendeshalb auszusprechen. Sie finden, daß die Polemik des Herrn Hennequin aus Paris gegen die Parzellirung des Grundbesitzes denselben mit den Autonomen in eine überraschende Harmonie bringt! Die Ueberraschung, sagt Aristoteles, ist der Anfang des Philosophirens. Sie haben beim Anfang geendet. Würde Ihnen sonst die überraschende Thatsache entgangen sein, daß communistische Grundsätze in Deutschland nicht von den Liberalen, sondern von Ihren reaktionären Freunden verbreitet werden?

Wer spricht von Handwerker-Corporationen? Die Reactionaire. Der Handwerkerstand soll einen Staat im Staat bilden. Finden Sie es auffallend, daß solche Gedanken, modern ausgedrückt, also lauten: „Der Staat soll sich in den Handwerker-Stand verwandeln"? Wenn dem Handwerker sein Stand der Staat sein soll, wenn aber der moderne Handwerker, wie jeder moderne Mensch, den Staat nur als die all seinen Mitbürgern gemeinsame Sphäre versteht und verstehen kann, wie wollen Sie anders beide Gedanken synthesiren als in einen Handwerker Staat?

Wer polemisirt gegen die Parzellirung des Grundbesitzes? Die Reactionäre. Man ist in einer ganz kurz erschienenen feudalistischen Schrift (Kosegarten über Parcellirung) so weit gegangen, das Privateigenthum ein Vorrecht zu nennen. Das ist Fouriers Grundsatz. Sobald man über die Grundsätze einig ist, läßt sich nicht über die Consequenzen und die Anwendung streiten?

Die „Rheinische Zeitung", die den communistischen Ideen in ihrer jetzigen Gestalt nicht einmal theoretische Wirklichkeit zugestehen, also noch weniger ihre praktische Verwirklichung wünschen oder auch nur für möglich halten kann, wird diese Ideen einer gründlichen Kritik unterwerfen. Daß aber Schriften, wie die von Leroux, Considerant und vor Allen das scharfsinnige Werk Proudhons nicht durch oberflächliche Einfälle des Augenblicks, sondern nur nach lang anhaltenden und tief eingehen-

Alter und Jugend.

Von

R. E. Prutz.

(Eingesandt vom Verfasser.)

Ihr könnt nicht uns verstehen,
Und wir nicht Euren Rath:
Wohlan, so laßt uns gehen,
Ein Jeder seinen Pfad.
Ihr legt die Stirn in Falten,
Ihr nennt Euch selbst die Alten,
Euch dünkt ein Spott der Thoren,
Was uns die Seele schwellt.
Ihr mögt nur immer sagen,
Kopfschütteln nur und fragen,
Besänftigen und klagen:
Uns packt es an und reißt es fort,
Nun sind wir hier, nun sind wir dort,
Wir wollen einmal wagen.

Lebt wohl! Zum letzten Male
Kreuzt uns're Bahn sich hier:
Ihr geht gemach im Thale,
Auf Klippen wandern wir.
Ruht aus in Abendgluthen.

Vom Main, 13. Oktober. Obschon der Herbst sich bereits in seinen fahlen Farben herniedersenkt, und das rege Leben der städtischen Gesellschaft wiedergekehrt ist, so sind die Taunusbäder um uns her doch noch immer von zahlreichen Fremden besucht. Davon ist jedoch der größere Theil mehr des Spieles wegen dort, als der Heilquellen. Viele der deutschen Badeorte gleichen Tempeln des Lasters, prächtig ausgeputzt und anlockend durch alle Künste der Verführung, und wer eintritt in den magischen Kreis der grünen Tische, ist verloren, läßt Geld und Freunde und oft seinen guten Namen dort zurück. Das Glücksspiel an der Bank ist etwas so tief Unmoralisches, daß bis heute nur wenige Stimmen es zu vertheidigen gewagt haben; und demungeachtet gibt es Regierungen, die es nicht nur dulden, sondern begünstigen; die es neu einführen an Orten, die sich bis jetzt von dieser Seuche frei gehalten. Und halten diese Regierungen vielleicht das Spiel für etwas Erlaubtes, Wohlthätiges? Nimmermehr; denn sie selbst verbieten ihren Unterthanen auf's Strengste, sich an der Bank blicken zu lassen. Also auf Fremde geht die Spekulation ihrer Verwaltungsbehörden; Nicht-Unterthanen mögen immerhin zu Grunde gerichtet werden, wenn

II.

Bemerkungen über die neueste preußische Censurinstruction.

Von einem Rheinländer.

Wir gehören nicht zu den Malcontenten, die schon vor der Erscheinung des neuen preußischen Censuredicts ausrufen: Timeo Danaos et dona ferentes. Vielmehr da in der neuen Instruction die Prüfung schon erlassener Gesetze, sollte sie auch nicht im Sinne der Regierung ausfallen, gebilligt wird, so machen wir sogleich einen Anfang mit ihr selbst. Die Censur ist die officielle Kritik; ihre Normen sind kritische Normen, die also am wenigsten der Kritik, mit der sie sich in ein Feld stellen, entzogen werden dürfen.

Die im Eingang der Instruction ausgesprochene allgemeine Tendenz wird gewiß Jeder nur billigen können: „um schon jetzt die Presse von unstatthaften, nicht in der allerhöchsten Absicht liegenden Beschränkungen zu befreien, haben Se. Majestät der König durch eine an das königl. Staats-Ministerium am 10. d. M. erlassene höchste Ordre jeden ungebührlichen Zwang der schriftstellerischen Thätigkeit ausdrücklich zu mißbilligen und unter Anerkennung des Werths und des Bedürfnisses einer freimüthigen und anständigen Publicität uns zu ermächtigen geruht, die Censoren zur angemessenen Beachtung des Art. 2 des Censuredicts vom 11. October 1819 von Neuem anzuweisen."

4

until a year later in Switzerland, where it appeared over the signature, "By a Rhinelander".

In May 1842 began Marx's collaboration with the *Rheinische Zeitung*, published in Cologne by a group of wealthy liberals. In mid-October of that year he accepted the offer of its shareholders and became its editor.

Under his guidance, the paper was a vehicle for the ideas of all democratic Germans.

5. Karl Marx, Communism and the Augsburg "Allgemeine Zeitung"
Rheinische Zeitung, *October 16, 1842*

In this article Marx examined communism as a crucial theoretical issue burgeoning upon the soil of reality. He was critical of any superficial approach to the subject, for communism, he said, was a topic that called for profound study.

6. *Cutting firewood*

7. *Karl Marx, "Proceedings of the Sixth Rhine Province Assembly. Third Article. Debates on the Law on Thefts of Wood"*
Supplement to the Rheinische Zeitung, *October 25, 1842*

Here Marx makes his first steps in the study of the class role of the monarchist feudal state as an instrument for the suppression of the exploited classes. He comes out as champion of the politically and socially downtrodden masses.

"IN 1842-43, AS EDITOR OF THE *RHEINISCHE ZEITUNG*, I FIRST FOUND MYSELF IN THE EMBARRASSING POSITION OF HAVING TO DISCUSS WHAT IS KNOWN AS MATERIAL INTERESTS. THE DELIBERATIONS OF THE RHINE PROVINCE ASSEMBLY ON THEFTS OF WOOD ... CAUSED ME IN THE FIRST INSTANCE TO TURN MY ATTENTION TO ECONOMIC QUESTIONS," Marx wrote later.

6

7

8

8. *Mosel peasant wine-growers at work*

9. *Karl Marx, "Justification of the Correspondent from the Mosel", Rheinische Zeitung, January 15, 1843*

An article by Marx championing the cause of the Mosel peasant wine-growers. The main idea of the article is that the reason for the misery of the people should be traced to the nature of the social system, the nature of the monarchy, in Prussia.

In the *Rheinische Zeitung* articles, Lenin observed, "WE SEE SIGNS OF MARX'S TRANSITION FROM IDEALISM TO MATERIALISM AND FROM REVOLUTIONARY DEMOCRACY TO COMMUNISM".

9

Ministerium der Geistlichen- Unterrichts- u. Medicinal-Angelegenheiten

Central-Büreau

Geheimes Staatsarchiv

Acta

betreffend

die Rheinische Zeitung.

Rep 76 I

vom October 1842.

Reponirt.
124 LL.

XII Abtheilung № 19.

10

10. The police file started in October 1842 concerning the Rheinische Zeitung

Dreading the increasing revolutionary impact made by the paper, the Prussian Government passed a decision in January 1843 to ban publication of the *Rheinische Zeitung* as from April 1, 1843. An especially rigid censorship was imposed in the intervening months. The last issue came out on March 31.

11. A cartoon portraying the Prussian ministry of the 1840s
The squirrel represents reactionary Minister of Education Eichhorn (the German word for squirrel)

11

Erklärung.

Unterzeichneter erklärt, daß er der jetzigen Censurverhältnisse wegen aus der Redaktion der "Rheinischen Zeitung" mit dem heutigen Tage ausgetreten ist.

Köln, den 17. März 1843.   Dr. Marx.

12. Marx's announcement of his resignation from the Rheinische Zeitung's editorial board
Published in the Rheinische Zeitung on March 18, 1843

"THE UNDERSIGNED DECLARES THAT, OWING TO THE PRESENT CONDITIONS OF CENSORSHIP, HE HAS RETIRED AS FROM TODAY FROM THE EDITORIAL BOARD OF THE RHEINISCHE ZEITUNG.
"COLOGNE, MARCH 17, 1843
"DR. MARX"

13. Petitions of Rheinische Zeitung readers to the King of Prussia protesting against the suppression of the paper
February 1843

Fifty-six petitions were submitted; they came from Cologne, Trier, Barmen, Bernkastel, the Mosel peasants, and so on

14

15

14. *Burial of the* Rheinische Zeitung

15. *Censor Saint-Paul's report on the activity of Karl Marx*

A page of the manuscript

"DR. MARX IS INCONTESTABLY THE THEORETICAL MASTERMIND OF THE NEWSPAPER, THE MOVING SPIRIT OF ITS THEORIES; I HAVE BECOME ACQUAINTED WITH HIM; HE IS INFINITELY FIRM IN HIS VIEWS, WHICH HAVE BECOME CONVICTIONS. OWING TO THE PRESENT CIRCUMSTANCES, HE HAS DECIDED TO LEAVE THE *RHEINISCHE ZEITUNG* AND LEAVE PRUSSIA."

16. *Prometheus Bound, an allegory on the prohibition of the* Rheinische Zeitung *by the Prussian Government*

,17

17. *Kreuznach (on the Rhine) in the mid-19th century*

In May 1843 Marx came to Kreuznach where his fiancée Jenny von Westphalen stayed with her mother, and resided there in the summer and autumn of 1843.

18. *Jenny von Westphalen (1814-1881)*

Jenny came from an aristocratic family. She had brains, character, and looks. Having fallen in love with Marx, she did not hesitate to throw her lot in with that of the young student from a family that was neither rich nor of the nobility. Karl and Jenny became secretly engaged in the summer of 1836, while their nuptials did not come until seven years later, on June 19, 1843 in Kreuznach. They lived in love and friendship as two kindred spirits for the rest of their lives. For Marx, Jenny was a loving wife, a good mother of his children, a secretary, sagacious adviser, and faithful companion.

"IF EVER WOMAN FOUND HER HIGHEST HAPPINESS IN RENDERING OTHERS HAPPY, THAT WOMAN WAS SHE."

FREDERICK ENGELS

19

21

19. Johann Ludwig von Westphalen (1770-1842), Jenny's father

Privy Councillor Ludwig von Westphalen was on friendly terms with Karl Marx's father. The children of the two families were playmates from an early age. Karl was a frequent guest of the Westphalens. A connoisseur and lover of literature, Westphalen read and knew Homer and Shakespeare in the original languages. He called Karl Marx's attention to the ideas of Saint-Simon. Karl responded with a most impetuous attachment and deep respect. It was to Ludwig von Westphalen, indeed, that he dedicated his doctoral dissertation, "To my dear fatherly friend ... as a token of filial love".

20. Caroline von Westphalen (1780-1856), Jenny's mother

21. The house in Salzwedel where Jenny was born

22. *The house in Trier where the Westphalens lived from 1816 to 1833. Marx was a frequent visitor*

23. *Marx's album of verse dedicated to Jenny, 1836*

NEVER CAN I DO IN PEACE
THAT WITH WHICH MY SOUL'S OBSESSED,
NEVER TAKE THINGS AT MY EASE;
I MUST PRESS·ON WITHOUT REST,

....

ALL THINGS I WOULD STRIVE TO WIN,
ALL THE BLESSINGS GODS IMPART,
GRASP ALL KNOWLEDGE DEEP WITHIN,
PLUMB THE DEPTHS OF SONG AND ART.

....

THEREFORE LET US RISK OUR ALL,
NEVER RESTING, NEVER TIRING;
NOT IN SILENCE DISMAL, DULL,
WITHOUT ACTION OR DESIRING;

NOT IN BROODING INTROSPECTION
BOWED BENEATH A YOKE OF PAIN,
SO THAT YEARNING, DREAM AND ACTION
UNFULFILLED TO US REMAIN.

24. *The marriage contract of Karl Marx and Jenny von Westphalen, dated June 12, 1843*

22

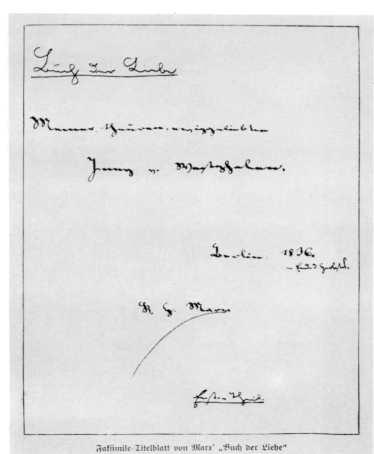

Faksimile-Titelblatt von Marx' „Buch der Liebe"

23

24

During his stay in Kreuznach, Marx did not cease his scientific studies. The main thing for him at that time was to analyse Hegel's ideas about the State and Law in a critical light.

25. Karl Marx, Contribution to the Critique of Hegel's Philosophy of Law. *Summer 1843*

A page of the manuscript

"THE FIRST WORK WHICH I UNDERTOOK TO DISPEL THE DOUBTS ASSAILING ME WAS A CRITICAL RE-EXAMINATION OF THE HEGELIAN PHILOSOPHY OF LAW... MY INQUIRY LED ME TO THE CONCLUSION THAT NEITHER LEGAL RELATIONS NOR POLITICAL FORMS COULD BE COMPREHENDED WHETHER BY THEMSELVES OR ON THE BASIS OF A SO-CALLED GENERAL DEVELOPMENT OF THE HUMAN MIND, BUT THAT ON THE CONTRARY THEY ORIGINATE IN THE MATERIAL CONDITIONS OF LIFE..."

KARL MARX

25

26

28

26. Books on the history of Britain, France, Germany, Sweden and the United States of America which Marx read in Kreuznach in the summer of 1843

Working on his critique of Hegel's philosophy of law, Marx was impelled to seek facts in world history to refute Hegel's constructions.

Seeing that the Prussian Government's reprisals ruled out revolutionary democratic activity, Marx decided to carry on abroad.

"I HAD BEGUN TO BE STIFLED IN THAT ATMOSPHERE," wrote Marx to Arnold Ruge. "IT IS A BAD THING TO HAVE TO PERFORM MENIAL DUTIES EVEN FOR THE SAKE OF FREEDOM; TO FIGHT WITH PINPRICKS, INSTEAD OF WITH CLUBS. I HAVE BECOME TIRED OF HYPOCRISY, STUPIDITY, GROSS ARBITRARINESS, AND OF OUR BOWING AND SCRAPING, DODGING, AND HAIR-SPLITTING OVER WORDS."

At the end of October 1843 Marx left Germany for Paris.

27. A cartoon exposing the persecution by the Prussian Government of those who engaged in revolutionary democratic activity

28. "Liberty in the Barricades"

29

29. *Uprising of the Lyons' weavers, 1831*

31

"FRANCE IS THE LAND WHERE, MORE THAN ANYWHERE ELSE, THE HISTORICAL CLASS STRUGGLES WERE EACH TIME FOUGHT OUT TO A DECISION... THIS WAS THE REASON WHY MARX NOT ONLY STUDIED THE PAST HISTORY OF FRANCE WITH PARTICULAR PREDILECTION, BUT ALSO FOLLOWED HER CURRENT HISTORY IN EVERY DETAIL, STORED UP THE MATERIAL FOR FUTURE USE."

FREDERICK ENGELS

30

30. *A view of Paris in the 1840s*

31. *A cartoon of Louis Philippe*

The 1830 bourgeois revolution in France placed Louis Philippe, King of the Bankers, at the helm of power. "IT WAS NOT THE FRENCH BOURGEOISIE THAT RULED UNDER LOUIS PHILIPPE," Marx wrote, "BUT *ONE FACTION OF IT*: BANKERS, STOCK-EXCHANGE KINGS, RAILWAY KINGS, OWNERS OF COAL AND IRON MINES AND FORESTS, A PART OF THE LANDED PROPRIETORS ASSOCIATED WITH THEM—THE SO-CALLED *FINANCE ARISTOCRACY*."

32

33

In Paris, Marx devoted much of his time studying the French Revolution of the end of the 18th century with the intention of writing a history of the Convention. This study contributed to the development of Marx's view of the class struggle as the crucial factor in the march of history.

32. *The French Revolution of the late 18th century. Capture of the Bastille on July 14, 1789*

33. *Summary of Levasseur's* Memoirs, *which Marx titled,* The Struggle Between the Montagnards and Girondists

34

35

34. *Maximilien Robespierre (1758-1794)—leader of the Jacobins and head of the revolutionary government (1793-94)*

35. *Camille Desmoulins (1760-1794)—French journalist, deputy to the Convention, a Jacobin*

36. *Rene Levasseur (1747-1834)—deputy to the Convention, a Jacobin, author of memoirs about the French Revolution of the late 18th century*

In Paris, Marx acquainted himself with the activity of the local revolutionary clubs, where Auguste Blanqui, who propagated utopian communism, was widely known at the time. In Paris, too, Marx set his mind to studying the works of the great utopian socialists—Saint-Simon, Fourier, and Owen—and the contemporary currents of utopian socialism and communism—those of Pierre Leroux, Étienne Cabet, and Théodore Dézamy. Later, he described them as theorists who had adroitly spotted and stigmatised the vices and crimes of bourgeois society, but were unable to show the proletariat a scientifically grounded way to emancipation.

37. Heine visiting Marx in Paris

Heinrich Heine, that great German poet, was a frequent guest of the Marxes. The poet himself confessed to the tremendous influence that Marx exercised over him. In February 1844 he wrote: "My new verse ... will now be imbued with a loftier politics."

38. The house at 38 Rue Vanneau in the Paris suburb of Saint-Germain

Here the Marxes resided from the end of October 1843 until January 1845. On May 1, 1844, their daughter Jenny, named after her mother, was born in this house.

40
41

39. Henri Saint-Simon (1760-1825)

40. Charles Fourier (1772-1837)

41. Robert Owen (1771-1858)

42. Books of the utopian socialists which Marx read in Paris in 1843 and 1844

43. Auguste Blanqui (1805-1881)

44. Pierre Leroux (1797-1871)

45. Étienne Cabet (1788-1856)

42

44
45

DEUTSCH-FRANZÖSISCHE

JAHRBÜCHER

herausgegeben

von

Arnold Ruge und Karl Marx.

1ste und 2te Lieferung.

PARIS,

IM BUREAU DER JAHRBÜCHER }
AU BUREAU DES ANNALES. } RUE VANNEAU, 22.

1844

46

46. Deutsch-Französische Jahrbücher, *the first double issue, Paris, 1844*

The only issue, a double number, of the journal came out in Paris at the end of February 1844. The determining part in drawing it up belonged to Karl Marx.

Further publication was not possible owing to the persecution by the Prussian Government (a substantial number of copies was confiscated when crossing the German border), and Marx's increasing ideological differences with co-publisher Arnold Ruge.

The double issue of the journal contained Marx's articles, "Contribution to the Critique of Hegel's Philosophy of Law. Introduction" and "On the Jewish Question", and a few of his letters; it also contained Engels's articles, "Outlines of a Critique of Political Economy" and "The Condition of England", verse by Heinrich Heine and Georg Herwegh, and other material. Marx's articles marked his final conversion from idealism to materialism and from revolutionary democracy to communism.

"MARX'S ARTICLES IN THIS JOURNAL SHOWED THAT HE WAS ALREADY A REVOLUTIONARY, WHO ADVOCATED 'MERCILESS CRITICISM OF EVERYTHING EXISTING', AND IN PARTICULAR THE 'CRITICISM BY WEAPON', AND APPEALED TO THE *MASSES* AND TO THE *PROLETARIAT*".

V. I. LENIN

47. *A meeting of Paris workers*

47

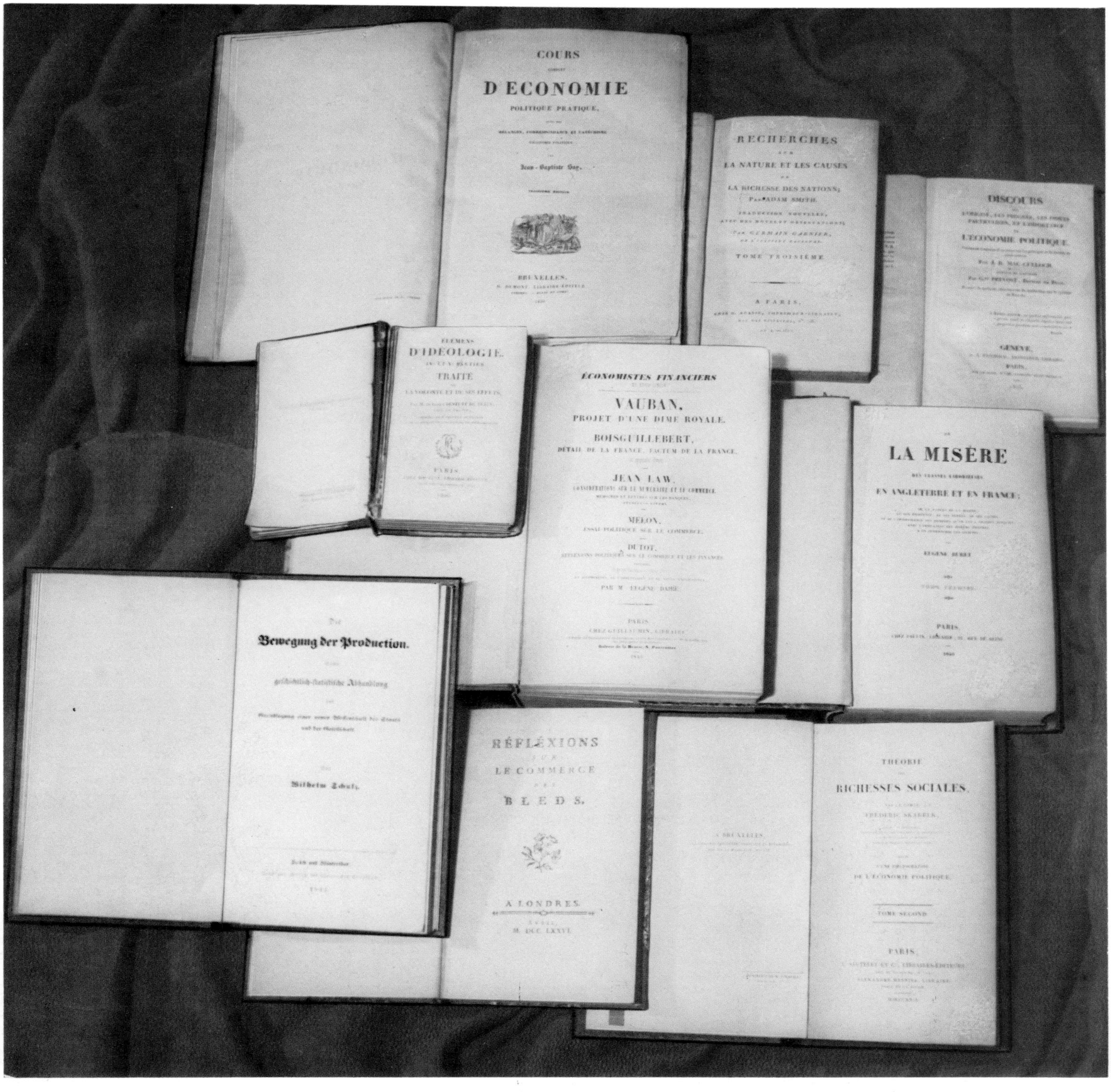

48

"YOU WOULD HAVE TO AT-
TEND ONE OF THE MEETINGS OF
THE FRENCH WORKERS TO AP-
PRECIATE THE PURE FRESH-
NESS, THE NOBILITY WHICH
BURSTS FORTH FROM THESE
TOIL-WORN MEN," Marx wrote to
Ludwig Feuerbach. "IT IS AMONG
THESE 'BARBARIANS' OF OUR
CIVILISED SOCIETY THAT HIS-
TORY IS PREPARING THE PRACTI-
CAL ELEMENT FOR THE EMANCI-
PATION OF MANKIND."

While in Paris, Marx made contact
with the League of the Just, an organisation of German émigré workers and
artisans founded in 1837, and with
secret societies which included the
foremost members of the proletariat of
Paris. But Marx joined none of the
existing secret societies, because he
was aware of the futility of their
projects and the sectarian nature of
their activity.

48. Books on political economy which
Marx read in Paris in 1843 and 1844

49

49. Karl Marx, Economic and Philosophic Manuscripts of 1844

A page of the manuscript

Ever since 1843, when Marx concluded that the anatomy of "civil society", that is, of social relations, should be traced in political economy, he accorded that subject a special place in his studies.

The results of his research of that period Marx set forth in what has come down to us as three uncompleted manuscripts written in April to August 1844. They were published for the first time in 1932 by the Institute of Marx-Engels-Lenin, of Moscow, under the title, *Economic and Philosophic Manuscripts of 1844.*

In these manuscripts Marx made it his purpose to produce a critique of private property and bourgeois political economy.

50

50. Uprising of the Silesian weavers, June 1844

51. Karl Marx, "Critical Marginal Notes on the Article 'The King of Prussia and Social Reform. By a Prussian'"
Vorwärts!, August 7, 1844

In the summer of 1844, Marx wrote prolifically for *Vorwärts!*, a German-language newspaper published in Paris. When a rising of weavers, the first open action of German workers, occurred in Silesia, *Vorwärts!* printed Marx's article, "Critical Marginal Notes on the Article 'The King of Prussia and Social Reform. By a Prussian'". Unlike the capitalist press, it stressed the immense significance the weavers' rising had for the future of the working-class movement.

"THE SILESIAN UPRISING *BEGINS* PRECISELY WITH WHAT THE FRENCH AND ENGLISH WORKERS' UPRISINGS *END*, WITH CONSCIOUSNESS OF THE NATURE OF THE PROLETARIAT...

"EVERY REVOLUTION DISSOLVES THE *OLD SOCIETY* AND TO THAT EXTENT IT IS *SOCIAL*. EVERY REVOLUTION OVERTHROWS THE *OLD POWER* AND TO THAT EXTENT IT IS *POLITICAL*."

KARL MARX

51

Frederick Engels espoused materialism and communism at the same time as Marx.

52. A view of Barmen in the 1840s

53. The house in Barmen where Engels was born on November 28, 1820

54. Frederick Engels, 1839

55

55. Engels's father, Friedrich Engels (1796-1860)

A wealthy cotton spinner, a strong-minded man of energy and enterprise, Engels's father was fiercely religious and conservative in his political outlook.

56. Engels's mother, Elisabeth Francisca Mauritzia Engels (1797-1873)

57. The birth certificate of Frederick Engels

Barmen, December 5, 1820, extract from the Barmen Register of Births, Deaths and Marriages.
"No. 659. Birth of Frederick Engels, November 28, 1820.
"In the year one thousand eight hundred and twenty, on December 5 at half past three in the afternoon, there appeared before me, *Peter Wichelhausen*, Deputy of the Parish of Barmen, the merchant Herr *Friedrich Engels* domiciled in Brucher Rotte to notify that on Tuesday, the 28th day of November at nine o'clock in the evening, his wife, *Elisabeth Francisca Mauritzia*, née *van Haar*, was delivered of a child of the male sex, to whom he gave the first name of *Friedrich*."

57

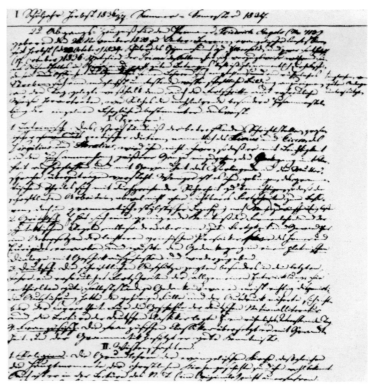

59

58. *The gymnasium in Elberfeld which Frederick Engels attended from 1834 to 1837*

59. *Reference issued to Prima Pupil Frederick Engels when he left school on September 25, 1837*

"Pupil of the Elberfeld Gymnasium since the autumn of 1834 (October 20th) and since the autumn of 1836 (October 17th) a member of the Prima of the same, has taken pains to be of *very good behaviour*, especially during his stay in the Prima form, has commended himself to his teachers particularly by his modesty, frankness and good-natured disposition, and equally displayed commendable *endeavour*, supported by good talents, to acquire the most comprehensive scientific education possible, for which reason also his *progress* has been gratifyingly conspicuous...

"The undersigned discharges with his best blessings a dear pupil ... on his going into business at the end of the school year (September 15th of this year), which he found himself induced to choose as his outward profession in life instead of the studies he had earlier intended...

"Elberfeld, September 25th, 1837
Dr. J. C. L. Hantschke "

60. *A page of Engels's exercise book on ancient history*

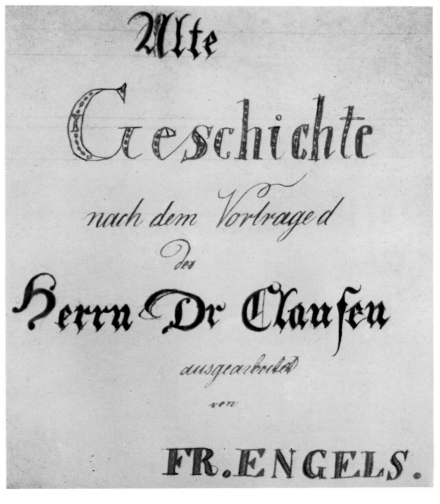

60

61. *A poem by Frederick Engels with his drawings on the margins, 1836*

62-63. *Views of Bremen in the 1840s*

Engels's father did not let his son finish the gymnasium and sent him to Bremen to learn commerce in a trading firm (1838-41).

62

Bremen von der Ostseite.

63

64. *Heinrich Heine (1797-1856)*

65. *Ludwig Bernays (1786-1837)*

Engels's vision of the world took shape under the influence of progressive ideas: he associated with a radical literary group, the Young Germany, which consisted of writers who considered themselves followers of revolutionary poet Heinrich Heine, and Ludwig Bernays, a progressive journalist.

"I MUST BECOME A YOUNG GERMAN, OF RATHER, I AM ONE ALREADY, BODY AND SOUL. I CANNOT SLEEP AT NIGHT, ALL BECAUSE OF THE IDEAS OF THE CENTURY," Engels wrote in a letter to his friend Friedrich Graeber.

Telegraph

für

Deutschland.

1839.   März.   № 49.

Briefe aus dem Wupperthal.*)

I.

Bekanntlich begreift man unter diesem bei den Freunden des Lichtes sehr verrufenen Namen die beiden Städte Elberfeld und Barmen, die das Thal in einer Länge von fast drei Stunden einnehmen. Der schmale Fluß ergießt bald rasch, bald stockend seine purpurnen Wogen zwischen rauchigen Fabrikgebäuden und garnbedeckten Bleichen hindurch; aber seine hochrothe Farbe rührt nicht von einer blutigen Schlacht her, denn hier streiten nur theologische Federn und wortreiche alte Weiber, gewöhnlich um des Kaisers Bart; auch nicht von Schaam über das Treiben der Menschen, obwohl dazu wahrlich Grund genug vorhanden ist, sondern einzig und allein von den vielen Türkischroth-Färbereien. Kommt man von Düsseldorf her, so tritt man bei Sonnborn in das heilige Gebiet; die Wupper kriecht träg und verschlammt vorbei und spannt durch ihre jämmerliche Erscheinung, dem eben verlassenen Rheine gegenüber, die Erwartungen bedeutend herab. Die Gegend ist ziemlich anmuthig; die nicht sehr hohen, bald sanft steigenden, bald schroffen Berge, über und über waldig, treten keck in die grünen Wiesen hinein, und bei schönem Wetter läßt der blaue, in der Wupper sich spiegelnde Himmel ihre rothe Farbe ganz verschwinden. Nach einer Biegung um einen Abhang sieht man die verschrobenen Thürme

*) Unsre Leser werden uns Dank wissen für diese authentische Schilderung einer Gegend, welche das wahre Zion der häßlichsten Form manchen Orten in Deutschland grassirenden und das Mark des ausmergelnden Pietismus ist.   X. d. R.

66. *Frederick Engels, "Letters from Wuppertal"*
Telegraph für Deutschland, *March 1839*

In "Letters from Wuppertal" Engels described the disastrous condition of workers and artisans: "Terrible poverty prevails among the lower classes, particularly the factory workers in Wuppertal... Diseases are so widespread as to be barely credible."

67

67. *A drawing by Frederick Engels in his letter to Wilhelm Graeber, c. April 28-30, 1839*

68. *Frederick Engels's letter to Wilhelm Graeber, c. April 28-30, 1839, written in nine languages*
A fragment of the manuscript

"WRITING A POLYGLOTIC LETTER, I WILL TAKE NOW THE ENGLISH LANGUAGE, BUT, NO, MY BEAUTIFUL ITALIAN, LOVELY AND PURE AS THE ZEPHYR, WITH WORDS LIKE FLOWERS FROM THE LOVELIEST OF GARDENS, AND SPANISH, A LANGUAGE LIKE THE WIND IN THE TREES, AND PORTUGUESE, LIKE THE RUSTLING OF THE SEA ON A SHORE OF FLOWERS AND MEADOWS, AND FRENCH, LIKE THE QUICK MURMUR OF A FOUNTAIN, VERY AMUSING, AND DUTCH, LIKE THE SMOKE FROM A PIPE OF TOBACCO, VERY COSY."

68

69

Schelling

und die

Offenbarung.

Kritik

des neuesten Reaktionsversuchs

gegen die

freie Philosophie.

Leipzig,
Robert Binder.
1842.

71

69. *The artillery brigade barracks in Berlin*

In 1841 and 1842 Engels did his military service in Berlin as a volunteer with a foot company of an artillery brigade.

In time free from military service, Engels attended lectures at Berlin University as an external student. Like Marx, he studied Hegelian philosophy, and engaged in what he called "intellectual battles" in the circle of Young Hegelians, who named themselves The Free.

70. *Title page of Frederick Engels's pamphlet* Schelling and Revelation, *Leipzig, 1842. Published without the author's name*

Here Engels comes out against the idealist philosophy of Friedrich Wilhelm Schelling who had been invited to Berlin University by the Prussian king to offset the influence of the Young Hegelians.

71. *Berlin University in the 1840s*

72. *Frederick Engels at his desk*

73

73. "The Insolently Threatened Yet Miraculously Rescued Bible or: The Triumph of Faith", a satirical poem
  Cover of the pamphlet published in Germany in 1842

The poem was written by Engels in collaboration with Edgar Bauer. It describes the Young Hegelians' struggle against a reactionary group of professors of theology in Bonn. Marx is portrayed in the poem in the following terms:

"A swarthy chap of *Trier*, a marked monstrosity.
He neither hops nor skips, but moves in leaps and bounds,
Raving aloud. As if to seize and then pull down
To Earth the spacious tent of Heaven up on high,
He opens wide his arms and reaches for the sky."

74. Engels lived in his Berlin Dorotheenstrasse lodgings from 1841 to 1842

75. *A caricature by Engels of the Berlin circle of Young Hegelians, known as "The Free", who indulged in hollow rhetoric instead of mounting a serious political offensive against Prussian authoritarianism, 1841-1842*

76. *The coffee-house in Berlin where Young Hegelians often congregated. Karl Marx and Frederick Engels visited the place too*

75

76

77

78

80

77. *Manchester in the 1840s*

On his father's insistence, Engels went to England. In Manchester he joined the cotton-spinnery "Ermen & Engels" as office clerk (1842-44).

78. Rheinische Zeitung, *No. 359, December 25, 1842, contains Engels's article, "The Condition of the Working-Class in England"*

"WHILE I WAS IN MANCHESTER," Engels wrote, "IT WAS TANGIBLY BROUGHT HOME TO ME THAT THE ECONOMIC FACTS, WHICH HAVE SO FAR PLAYED NO ROLE OR ONLY A CONTEMPTIBLE ONE IN THE WRITING OF HISTORY, ARE, AT LEAST IN THE MODERN WORLD, A DECISIVE HISTORICAL FORCE; THAT THEY FORM THE BASIS OF THE ORIGINATION OF THE PRESENT-DAY CLASS ANTAGONISMS; THAT THESE CLASS ANTAGONISMS, IN THE COUNTRIES WHERE THEY HAVE BECOME FULLY DEVELOPED, THANKS TO LARGE-SCALE INDUSTRY, HENCE ESPECIALLY IN ENGLAND, ARE IN THEIR TURN THE BASIS OF THE FORMATION OF POLITICAL PARTIES AND OF PARTY STRUGGLES, AND THUS OF ALL POLITICAL HISTORY. MARX HAD NOT ONLY ARRIVED AT THE SAME VIEW, BUT HAD ALREADY [GENERALISED IT] IN THE *GERMAN-FRENCH ANNUALS*."

79. Dwelling of an English worker in *the early half of the 19th century*

80. The Riot Act read in Manchester *during a workers' strike in August 1842*

81

82

83

UMRISSE

zu

EINER KRITIK DER NATIONALŒKONOMIE

von

Friedrich Engels in Manchester.

—

Die Nationalökonomie entstand als eine natürliche Folge der Ausdehnung des Handels, und mit ihr trat an die Stelle des einfachen, unwissenschaftlichen Schachers ein ausgebildetes System des erlaubten Betrugs, eine komplete Bereicherungswissenschaft.

Diese, aus dem gegenseitigen Neid und der Habgier der Kaufleute entstandene Nationalökonomie oder Bereicherungswissenschaft trägt das Gepräge der ekelhaftesten Selbstsucht auf der Stirne. Man lebte noch in der naiven Anschauung, dass Gold und Silber der Reichthum sei, und hatte also nichts Eiligeres zu thun, als überall die Ausfuhr der « edlen » Metalle zu verbieten. Die Nationen standen sich gegenüber wie Geizhälse, deren Jeder seinen theuren Geldsack mit beiden Armen umschliesst und mit Neid und Argwohn auf seine Nachbarn blickt. Alle Mittel wurden aufgeboten, um den Völkern, mit denen man im Handelsverkehr stand, so viel baares Geld wie möglich abzulocken, und das glücklich Hereingebrachte hübsch innerhalb der Mauthlinie zu behalten.

Die konsequenteste Durchführung dieses Prinzips hätte den Handel getödtet. Man fing also an, diese erste Stufe zu überschreiten; man sah ein, dass das Kapital im Kasten todt da liegt, während es in der Cirkulation sich stets vermehrt. Man wurde also menschenfreundlicher, man schickte seine Dukaten als Lockvögel aus, damit

81. *Striking workers clash with troops in Preston, August 1842*

82. *The Hall of Science in Manchester*

Here, in 1843, Engels attended the Sunday meetings of the followers of utopian socialist Robert Owen.

83. *Karl Marx, "Summary of Frederick Engels's article, 'Outlines of a Critique of Political Economy'", published in the* Deutsch-Französische Jahrbücher
A page of the manuscript

Marx set high value on this piece by the 24-year-old Engels. He referred to it in later years, notably in his *Capital.*

84. *Frederick Engels, "Outlines of a Critique of Political Economy"*
From the Deutsch-Französische Jahrbücher, *Paris, 1844*

Here Engels "EXAMINED THE PRINCIPAL PHENOMENA OF THE CONTEMPORARY ECONOMIC ORDER FROM A SOCIALIST STANDPOINT, REGARDING THEM AS NECESSARY CONSEQUENCES OF THE RULE OF PRIVATE PROPERTY".

V. I. LENIN

Karl Marx. His Life and Work

7. *House 5-7 on Rue de l'Alliance*

Karl Marx lived in house No. 5 from May 1845 to May 1846. His daughter Laura was born here on September 26, 1845. Frederick Engels lived in house No. 7 till June 1846.

The Belgian authorities prohibited Marx to write for the press on topics of current policy, thus denying him a chance to earn his livelihood by writing. But despite the hardships of life in exile, Marx's home was a favourite meeting place for emigrant revolutionaries and Belgian democrats.

8. *Jenny Marx in the first years after her marriage*

9. *Helene Demuth (1823-1890), devoted maid and friend of the Marx family*

In the spring of 1845, Caroline von Westphalen, Jenny's mother, sent her 22-year-old maid Helene Demuth to help her daughter. Helene took over the management of the house. All members of the Marx family were fond of her and treated her with deep respect.

10. *A page of Marx's notebook which he used in Paris and Brussels in 1844-47*

Five pages of the notebook contain eleven philosophical principles that were by all evidence put down by Marx in April 1845. Engels discovered them after Marx's death and gave them the title, "Theses on Feuerbach".

THIS WAS "THE FIRST DOCUMENT IN WHICH IS DEPOSITED THE BRILLIANT GERM OF THE NEW WORLD OUTLOOK."

FREDERICK ENGELS

"THE COINCIDENCE OF THE CHANGING OF CIRCUMSTANCES AND OF HUMAN ACTIVITY OR SELF-CHANGE CAN BE CONCEIVED AND RATIONALLY UNDERSTOOD ONLY AS *REVOLUTIONARY PRACTICE*."

FROM THESIS 3

"THE ESSENCE OF MAN ... IS THE ENSEMBLE OF THE SOCIAL RELATIONS."

FROM THESIS 6

"THE PHILOSOPHERS HAVE ONLY *INTERPRETED* THE WORLD IN VARIOUS WAYS; THE POINT IS TO *CHANGE* IT."

FROM THESIS 11

11. *A view of London in the 1840s*

In July-August 1845 Marx paid his first visit to England. He and Engels went to London and Manchester. The purpose of the visit was to study economic literature and to have a first-hand look at the most advanced of the capitalist countries and its working-class movement.

12. *The London docks*

13. *A street of the London poor*

11

13

14

14. *A view of Manchester in the 1840s*

15. *Chetham's Library in Manchester*

16. *The reading-room in Chetham's Library where Marx and Engels spent* *most of their time during their stay in Manchester in 1845*

In Chetham's Library Marx and Engels chiefly examined the works of the classics of British political economy and the utopian socialists. Later, Engels recalled those times: "In the last few days, I have often been sitting in the small bow-window where we sat 24 years ago; I like this place very much; because of its coloured window the weather is always fine there."

15

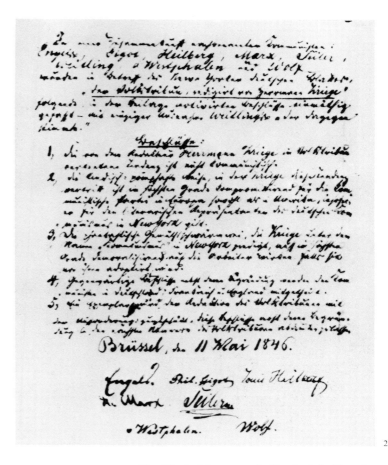

28

In early 1845 in Brussels, Marx and Engels founded the Communist Correspondence Committee. Its purpose was to establish ties and regular correspondence with socialists and other members of the labour movement in various countries. Through exchanges of opinion and criticism of mistaken views Marx and Engels strove to rally them to their scientific programme and prepare the ground for the founding of a proletarian party.

By the middle of 1846, the Brussels Communist Correspondence Committee managed to establish contacts with the Chartists in Britain, the London leadership of the League of the Just, the Paris communities of that League, and with some communist groups in Cologne and Elberfeld, and in Westphalia, Silesia, and elsewhere in Germany.

23. Wilhelm Wolff (1809-1864), member of the Brussels Communist Correspondence Committee

24. Roland Daniels (1819-1855) headed a group of Cologne Communists connected with the Brussels Communist Correspondence Committee

25. Joseph Weydemeyer (1818-1866) headed a communist group in Bielefeld connected with the Brussels Communist Correspondence Committee

26. George Julian Harney (1817-1897), member of the London Communist Correspondence Committee, a leader of the left-wing Chartists

27. Edgar von Westphalen (1819-1890), member of the Brussels Communist Correspondence Committee, Jenny Marx's brother

28. Karl Marx and Frederick Engels, "Circular against Kriege"
The Circular was adopted by the Brussels Communist Correspondence Committee on May 11, 1846
A page of the manuscript

In the "Circular", Marx and Engels criticised the German "true socialism", whose ideologists preached class peace resting on universal love of man. "The fantastic emotionalism which Kriege is preaching in New York under the name of 'communism'," Marx and Engels said, "must have an extremely damaging effect on the workers' morale if it is adopted by them."

29

29. *A workers' meeting in a tavern*

30. *Wilhelm Weitling (1808-1871), one of the early leaders of the working-class movement in Germany, theoretician of utopian egalitarian communism, a tailor*

31. *Wilhelm Weitling, Guarantees of Harmony and Freedom, 1842*
The title page

In his book, Weitling was sharply critical of capitalist society. But he did not understand the role of the class struggle, and refuted the importance of having a proletarian party or a scientific proletarian theory.

Weitling's nihilistic attitude, wrote a Russian contemporary writer, Pyotr Annenkov, in his memoirs, was likened by Marx to "a vain, dishonest posing as preacher suggesting an inspired prophet, on the one side, and on the other, only credulous asses."

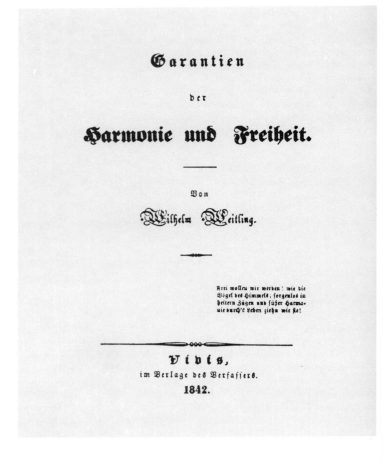

Garantien

der

Harmonie und Freiheit.

Von

Wilhelm Weitling.

Frei wollen wir werden! wie die
Vögel des Himmels; sorgenlos in
heitern Zügen und süßer Harmonie durch's Leben ziehn wie Sie!

Vivis,
im Verlage des Verfassers.
1842.

30

32

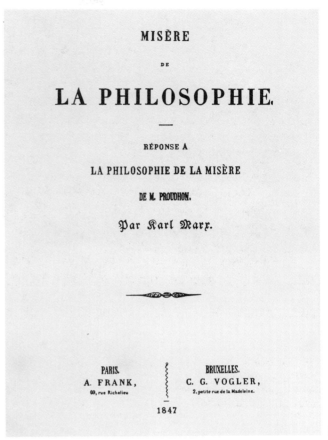

MISÈRE

DE

LA PHILOSOPHIE.

—

RÉPONSE A

LA PHILOSOPHIE DE LA MISÈRE

DE M. PROUDHON.

Par Karl Marx.

PARIS.
A. FRANK,
69, rue Richelieu

BRUXELLES.
C. G. VOGLER,
2, petite rue de la Madeleine.

1847

33

32. Pierre Joseph Proudhon (1809-1865), French petty-bourgeois socialist, theorist of anarchism

33. Karl Marx, The Poverty of Philosophy. Answer to the "Philosophy of Poverty" by M. Proudhon, *Paris-Brussels, 1847*
The title page of the first edition

The Poverty of Philosophy is one of the most important of Marx's works. It contains a scientific analysis of capitalist society's economic pillars, and a profound critique of the French petty-bourgeois socialist Proudhon's views. It also expounds for the first time the basic principles of the materialist doctrine on the objective laws of social development. The book, Marx wrote later, "contains the seeds of the theory developed after twenty years' work in *Capital*".

34. A cartoon of Pierre Joseph Proudhon

34

35

Statuten des Bundes der Kommunisten.

Proletarier aller Länder vereinigt Euch!

Abschnitt I. Der Bund.

Art. 1. Der Zweck des Bundes ist der Sturz der Bourgeoisie, die Herrschaft des Proletariats, die Aufhebung der alten, auf Klassengegensätzen beruhenden bürgerlichen Gesellschaft und die Gründung einer neuen Gesellschaft ohne Klassen und ohne Privateigentbum

Art. 2. Die Bedingungen der Mitgliedschaft sind:

A) diesem Zweck entsprechende Lebensweise und Wirksamkeit;

B) revolutionaire Energie und Eifer der Propaganda;

C) Bekenntung des Kommunismus;

D) Enthaltung der Theilnahme an jeder antikommunistischen, politischen oder nationalen Gesellschaft und Anzeige der Theilnahme an irgend welcher Gesellschaft bei der vorgesetzten Behörde;

E) Unterwerfung unter die Beschlüsse des Bundes;

F) Verschwiegenheit über das Bestehen aller Angelegenheiten des Bundes;

G) einstimmige Aufnahme in eine Gemeinde.

Wer diesen Bedingungen nicht mehr entspricht, wird ausgeschlossen. (Siehe Abschnitt VIII.)

Art. 3. Alle Mitglieder sind gleich und Brüder und als solche sich Hülfe in jeder Lage schuldig.

Art. 4. Die Mitglieder führen Bundesnamen.

Art. 5. Der Bund ist organisirt in Gemeinden, Kreisen, leitenden Kreisen, Centralbehörde und Kongresse.

36

35. The official instructions issued to Joseph Moll on January 20, 1847 by the London Committee of the League of the Just and the London Communist Correspondence Committee to negotiate the reorganisation of the League of the Just with Karl Marx and Frederick Engels

"TO THE BRUSSELS COMMUNIST CORRESPONDENCE COMMITTEE.

"THE UNDERSIGNED MEMBERS OF THE LONDON COMMUNIST CORRESPONDENCE COMMITTEE HAVE HEREBY EMPOWERED CITIZEN JOSEPH MOLL TO ENTER INTO NEGOTIATIONS WITH THE COMMUNIST CORRESPONDENCE COMMITTEE IN BRUSSELS ON THEIR BEHALF AND TO GIVE AN ORAL ACCOUNT OF THE STATE OF AFFAIRS IN LONDON.

"KARL SCHAPPER, HEINRICH BAUER, KARL PFÄNDER, FRIEDRICH DOEPEL, ALBERT LEHMANN, CHARLES MOLL, JOHANN GOEBEL"

Leaders of the League of the Just were persuaded that the ideas of Marx and Engels provided the right bearings for revolutionary action. In early 1847 they delegated Joseph Moll to offer Marx and Engels to join the League and help reorganise it in line with the principles of the new revolutionary theory. Marx and Engels consented.

"FOR THE PROLETARIAT TO BE STRONG ENOUGH TO WIN ON THE DECISIVE DAY IT MUST— AND MARX AND I HAVE ADVO-

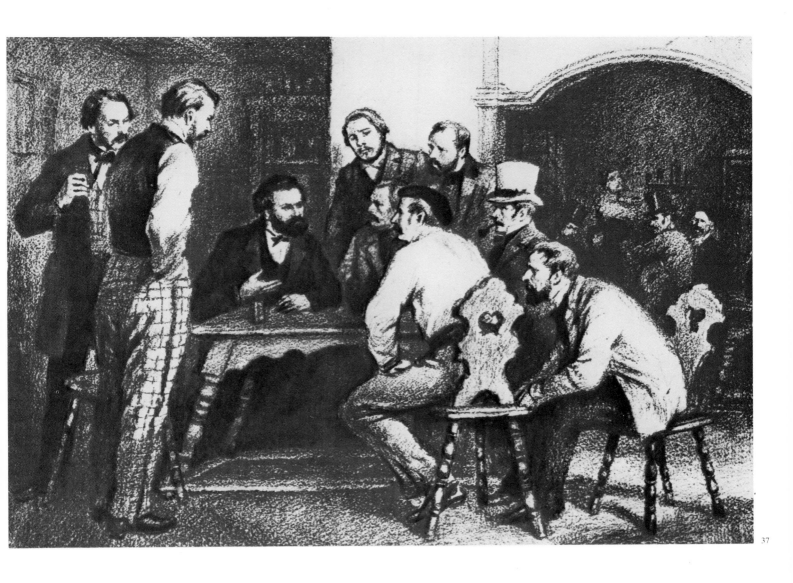

37

CATED THIS EVER SINCE 1847—
FORM A SEPARATE PARTY DIS-
TINCT FROM ALL OTHERS AND
OPPOSED TO THEM, A CON-
SCIOUS CLASS PARTY."

FREDERICK ENGELS

*36. A page of the first edition of the
Rules of the Communist League*

"THE AIM OF THE LEAGUE
IS THE OVERTHROW OF THE
BOURGEOISIE, THE RULE OF THE
PROLETARIAT, THE ABOLITION
OF THE OLD BOURGEOIS SOCIE-
TY WHICH RESTS ON THE AN-
TAGONISM OF CLASSES, AND
THE FOUNDATION OF A NEW
SOCIETY WITHOUT CLASSES AND
WITHOUT PRIVATE PROPERTY."

RULES, SECTION I, ART. 1

At the congress in June 1847, the
League of the Just was radically reor-
ganised. A new proletarian international organisation was inaugurated, named
the Communist League.

Frederick Engels and Wilhelm Wolff
came to the Congress, while Marx was
prevented from doing so by financial
difficulties.

The First Congress approved the
draft Rules of the Communist League,
which were thereupon forwarded for
discussion to communities and members of the League. The League of the
Just motto, All Men Are Brethren!,
was superseded by the rallying cry,
Working Men of All Countries, Unite!
which expressed the internationalist
and class nature of the workers' movement.

37. Marx and Engels among workers

38

Both Marx and Engels took part in the Second Congress. In the several days of discussion they stood up for the principles of scientific communism, which, indeed, prevailed. The Congress adopted the Rules unanimously, and Marx and Engels were asked to work out the Programme of the Communist League. This completed the founding of the League, the first international revolutionary party of the working class espousing scientific communism.

Friedrich Lessner, a veteran of the working-class movement and member of the League, who was present at the Congress, was deeply impressed by Marx:

"MARX WAS THEN STILL A YOUNG MAN OF 28 OR 30. HE WAS OF MEDIUM HEIGHT, BROAD-SHOULDERED, STURDILY BUILT, ENERGETIC, WITH A LARGE NOBLE FOREHEAD, THICK COAL-BLACK HAIR, AND A PENETRATING GLANCE. HIS LIPS ALREADY HAD THAT SARCASTIC TWIST WHICH HIS OPPONENTS FEARED. MARX WAS A BORN LEADER OF THE PEOPLE. HIS SPEECH WAS CURT, COHERENT, AND COMPELLINGLY LOGICAL; HE NEVER SAID A SUPERFLUOUS WORD; EACH SENTENCE WAS A THOUGHT, AND EVERY THOUGHT A NECESSARY LINK IN THE CHAIN OF HIS REASONING."

42

38. *Red Lion Hotel, Great Windmill Street, London, where the Second Congress of the Communist League was held from November 28 to December 8, 1847*

39. *The* Deutsche-Brüsseler Zeitung

Marx and Engels became its contributors from this issue on. It appeared until February 1848, and became an unofficial organ of the Communist League.

40. *A cartoon by Engels of King Frederick William IV of Prussia making his speech at the opening of the United Provincial Diet in Berlin, April 11, 1847*

Published as a supplement to the Deutsche-Brüsseler Zeitung *of May 6, 1847*

41. *Letter of the Central Authority of the Communist League to the Brussels District Committee dated October 18, 1847, requesting it to delegate Karl Marx to the League's Second Congress*
A fragment of the manuscript

42. *Marx and Engels writing the* Manifesto of the Communist Party

43. *Karl Marx and Frederick Enge...*
Manifesto of the Communist Part...
London, 1848
Cover of the first editi...

Engels described the *Manifesto of t...
Communist Party* as "THE MOS...
WIDESPREAD, THE MOST INTE...
NATIONAL PRODUCTION OF AL...
SOCIALIST LITERATURE, TH...
COMMON PLATFORM ACKNOW...
EDGED BY MILLIONS OF WOR...
ING MEN FROM SIBERIA T...
CALIFORNIA".

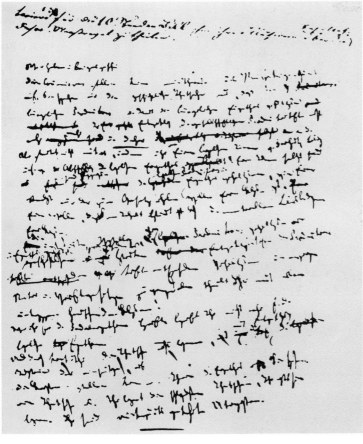

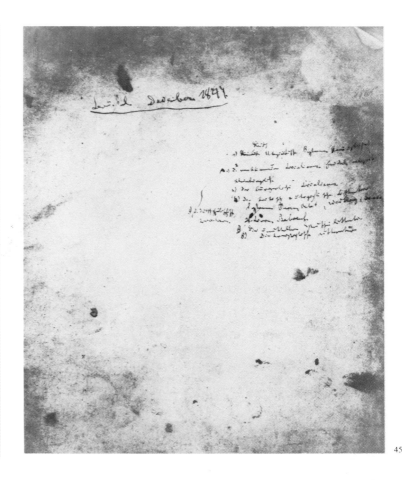

45

"THIS LITTLE BOOKLET IS WORTH WHOLE VOLUMES: TO THIS DAY ITS SPIRIT INSPIRES AND GUIDES THE ENTIRE ORGANISED AND FIGHTING PROLETARIAT OF THE CIVILISED WORLD."

V. I. LENIN

"WITH THE CLARITY AND BRILLIANCE OF GENIUS, THIS WORK OUTLINES A NEW WORLD-CONCEPTION, CONSISTENT MATERIALISM, WHICH ALSO EMBRACES THE REALM OF SOCIAL LIFE; DIALECTICS, AS THE MOST COMPREHENSIVE AND PROFOUND DOCTRINE OF DEVELOPMENT; THE THEORY OF THE CLASS STRUGGLE AND OF THE WORLD-HISTORIC REVOLUTIONARY ROLE OF THE PROLETARIAT—THE CREATOR OF A NEW, COMMUNIST SOCIETY."

V. I. LENIN

44. A page of the rough copy of the Manifesto of the Communist Party. *The first two lines were in Jenny Marx's hand*

45. *Outline plan for the third section of the* Manifesto of the Communist Party

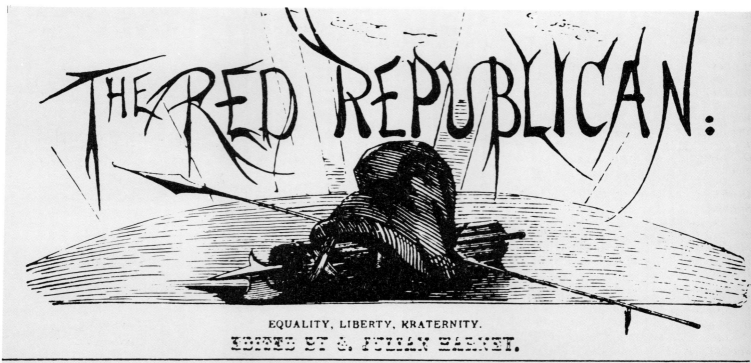

THE RED REPUBLICAN.

EQUALITY, LIBERTY, KRATERNITY.
EDITED BY G. JULIAN HARNEY.

No. 21.—Vol. I.]   SATURDAY, NOVEMBER 9, 1850.   [PRICE ONE PENNY.

German Communism.

MANIFESTO OF THE GERMAN
COMMUNIST PARTY.

(Published in February, 1848.)

Two things appear on considering these facts.
I. The ruling Powers of Europe acknowledge
Communism to be also a Power. II. It is time for
the Communists to lay before the world an account
of their aims and tendencies, and to oppose these
silly fables about the bugbear of Communism, by a
manifesto of the Communist Party.

ments of the modern Bourgeoisie. The discover
of the New World, the circumnavigation of Africa
gave the Middleclass—then coming into being—
new fields of action. The colonization of America
the opening up of the East Indian and Chinese
Markets, the Colonial Trade, the increase of com
modities generally and of the means of exchang
gave an impetus, hitherto unknown, to Commerce

46

47

Kommunismens

Röst.

Förklaring af det Kommunistiska Partiet,
offentliggjord i Februari 1848.

Folkets Röst är Guds Röst.

Pris: 8 ß. Banko.

SE PUBLICA TODOS LOS SÁBADOS.

LA EMANCIPACION.

PERIODICO SOCIALISTA

DEFENSOR DE LA INTERNACIONAL.

No mas derechos sin deberes:
No mas deberes sin derechos.

La emancipacion de los trabajadores
debe ser obra de los trabajadores mismos.

Año II.	Precio de suscricion: 4 rs. trimestre. Administracion: San Pedro, 16, 3.°	MADRID 2 DE NOVIEMBRE DE 1872.	Para suscriciones dirigirse á la librería de San Martin, Puerta del Sol.	Núm. 73.

proletariado tuvo por primera vez durante dos meses el poder político en
sus manos; esto lo esto, decimos, el programa revolucionario contenido
en el Manifiesto ha resultado en muchos de sus partes. Nos contentaremos
con citar un hecho: la Commune de Paris ha probado que «la clase obrera no
puede limitarse á entrar en posesion de la maquina del Estado completamente montada para hacerla funcionar á beneficio de sus propios fines.»
(Vid. La Guerra civil en Francia, manifiesto del Consejo general de la
Asociacion Internacional de los Trabajadores, edicion francesa de Bruselas,
pág. 17) donde está tratada esta materia mas ampliamente desarrollada). Ademas,
como se debe decir que la critica de la literatura revolucionaria está incompleta en la ac-
tualidad, puesto que solo llega hasta el año 1847, y que las observaciones
sobre la posicion de los comunistas con respecto á los diversos partidos de
la oposicion oficial (capítulo IV), bien que justas hoy todavía en sus rasgos
principales, no tienen ya ningun valor práctico, porque la situacion política
ha cambiado completamente y porque el movimiento histórico ha barrido
la mayor parte de los partidos políticos que se enumeran en el Manifiesto.

Con todo, el Manifiesto es un documento histórico, en el cual no nos
creemos con derecho á introducir alteraciones. Quizás salga á luz otra edicion acompañada de una introduccion que tendrá por objeto llenar el vacío
que separa ahora el año de 1847 del año de 1872.

K. Marx.—F. Engels.

Lóndres 24 de junio de 1872.

MANIFIESTO DEL PARTIDO COMUNISTA.

Europa está acosada por un fantasma, por el fantasma del comunismo.
Todos los poderes de la vieja Europa se han unido en santa cruzada con-
tra este fantasma: el papa y el czar, Metternich y Guizot, los radicales fran-
ceses y los polizontes alemanes. ¿Dónde está la oposicion que no haya sido
acusada de comunismo por sus enemigos en el poder? ¿Y dónde está la op-
sicion que no haya lanzado esta acusacion al rostro de sus opositores mas
avanzados, lo mismo que de sus enemigos reaccionarios? Dos cosas se des-
prenden de la consideracion de estos hechos:

I. Las potencias oficiales de Europa reconocen el comunismo como una
potencia.

II. Es hora ya, para los comunistas, de proclamar abiertamente ante el
mundo sus miras, sus tendencias y sus fines; de oponer á esos fabulas ri-
dículas sobre el espantajo del comunismo con un Manifiesto del partido co-
munista.

Con este objeto, los comunistas de diferentes nacionalidades se han
reunido en Lóndres y han redactado el Manifiesto siguiente, que será publi-

46. The first edition of the Manifesto in English

Printed in the Chartist Red Republican in 1850. The introduction by Julian Harney, the journal's editor, first named the authors of the Manifesto—Marx and Engels

47. The first edition of the Manifesto in Swedish, put out in Stockholm in 1848 under the title Voice of Communism. *Declaration of the Communist Party made in February 1848*

48. The first edition of the Manifesto in Spanish

It appeared in La Emancipacion, organ of the First International, in Madrid in 1872. The translator was José Mesa, a member of the First International

49. A Russian-language edition of the Manifesto appeared in Geneva in 1882 in a translation by Georgi Plekhanov

Marx and Engels wrote a preface specially for it

50. An edition of the Manifesto in Italian with a preface by Engels. It was published in Milan in 1893 in a translation by P. Bettini

51. The Manifesto in Polish, with a preface by Engels. Put out in London in 1892

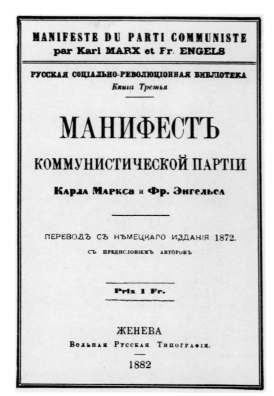

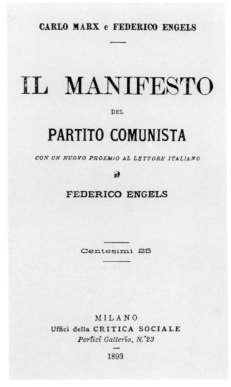

52. The first edition of the Manifesto in French between separate covers. Paris, 1895

Translated by Laura Lafargue, Marx's daughter. The edition was revised by Engels

53. The Manifesto in Czech, put out in Vienna in 1893. The translation was by A. Radimski, a Czech Social-Democrat. The facsimile is of a copy presented to Frederick Engels by the Czech Socialists

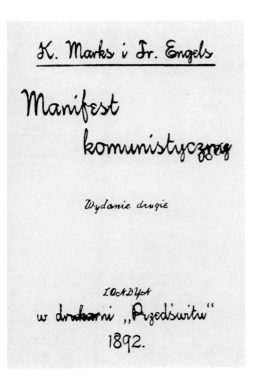

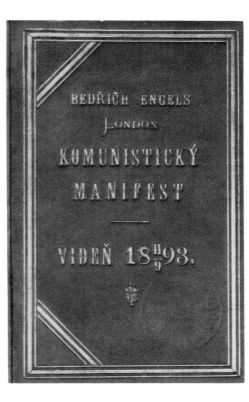

54. *Marx's portrait with a page of the* Manifesto of the Communist Party *as the background*

A leaflet

The leaflet was circulated among participants in the revolutionary movement in Russia.

56. *Karl Marx, "Wages", 1847*
A fragment of the manuscript

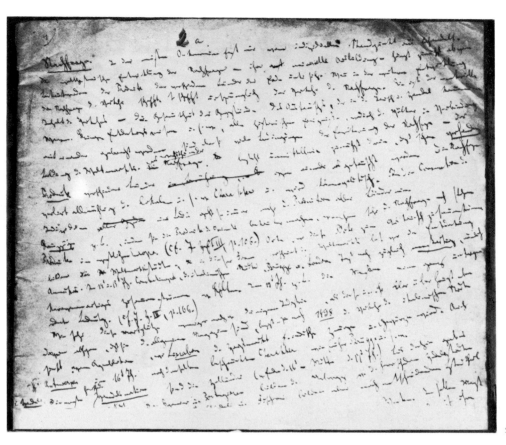

DISCOURS

SUR LA QUESTION

DU LIBRE ÉCHANGE,

PRONONCÉ A

L'ASSOCIATION DÉMOCRATIQUE

DE BRUXELLES,

Dans la Séance Publique du 9 Janvier 1848,

PAR CHARLES MARX.

———

Imprimé aux frais de l'Association Démocratique.

———

Messieurs,

L'abolition des lois céréales en Angleterre est le plus grand ...omphe que le libre échange ait remporté au 19ᵐᵉ siècle. Dans ...us les pays où les fabricants parlent de libre échange ils ont ...incipalement en vue le libre échange des grains et des matières ...emières en général. Frapper de droits protecteurs les grains ...rangers, c'est infâme, c'est spéculer sur la famine des peuples.

To maintain contact with the workers, Marx held, the secret organisation of the Communist League had to have a network of legal workers' associations. "The League standing behind the public educational associations, and guiding them," Marx wrote later, "found them to be a most convenient forum for public propaganda, and also a reservoir whose most useful members could replenish and swell its own ranks."

On the initiative of Marx and Engels, a German Workers' Society was organised in Brussels at the end of August 1847. The leading part in it was played by members of the Communist League. Marx was among the most active of them. In the latter half of December he delivered a series of lectures at the Society on political economy. What was evidently a rough outline of the unpublished part of these lectures, a manuscript entitled "Wages", is extant.

55. *The house on Rue de la Tête d'Or in Brussels where the Democratic Association was founded in September 1847*

The Democratic Association, which encompassed proletarian revolutionaries and the foremost of the bourgeois and petty-bourgeois democrats, was founded in Belgium, the refuge of émigrés from all over Europe. Marx and Engels took a most conspicuous part in launching the Association. Indeed, Marx was its vice-president.

57. *Karl Marx,* Speech on the Question of Free Trade, *published in Brussels in early February 1848*

The title page

This speech was delivered at a public meeting of the Brussels Democratic Association on January 9, 1848.

1848-1849

In the activities of Marx and Engels the period of their participation in the mass revolutionary struggle of 1848-49 stands out as the central point.

V. I. Lenin

Revolutions are the locomotives of history.

Karl Marx

1. *Clashes at the approaches to the royal palace in Paris. Capture of the Château d'Eau on February 24, 1848*

2

3

On February 24, 1848, the people of Paris overthrew Louis Philippe, King of the Bankers, and France became a republic.

On March 13, a revolution erupted in Vienna, and on March 18 barricades were thrown up in Berlin, capital of Prussia. The people of Milan, Venice, Piedmont and Rome were in open rebellion. Revolutionary movements sprang up in Spain, Hungary, Bohemia, and Poland.

2. Insurgents overturn the royal throne in the Tuileries on February 24, 1848

3. A cartoon of Louis Philippe fleeing on February 24, 1848

4. Students, workers and craftsmen demand Metternich's resignation. Vienna, March 13, 1848

5. Fighting on barricades in Berlin on March 18 and 19, 1848

4

5

6. Italian national flag being raised in Venice on March 17, 1848, as revolution erupts in Italy

7. People demonstrating in Pest in March 1848, as revolution seizes Hungary

8. Revolution in Spain. Madrid, May 7, 1848

9. Chartists demonstrate in London on April 10, 1848 demanding adoption of the People's Charter

Word of the outbreak of a revolution in France reached Marx and Engels in Brussels. Engels wrote as follows of the sentiment that prevailed in the Belgian capital: "The excitement and inquietude was universal in this town on the evening of that day... The railway station was crowded with people of all classes, anxious for the arrival of news... At half-past twelve at night, the train arrived, with the glorious news of Thursday's revolution, and the whole mass of people shouted, in one sudden outburst of enthusiasm: *Vive la République!* The news spread rapidly all over the town."

Friedrich Lessner, a German worker and member of the Communist League, recollected: "We were in a state of elation and delight. We had just one urge and thought: To sacrifice everything for the liberation of humankind!"

7

8

9

A large part of the inheritance he had received on his father's death, Marx contributed for the purchase of arms for the Brussels workers.

The Belgian government, like the Prussian and French governments before it, organised police reprisals against Marx. He and his wife were arrested and put in Amigo prison. After being interrogated, they were released and ordered out of Belgium along with other émigrés. By that time the reactionary French government had been deposed, and Marx set out for revolutionary Paris.

Samedi 4 Mars 1848.

LA REFORME

PRIX DE L'ABONNEMENT.

PRIX DES INSERTIONS.

Aux citoyens membres du Gouvernement provisoire de la République française.

Bruxelles, le 28 février 1848.

Citoyens,

L'association démocratique ayant pour but l'union et la fraternité de tous les peuples, établie depuis quelque temps à Bruxelles et composée des membres de plusieurs nations de l'Europe jouissant avec les Belges, sur le sol de ceux-ci, d'institutions qui permettent déjà depuis longtemps l'expression libre et publique de toutes les opinions politiques et religieuses, cette association vient vous offrir l'hommage de ses félicitations pour la grande tâche que vient d'accomplir la nation française, et de sa gratitude pour l'immense service que cette nation vient de rendre à la cause de l'humanité.

Nous avons eu déjà l'occasion de féliciter les Suisses d'avoir préludé, comme ils l'ont fait naguère, à l'œuvre de l'émancipation des peuples, qu'il vous appartenait de poursuivre avec la vigueur que l'héroïque population de Paris déploie toujours lorsque son tour est venu. Nous comptions bien en avoir sans grand retard le droit de renouveler auprès des Français notre démarche auprès des Suisses. Mais la France a devancé de beaucoup le temps où nous espérions avoir à nous adresser à elle. Ce n'est, au reste, qu'une raison pour que toutes les nations hâtent désormais le pas pour vous suivre.

Nous croyons pouvoir conjecturer avec certitude que celles qui touchent le plus près la France seront les premières à la suivre dans la carrière où elle vient d'entrer.

Cette conjecture est d'autant plus certaine que la France vient de faire une Révolution destinée bien plus à resserrer les liens qui la joignent à toutes les nations, qu'à menacer aucune de celles-ci dans son indépendance. C'est l'exemple des peuples que nous saluons dans la France de février 1848, et non leur puissance. La France désormais n'attendra plus d'autre hommage.

Nous voyons déjà la grande nation dont vous dirigez aujourd'hui les destinées avec la seule autorité de la confiance de tous; nous la voyons déjà, citoyens, renouer même avec les peuples qu'elle a considérés longtemps comme des rivaux de puissance, une alliance que l'odieuse politique de quelques hommes était seule parvenue à ébranler. L'Angleterre, l'Allemagne, tendent de nouveau la main à votre grand pays. L'Espagne, l'Italie, la Suisse, la Belgique vont ou se relever ou se reposer tranquilles et libres sous votre égide. La Pologne ressuscitera comme Lazare à l'appel que vous allez faire dans un triple langage.

Il est impossible que la Russie elle-même n'y vienne pas mêler enfin des accens que l'oreille des peuples occidentaux et méridionaux ne connaît encore qu'imparfaitement. A vous, Français, à vous l'honneur, à vous la gloire d'avoir jeté les principaux fondemens de cette alliance des peuples si prophétiquement chantée par votre immortel Béranger.

Nous vous offrons, citoyens, dans toute l'effusion des sentimens d'une fraternité immuable, le tribut de notre plus profonde reconnaissance.

Le comité de l'association démocratique ayant pour but l'union et la fraternité de tous les peuples, établi à Bruxelles.

Signé : Jottrand, avocat, président; Ch. Marx, vice-président; général Mellinet, président d'honneur; Spilthoorn, avocat, président de la société démocratique de Gand; Maynz, professeur à l'université de Bruxelles; Lelewel; Bailliu, trésorier; Bataille, vice-secrétaire; Pelerning, ouvrier; Loriau, négociant.

Cette adresse a été présentée ce matin au Gouvernement provisoire de la République française, par MM. Spilthoorn, délégué de la démocratie belge, et Braas, avocat démocrate à Namur.

10. *Rescript of Leopold I, King of the Belgians, for Marx's expulsion from Belgium*

11. *Marx arrested in Brussels*

12. *Amigo prison in Brussels, where Marx and his wife were detained*

13. *The courthouse in Brussels where Jenny Marx was interrogated on March 4, 1848*

14. *An address signed by Marx, hailing the French Republic*
   La Reforme, *March 4, 1848*

15. *A detachment of volunteers in one of the chambers of the Hôtel de Ville in Paris, 1848*

16

17

16. *The letter from Ferdinand Flocon, member of the Provisional Government of the French Republic, inviting Marx to return to France*

"PARIS, MARCH 1, 1848
"HONEST AND WORTHY MARX,
"THE SOIL OF THE FRENCH REPUBLIC IS A PLACE OF ASYLUM FOR ALL FRIENDS OF FREEDOM. TYRANNY EXPELLED YOU, A FREE FRANCE OPENS ITS DOORS TO YOU ONCE MORE."

17. *A mass demonstration in the square outside the Hôtel de Ville in Paris on March 17, 1848*

18. *A page of the minutes of a sitting of the Paris communities of the Communist League on March 8 and 9, 1848, in Marx's handwriting*

19. *The letter which Marx and Engels sent Étienne Cabet, a French journalist, at the end of March 1848*

In the letter Marx and Engels object against the activity of the German Democratic Society in Paris and its plans to "export" revolution to Germany.

19

Forderungen der Kommunistischen Partei in Deutschland.

„Proletarier aller Länder vereinigt Euch!"

1. Ganz Deutschland wird zu einer einigen, untheilbaren Republik erklärt.

2. Jeder Deutsche, der 21 Jahre alt ist, ist Wähler und wählbar, vorausgesetzt daß er keine Kriminalstrafe erlitten hat.

3. Die Volksvertreter werden besoldet, damit auch der Arbeiter im Parlament des deutschen Volkes sitzen könne.

4. Allgemeine Volksbewaffnung. Die Armeen sind in Zukunft zugleich Arbeiter-Armeen, so daß das Heer nicht blos, wie früher, verzehrt, sondern noch mehr produzirt, als seine Unterhaltungskosten betragen.
Dieß ist außerdem ein Mittel zur Organisation der Arbeit.

5. Die Gerechtigkeitspflege ist unentgeltlich.

6. Alle Feudallasten, alle Abgaben, Frohnden, Zehnten, etc., die bisher auf dem Landvolke lasteten, werden ohne irgend eine Entschädigung abgeschafft.

7. Die fürstlichen und andern feudalen Landgüter, alle Bergwerke, Gruben, u. s. w., werden in Staatseigenthum umgewandelt. Auf diesen Landgütern wird der Ackerbau im Großen und mit den modernsten Hilfsmitteln der Wissenschaft zum Vortheil der Gesamtheit betrieben.

8. Die Hypotheken auf den Bauerngütern werden für Staatseigenthum erklärt. Die Zinsen für jene Hypotheken werden von den Bauern an den Staat gezahlt.

9. In den Gegenden, wo das Pachtwesen entwickelt ist, wird die Grundrente oder der Pachtschilling als Steuer an den Staat gezahlt.

Alle diese unter 6, 7, 8 und 9 angegebenen Maaßregeln werden gefaßt, um öffentliche und andere Lasten der Bauern und kleinen Pächter zu vermindern, ohne die zur Bestreitung der Staatskosten nöthigen Mittel zu schmälern und ohne die Produktion selbst zu gefährden.

Der eigentliche Grundeigenthümer, der weder Bauer noch Pächter ist, hat an der Produktion gar keinen Antheil. Seine Konsumtion ist daher ein bloßer Mißbrauch.

10. An die Stelle aller Privatbanken tritt eine Staatsbank, deren Papier gesetzlichen Kurs hat.
Diese Maaßregel macht es möglich, das Kreditwesen im Interesse des ganzen Volkes zu regeln und untergräbt damit die Herrschaft der großen Geldmänner. Indem sie nach und nach Papiergeld an die Stelle von Gold und Silber setzt, verwohlfeilert sie das unentbehrliche Instrument des bürgerlichen Verkehrs, das allgemeine Tauschmittel, und erlaubt, das Gold und Silber nach außen hin wirken zu lassen. Diese Maaßregel ist schließlich nothwendig, um die Interessen der konservativen Bourgeois an die Revolution zu knüpfen.

11. Alle Transportmittel: Eisenbahnen, Kanäle, Dampfschiffe, Wege, Posten, ꝛc., nimmt der Staat in seine Hand. Sie werden in Staatseigenthum umgewandelt und der unbemittelten Klasse zur unentgeltlichen Verfügung gestellt.

12. In der Besoldung sämmtlicher Staatsbeamten findet kein anderer Unterschied statt, als der, daß diejenigen mit Familie, also mit mehr Bedürfnissen, auch ein höheres Gehalt beziehen als die Uebrigen.

13. Völlige Trennung der Kirche vom Staate. Die Geistlichen aller Konfessionen werden lediglich von ihrer freiwilligen Gemeinde besoldet.

14. Beschränkung des Erbrechts.

15. Einführung von starken Progressivsteuern und Abschaffung der Konsumtionssteuern.

16. Errichtung von Nationalwerkstätten. Der Staat garantirt allen Arbeitern ihre Existenz und versorgt die zur Arbeit Unfähigen.

17. Allgemeine, unentgeltliche Volkserziehung.

Es liegt im Interesse des deutschen Proletariats, des kleinen Bürger- und Bauernstandes, mit aller Energie an der Durchsetzung obiger Maaßregeln zu arbeiten. Denn nur durch Verwirklichung derselben können die Millionen, die bisher in Deutschland von einer kleinen Zahl ausgebeutet wurden und die man weiter in der Unterdrückung zu erhalten suchen wird, zu ihrem Recht und zu derjenigen Macht gelangen, die ihnen, als den Hervorbringern alles Reichthums, gebührt.

Das Comite:
Karl Marx. Karl Schapper. H. Bauer. F. Engels.
J. Moll. W. Wolff.

20

On receiving word of the events that had erupted in Germany, Marx and Engels, who were in Paris, worked out a concrete, scientifically based programme for the German proletariat in the bourgeois-democratic revolution, entitled, *Demands of the Communist Party in Germany.* Published as a leaflet, it was popularised at meetings of workers' associations and distributed among workers and craftsmen.

The main demands, consonant with the historical objectives of the German revolution, were: to put an end to the aftermaths of feudalism, to do away with large landed estates, to form a single and indivisible German republic, to democratise the political system through the establishment of people's representative bodies, to arm the people, to introduce free education, to nationalise feudal estates, mines, and transport, and to take appropriate action in order to provide all workers with jobs.

21

22

23

20. Demands of the Communist Party in Germany—*the political platform of the Communist League in the German revolution*

Written by Marx and Engels in March 1848 and printed as a leaflet in Paris at the end of March 1848

21. *Barricades on the Kronen- and Friedrichstrasse, Berlin, on March 18, 1848*

22. *A view of Cologne in the mid-19th century*

23. *Unter Hutmacher, the street in the old part of Cologne where the* Neue Rheinische Zeitung *had its editorial offices and printing plant*

In April 1848, Marx and Engels went to Cologne to take direct part in the German revolution.

There had already been a strong community of the Communist League in that city when the revolution broke out, and thanks to the *Code Napoléon* that was operating in Rhine Province, the press there had more freedom than anywhere else in Germany. This was why Cologne was picked as the seat of the Communist League's Central Authority, where it would launch a daily revolutionary newspaper. The daily was given the name *Neue Rheinische Zeitung*, whose first issue came out on June 1, 1848.

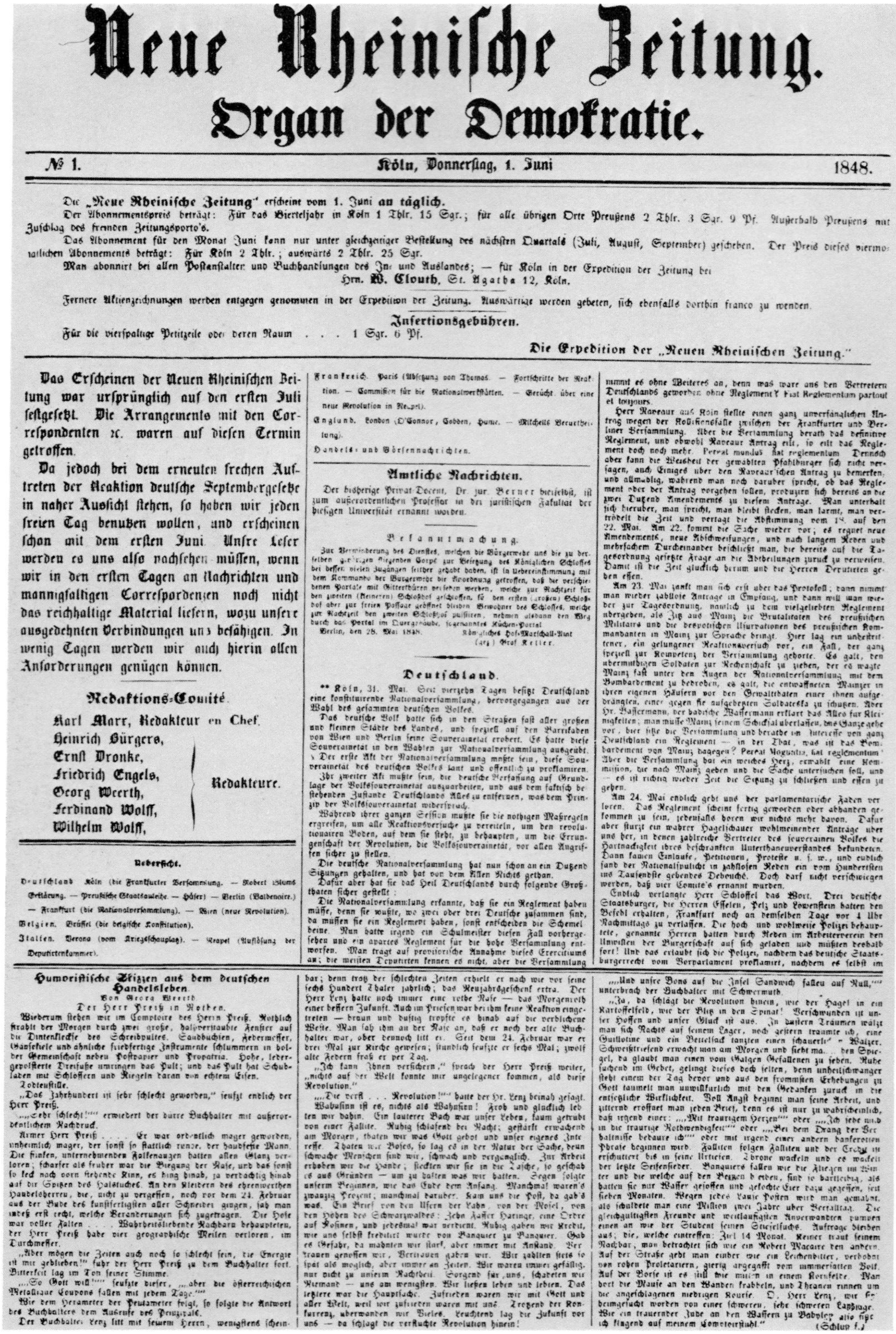

Neue Rheinische Zeitung.
Organ der Demokratie.

№ 1. Köln, Donnerstag, 1. Juni 1848.

Die „Neue Rheinische Zeitung" erscheint vom 1. Juni an täglich.

Der Abonnementspreis beträgt: Für das Vierteljahr in Köln 1 Thlr. 15 Sgr.; für alle übrigen Orte Preußens 2 Thlr. 3 Sgr. 9 Pf. Außerhalb Preußens mit Zuschlag des fremden Zeitungsporto's.

Das Abonnement für den Monat Juni kann nur unter gleichzeitiger Bestellung des nächsten Quartals (Juli, August, September) geschehen. Der Preis dieses viermonatlichen Abonnements beträgt: Für Köln 2 Thlr.; auswärts 2 Thlr. 25 Sgr.

Man abonnirt bei allen Postanstalten und Buchhandlungen des In- und Auslandes; — für Köln in der Expedition der Zeitung bei Hrn. W. Clouth, St. Agatha 12, Köln.

Fernere Aktienzeichnungen werden entgegen genommen in der Expedition der Zeitung. Auswärtige werden gebeten, sich ebenfalls dorthin franco zu wenden.

Insertionsgebühren.

Für die vierspaltige Petitzeile oder deren Raum . . . 1 Sgr. 6 Pf.

Die Expedition der „Neuen Rheinischen Zeitung."

Das Erscheinen der Neuen Rheinischen Zeitung war ursprünglich auf den ersten Juli festgesetzt. Die Arrangements mit den Correspondenten rc. waren auf diesen Termin getroffen.

Da jedoch bei dem erneuten frechen Auftreten der Reaktion deutsche Septembergesetze in naher Aussicht stehen, so haben wir jeden freien Tag benutzen wollen, und erscheinen schon mit dem ersten Juni. Unsre Leser werden es uns also nachsehen müssen, wenn wir in den ersten Tagen an Nachrichten und mannigfaltigen Correspondenzen noch nicht das reichhaltige Material liefern, wozu unsere ausgedehnten Verbindungen uns befähigen. In wenig Tagen werden wir auch hierin allen Anforderungen genügen können.

Redaktions-Comité.

Karl Marx, Redakteur en Chef.
Heinrich Bürgers,
Ernst Dronke,
Friedrich Engels,
Georg Weerth,
Ferdinand Wolff,
Wilhelm Wolff, — Redakteure.

Uebersicht.

Deutschland. Köln (die Frankfurter Versammlung. — Robert Blums Erklärung. — Preußische Staatsanleihe. — Hüser) — Berlin (Baldenaire.) — Frankfurt (die Nationalversammlung). — Wien (neue Revolution).

Belgien. Brüssel (die belgische Konstitution).

Italien. Verona (vom Kriegsschauplatz). — Neapel (Auflösung der Deputirtenkammer).

Frankreich. Paris (Absetzung von Thomas. — Fortschritte der Reaktion. — Commission für die Nationalwerkstätten. — Gerücht über eine neue Revolution in Neapel).

England. London (O'Connor, Cobden, Hume. — Mitchells Verurtheilung).

Handels- und Börsennachrichten.

Amtliche Nachrichten.

Bekanntmachung.

Deutschland.

Humoristische Skizzen aus dem deutschen Handelsleben.
Von Georg Weerth.
Der Herr Preiß in Rothen.

24. *The first issue of the* Neue Rheinische Zeitung. Organ der Demokratie, *June 1, 1848*

The paper appeared daily from June 1, 1848 to May 19, 1849. Lenin described it as "the finest and unsurpassed organ of the revolutionary proletariat". Marx was its editor-in-chief.

"THE EDITORIAL CONSTITUTION WAS SIMPLY THE DICTATORSHIP OF MARX. A BIG DAILY PAPER, WHICH HAS TO BE READY AT A DEFINITE HOUR, CANNOT OBSERVE A CONSISTENT POLICY WITH ANY OTHER CONSTITUTION. MOREOVER, MARX'S DICTATORSHIP WAS A MATTER OF COURSE HERE, WAS UNDISPUTED AND WILLINGLY RECOGNISED BY ALL OF US. IT WAS PRIMARILY HIS CLEAR VISION AND FIRM ATTITUDE THAT MADE THIS PUBLICATION THE MOST FAMOUS GERMAN NEWSPAPER OF THE YEARS OF REVOLUTION."

FREDERICK ENGELS

Editors of the *Neue Rheinische Zeitung*

25. *Karl Marx, editor-in-chief*

26. *Frederick Engels, Marx's closest assistant*

27. *Wilhelm Wolff (1809-1864), member of the Central Authority of the Communist League and assistant editor*

28. *Georg Weerth (1822-1856), German proletarian poet and journalist, member of the Communist League*

29. *Ernst Dronke (1822-1891), German journalist, member of the Communist League*

25
26

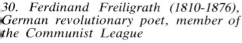

28
29

30. *Ferdinand Freiligrath (1810-1876), German revolutionary poet, member of the Communist League*

31. *Heinrich Bürgers (1820-1878), German journalist, member of the Communist League*

In many ways, the editorial staff of the *Neue Rheinische Zeitung* exercised the functions of the Communist League's Central Authority. It set and explained the tasks of the proletariat in the revolution, and directed League members taking part in the revolutionary events in various other cities of Germany as to what they were expected to do.

30
31

32

33

In their articles in the *Neue Rheinische Zeitung*, Marx and Engels exposed the counter-revolutionary postures of the German bourgeoisie, which had, as one article said, "concluded a defensive and offensive alliance with the reactionary forces, because it was afraid of the people". They called on the mass of the people to carry on with the revolution and to reach deeper. They told the workers that "the present movement is only the prologue to another movement a thousand times more serious, in which the issue will concern their own, the workers', most vital interests".

32. Capture of the armoury in Berlin on June 14, 1848

On June 10, the majority in the Prussian National Assembly opposed official acknowledgement of the results of the March 18 revolution. This angered the workers and petty-bourgeois democrats in Berlin.

On June 14, 1848, Berlin's workers and craftsmen captured the armoury, so as to defend the gains of the revolution with arms in hand.

33. Karl Marx, Rough outline of the fourth of his series of articles, The Bourgeoisie and the Counter-Revolution, *which appeared in the* Neue Rheinische Zeitung *on December 31, 1848*
Facsimile of a page of the manuscript

34. "To my beloved Berliners..."

A cartoon of Prussian King Frederick William IV, who addressed a hypocritical appeal to the people at the time of the June uprising in Berlin.

34

35

35. Engels's cartoon of the Prussian bourgeoisie and Frederick William IV. January 1849

36

Neue Rheinische Zeitung.
Organ der Demokratie.

№ 7.   Köln, Mittwoch 7. Juni   1848.

Deutschland.

** Köln, 6. Juni. Wir haben unſern Leſern geſtern das „mo-
tivirte Maniſeſt der radikal-demokratiſchen Partei in der konſtitui-
renden Nationalverſammlung zu Frankfurt am Main" mitgetheilt.
Unter der Rubrik Frankfurt finden ſie heute das Maniſeſt der Lin-
ken. Beide Maniſeſte ſcheinen ſich auf den erſten Blick kaum anders zu unterſcheiden als formell, indem die radikal-demokratiſche
Partei einen unbeholfenen und die Linke einen gewandten Redakteur

37

38

Marx and Engels resorted to satire, a weapon of
devastating power, to attack and expose the all-German
National Assembly in Frankfort on the Main, which had
been convened to create a united German state and work
out an all-German Constitution. The Assembly, which
dreaded the revolution, stood aloof from the democratic
movement and proved incapable of unifying Germany.
Engels wrote later: "We exposed the parliamentary cretin-
ism ... of the various so-called National Assemblies."

36. *Three professors drafting the Imperial Constitution*
    A cartoon on the work of the Frankfurt Assembly

37. Neue Rheinische Zeitung, *June 7, 1848. This issue
contained Marx's and Engels's article, "The Programmes of
the Radical-Democratic Party and of the Left at Frankfurt"*

"A Constituent National Assembly must above all be an
active, revolutionary active assembly. The Assembly at
Frankfurt is engaged in schoolbook parliamentary exercises
and leaves it to the governments to act."

Karl Marx and Frederick Engels

38. *The Frankfurt National Assembly*

For the revolution to make headway, Marx and Engels
held, it had to involve the mass of peasants in the battle
against the surviving elements of feudalism in Germany.
The *Neue Rheinische Zeitung* called on the peasants to
fight for the complete and uncompensated abolition of all
feudal duties.

39

41

In the *Neue Rheinische Zeitung*, Marx and Engels came out in support of progressive national liberation movements abroad. They pointed out that the struggle for the liberation of oppressed nationalities was part of the general democratic struggle, and an asset of the European revolution.

41. *Fighting in Milan on March 22, 1848*

42. *Marx's letter to the editor of* L'Alba, *an Italian democratic newspaper. It was published in the paper on June 29, 1848*

"WE SHALL DEFEND THE CAUSE OF ITALIAN INDEPENDENCE, WE SHALL FIGHT TO THE DEATH AUSTRIAN DESPOTISM IN ITALY AS IN GERMANY AND POLAND."

KARL MARX

43. *Giuseppe Garibaldi (1807-1882) headed the struggle for Italy's national liberation*

44. *Garibaldi's detachment in battle*

45. *Alexander Herzen,* Letters from France and Italy, *London, 1855*

46. *Alexander Herzen (1812-1870), Russian revolutionary democrat, materialist philosopher, journalist and writer*

A witness of the events in France and Italy, Herzen described the revolutionary developments in those countries in his *Letters*. His account abounds in stirring character studies of the more conspicuous revolutionaries.

44

ПИСЬМА

ИЗЪ ФРАНЦІИ И ИТАЛІИ

(1847—1852)

ИСКАНДЕРА

ЛОНДОНЪ

TRÜBNER & Co.
12, Paternoster Row,
CITY

FRANZ THIMM
3, Brook Street, Grosvenor
Square

1855.

45

46

47

48

The *Neue Rheinische Zeitung* championed the cause of the uprising in Posen, exposing the disgraceful behaviour of the Prussian government, which had launched full-scale military operations against practically unarmed Poles. The paper wrote angrily of how brutally Prussian troops shot down insurgent peasants.

The *Neue Rheinische Zeitung* also took the side of the Czechs and Hungarians fighting for national liberation.

47. Battle between Polish insurgents and the Prussian army at Rogalin, May 8, 1848

48. Neue Rheinische Zeitung, July 3, 1848
This issue contains Engels's article, "Germany's Foreign Policy"

"GERMANY WILL LIBERATE HERSELF TO THE EXTENT TO WHICH SHE SETS FREE NEIGHBOURING NATIONS."

FREDERICK ENGELS

49. A barricade beside the bridge tower on the Old Town side of the Vltava, during the Prague uprising of June 12-17, 1848

50. Josef Vaclav Frič (1829-1890), Czech revolutionary democrat, a leader of the Prague uprising in 1848

50

51. *Frederick Engels, "The Democratic Character of the Uprising"*
From the Neue Rheinische Zeitung, *June 25, 1848*

The article is devoted to the Prague uprising of June 12-17, 1848.

"THE UPRISING ... WAS AIMED AS MUCH AGAINST THE CZECH FEUDAL LORDS AS AGAINST THE AUSTRIAN TROOPS.
"THE AUSTRIANS ATTACKED THE PEOPLE NOT BECAUSE THEY WERE CZECHS, BUT BECAUSE THEY WERE *REVOLUTIONARIES*."

FREDERICK ENGELS

49

51

52

On June 23-26, the workers of Paris took up arms against the bourgeois government, which was impinging upon the social gains of the February revolution. Some 45,000 fought on barricades against 250,000 well-armed government troops. The *Neue Rheinische Zeitung* supported the June uprising all down the line. Marx and Engels said it was a cause of the international proletariat. They wrote in the *Neue Rheinische Zeitung* of the insurgents' admirable heroism, dedication, and single-heart-endness.

53

54

52. A meeting of the revolutionary club in Paris

53. Arms are issued to Paris workers, April 16, 1848

54. Blanqui, Barbes, Albert and Raspail, leaders of the Paris workers' revolutionary action of May 15, 1848, placed under arrest

55. The fighting in Faubourg Saint-Antoine, Paris, June 1848

"IT WAS A FIGHT FOR THE PRESERVATION OR ANNIHILATION OF THE *BOURGEOIS* ORDER."

KARL MARX

56

57

56. *Capture of Faubourg Saint-Antoine,
Paris, by government troops, June 26,
1848*

57. *Captured insurgents led through the
streets*

"THE PLEBEIANS ARE TOR-
MENTED BY HUNGER, ABUSED
BY THE PRESS, FORSAKEN BY
THE DOCTORS, CALLED THIE-
VES, INCENDIARIES AND GAL-
LEY-SLAVES BY THE RESPEC-
TABILITIES; THEIR WIVES AND
CHILDREN ARE PLUNGED INTO
STILL GREATER MISERY AND
THE BEST OF THOSE WHO HAVE
SURVIVED ARE SENT OVERSEAS.
IT IS THE *RIGHT* AND THE
*PRIVILEGE OF THE DEMOCRATIC
PRESS* TO PLACE LAURELS ON
THEIR CLOUDED THREATENING
BROW."

KARL MARX

59

58. *Louis Auguste Blanqui (1805-1881), French revolution-ary, utopian communist; took part in the 1848 revolution, devotee of conspiratorial tactics*

59. *Joachim Kersausie (1798-1874) drew up the operational plan of the June uprising. Engels called him "first commander-in-chief of barricade fighting"*

60. *June insurgents face a military tribunal in Paris*

61. *A cartoon of General Cavaignac, hangman of the June insurrection*

61

62

62. *Marx and Engels in the printshop of
the* Neue Rheinische Zeitung

63. *Karl Marx, "The June Revolution"*
Neue Rheinische Zeitung, *June 29,
1848*

The article is devoted to the heroic
uprising of the Paris proletariat.

"NONE OF THE NUMEROUS
REVOLUTIONS OF THE FRENCH
BOURGEOISIE SINCE 1789 AS-
SAILED THE EXISTING *ORDER*,
FOR THEY RETAINED THE CLASS
RULE, THE SLAVERY OF THE
WORKERS, THE *BOURGEOIS OR-
DER...* THE JUNE UPRISING DID
ASSAIL THIS *ORDER*."

KARL MARX

Neue Rheinische Zeitung.

Organ der Demokratie.

№ 29. Köln, Donnerstag 29. Juni 1848.

Die „Neue Rheinische Zeitung" erscheint vom 1. Juni an täglich. Bestellungen für das nächste Quartal, Juli bis September, wolle man baldigst machen.

Alle Postämter Deutschlands nehmen Bestellungen an.

Für Frankreich übernehmen Abonnements Herr **G. A. Alexandre**, Nr. 28, Brandgasse in Straßburg, und 23, rue Notre Dame de Nazareth in Paris; so wie das königliche Ober-Post-Amt in Aachen. Für England die HH. **J. J. Ewer** & Comp. 72, Newgate Street in London. Für Belgien und Holland die respekt. königlichen Briefpost-Aemter und das Postbüreau zu Lüttich.

Abonnementspreis in Köln vierteljährlich 1 Thlr. 15 Sgr., in allen übrigen Orten Preußens 2 Thlr. 3 Sgr. 9 Pf. Außerhalb Preußens mit Zuschlag des fremden Zeitungsportos. Inserate: die vierspaltige Petitzeile oder deren Raum 1 Sgr. 6 Pf.

Anzeigen aller Art erlangen durch die großen Verbindungen der Zeitung die weiteste Verbreitung.

Zu Nr. 28 der „Neuen Rheinischen Zeitung" ist am 28. Juni Morgens eine außerordentliche Beilage ausgegeben und versandt worden.

Französische Republik.

** Die Pariser Arbeiter sind erdrückt worden von der Uebermacht, sie sind ihr nicht erlegen. Sie sind geschlagen, aber ihre Gegner sind besiegt. Der augenblickliche Triumph der brutalen Gewalt ist erkauft mit der Vernichtung aller Täuschungen und Einbildungen der Februar-Revolution, mit der Auflösung der ganzen alt-republikanischen Partei, mit der Zerklüftung der französischen Nation in zwei Nationen, die Nation der Besitzer und die Nation der Arbeiter. Die trikolore Republik trägt nur mehr Eine Farbe, die Farbe der Geschlagenen, die Farbe des Bluts. Sie ist zur rothen Republik geworden.

Keine republikanische Reputation, sei es vom National, sei es von der Reforme auf Seite des Volks! Ohne andre Führer, ohne andre Mittel als die Empörung selbst, widerstand es der vereinigten Bourgeoisie und Soldateska länger, als je eine französische Dynastie, mit allem militärischen Apparat versehn, einer mit dem Volk vereinigten Fraktion der Bourgeoisie widerstand. Damit die letzte Illusion des Volks verschwinde, damit gänzlich mit der Vergangenheit gebrochen werde, mußte auch die gewohnte poetische Zuthat der französischen Emeute, die enthusiastische Bourgeoisjugend, die Zöglinge der école polytechnique, die dreikrampigen Hüthe auf der Seite der Unterdrücker stehn. Die Zöglinge der medizinischen Fakultät mußten den verwundeten Plebejern die Hülfe der Wissenschaft versagen. Die Wissenschaft existirt nicht für den Plebejer, der das unsagbare, das unsägliche Verbrechen beging, sich einmal für seine eigne Existenz in die Schanze zu schlagen, statt für Louis Philippe oder für Herrn Marrast.

Der letzte offizielle Rest der Februar-Revolution, die exekutive Kommission ist vor dem Ernst der Ereignisse wie ein Nebelbild zerflossen. Lamartine's Leuchtkugeln haben sich verwandelt in die Brandraketen Cavaignac's.

Die Fraternité, die Brüderlichkeit der entgegengesetzten Klassen, von denen die eine die andere exploitirt, diese Fraternité, im Februar proklamirt, mit großen Buchstaben auf die Stirne von Paris geschrieben, auf jedes Gefängniß, auf jede Kaserne — ihr wahrer, unverfälschter, ihr prosaischer Ausdruck, das ist der — Bürgerkrieg, der Bürgerkrieg in seiner fürchterlichsten Gestalt, der Krieg der Arbeit und des Kapitals. Diese Brüderlichkeit flammte vor allen Fenstern von Paris am Abend des 25. Juni, als das Paris der Bourgeoisie illuminirte, während das Paris des Proletariats verbrannte, verblutete, verächzte.

Die Brüderlichkeit währte grade so lang, als das Interesse der Bourgeoisie mit dem Interesse des Proletariats verbrüdert war. Pedanten der alten revolutionären Ueberlieferung von 1793, socialistische Systematiker, die bei der Bourgeoisie für das Volk bettelten und denen erlaubt wurde, lange Predigten zu halten und sich so lange zu compromittiren, als der proletarische Löwe in Schlaf gelullt werden mußte, Republikaner, welche die ganze alte bürgerliche Ordnung mit Abzug des gekrönten Kopfes verlangten, dynastische Oppositionelle, denen der Zufall an die Stelle eines Ministerwechsels den Sturz einer Dynastie unterschob, Legitimisten, welche die Livrée nicht abwerfen, sondern ihren Schnitt verändern wollten, das waren die Bundesgenossen, womit das Volk seinen Februar machte. Was es in Louis Philipp instinktmäßig haßte, war nicht Louis Philippe, sondern die gekrönte Herrschaft einer Klasse, das Kapital auf dem Throne. Aber wie immer großmüthig, wähnt es seinen Feind vernichtet zu haben, nachdem es den Feind seiner Feinde, den gemeinschaftlichen Feind gestürzt hat.

Die Februarrevolution war die schöne Revolution, die Revolution der allgemeinen Sympathie, weil die Gegensätze, die in ihr gegen das Königthum eklatirten, unentwickelt, einträchtig neben einander schlummerten, weil der sociale Kampf, der ihren Hintergrund bildete, nur eine luftige Existenz gewonnen hatte, die Existenz der Phrase, des Worts. Die Junirevolution ist die häßliche Revolution, die abstoßende Revolution, weil an die Stelle der Phrase die Sache getreten ist, weil die Republik das Haupt des Ungeheuers selbst entblößte, indem sie ihm die schirmende und versteckende Krone abschlugen.

Ordnung! war der Schlachtruf Guizots! Ordnung! schrie Sebastiani, der Guizotin, als Warschau russisch wurde. Ordnung! schreit Cavaignac, das brutale Echo der französischen Nationalversammlung und der republikanischen Bourgeoisie.

Ordnung! donnerten seine Kartätschen, als sie den Leib des Proletariats zerrissen.

Keine der zahllosen Revolutionen der französischen Bourgeoisie seit 1789 war ein Attentat auf die Ordnung, denn sie ließ die Herrschaft der Klasse, sie ließ die Sklaverei der Arbeiter, sie ließ die bürgerliche Ordnung bestehen, so oft auch die politische Form dieser Herrschaft und dieser Sklaverei wechselte. Der Juni hat diese Ordnung angetastet. Wehe über den Juni!

Unter der provisorischen Regierung war es Anstand und noch mehr, es war Nothwendigkeit, den großmüthigen Arbeitern, die, wie man in tausend von offiziellen Plakaten abdrucken ließ: „Drei Monat Elend zur Verfügung der Republik bereit stellten", es war Politik und Schwärmerei zugleich, ihnen vor zu predigen, die Februarrevolution sei in ihrem eigenen Interesse gemacht und es handle sich in der Februarrevolution vor allem um die Interessen der Arbeiter. Seit der Eröffnung der Nationalversammlung — wurde man prosaisch. Es handelte sich nur noch darum, — die Arbeit auf ihre alten Bedingungen, wie der Minister Trélat sagte, zurückzuführen. Also die Arbeiter hatten sich im Februar geschlagen, um in eine industrielle Crise geworfen zu werden.

Das Geschäft der Nationalversammlung besteht darin, den Februar ungeschehen zu machen, wenigstens für die Arbeiter und sie in die alten Verhältnisse zurückzuwerfen. Aber selbst das geschah nicht, weil es so wenig in der Gewalt einer Versammlung, wie eines Königs steht, einer industriellen Krise von universellem Charakter zuzurufen: bis hierhin! Die Nationalversammlung, im brutalen Eifer zu enden mit den verdrießlichen Februarredensarten, ergriff selbst die Maßregeln nicht, die auf dem Boden der alten Verhältnisse möglich waren. Die Pariser Arbeiter von 17—25 Jahr preßt sie für die Armee oder wirft sie auf das Pflaster; die auswärtigen verweist sie aus Paris in die Sologne, ohne ihnen selbst die zum Laufpaß gehörigen Gelder auszuzahlen; den erwachsenen Parisern versichert sie provisorisch ein Gnadenbrod in militärisch organisirten Werkstätten, unter der Bedingung, daß sie an keiner Volksversammlung Theil nehmen, d. h. unter der Bedingung, daß sie aufhören Republikaner zu sein. Nicht die sentimentale Rhetorik nach dem Februar reichte aus, nicht die brutale Legislatur nach dem 15. Mai. Faktisch, praktisch mußte entschieden werden. Habt ihr Canaillen die Februarrevolution für Euch gemacht, oder für Uns?

Die Bourgeoisie stellte die Frage so, daß sie den Juni beantwortet werden mußte — mit Kartätschen und Barrikaden.

Und dennoch schlägt, wie ein Volksrepräsentant am 25. Juni sagt, der Stupor die ganze Nationalversammlung. Sie ist betäubt, als Frage und Antwort das Pflaster von Paris in Blut ertränken, betäubt, die Einen, weil ihre Illusionen im Pulverdampf zerrinnen, die andern, weil sie nicht begreifen, wie das Volk es wagen kann, seine allereigensten Interessen selbstständig zu vertreten. Russisches Geld, englisches Geld, der bonapartische Adler, die Lilie, Amulette aller Art müssen dies sonderbare Ereigniß ihrem Verstande vermitteln. Beide Theile der Versammlung aber fühlen, daß eine unermeßliche Kluft sie von dem Volke trennt. Keine wagt, sich für das Volk zu erheben.

Sobald der Stupor vorüber ist, bricht die Raserei aus und mit Recht zischt die Majorität jene elenden Utopisten und Heuchler aus, die den Anachronismus begehen, noch die Phrase Fraternité, Brüderlichkeit im Mund zu führen. Es handelte sich ja eben um die Abschaffung dieser Phrase und der Illusionen, die ihr vieldeutiger Schoos verbirgt. Als Larochejaquelin, der Legitimist, der ritterliche Schwärmer gegen die Infamie eiferte, mit der man Vae victis! Weh den Besiegten! ausruft, geräth die Majorität der Versammluug in Veitstänze, als wäre sie von der Tarantel gestochen. Sie schreit Weh! über die Arbeiter, um zu verbergen, daß Niemand anders der „Besiegte" ist, als sie selbst. Entweder sie muß jetzt untergehen oder die Republik. Und darum heult sie krampfhaft: Es lebe die Republik!

Der tiefe Abgrund, der sich vor uns eröffnet hat, darf er die Demokraten irren, darf er uns wähnen lassen, die Kämpfe um die Staatsform seien inhaltlos, illusorisch, null?

Nur schwache feige Gemüther können die Frage aufwerfen. Die Kollisionen, welche aus den Bedingungen der bürgerlichen Gesellschaft selbst hervorgehen, sie müssen durchkämpft, sie können nicht wegphantasirt werden. Die beste Staatsform ist die, worin die gesellschaftlichen Gegensätze nicht verwischt, nicht gewaltsam, also nur künstlich, also nur scheinbar gefesselt werden. Die beste Staatsform ist die, worin sie zum freien Kampf und damit zur Lösung kommen.

Man wird uns fragen, ob wir keine Thräne, keinen Seufzer, kein Wort für die Opfer haben, welche vor der Wuth des Volkes fielen, für die Nationalgarde, die Mobilgarde, die republikanische Garde, die Linie?

Der Staat wird ihre Wittwen und Waisen pflegen, Dekrete werden sie verherrlichen, feierliche Leichenzüge werden ihre Reste zur Erde bestatten, die offizielle Presse wird sie unsterblich erklären, die europäische Reaktion wird ihnen huldigen vom Osten bis zum Westen.

Aber die Plebejer, vom Hunger zerrissen, von der Presse geschmäht, von den Aerzten verlassen, von den Honnetten Diebe gescholten, Brandstifter, Galeerensklaven, ihre Weiber und Kinder in noch gränzenloseres Elend gestürzt, ihre besten Lebenden über die See deportirt, — ihnen den Lorbeer um die drohend finstere Stirn zu winden, das ist das Vorrecht, das ist das Recht der demokratischen Presse.

Der 25. Juni.

* Mit jedem Tage nahm die Heftigkeit, die Erbitterung, die Wuth des Kampfes zu. Die Bourgeoisie wurde immer fanatisirter gegen die Insurgenten, je weniger ihre Brutalitäten sofort zum Ziele führten, je mehr sie selbst im Kampf, Nachtwachen und Bivouakiren ermattete, je näher sie ihrem endlichen Siege rückte. Die Bourgeoisie erklärte die Arbeiter nicht für gewöhnliche

Westphalen.

(darunter die türkischen Stämme) werden jenseits des Sauerlandes auf Mainz und Köln, die Russen aber auf Paderborn und Minden vordringen.

Unter Gottes Beistand und mit Beihülfe der mit uns verbündeten Franzosen und Belgier werdet Ihr hoffentlich die Russen überwinden. Die Südwestdeutschen u. s. w. werden mit den

Allein auch darüber seid Ihr einigermaßen belehrt worden; Kinder und erwachsene Leute sollen in dem höhern Theile des Paderborner Landes gesehen haben, wie fremde Truppen Gerste abmäheten.

Ich wende mich daher an Euch Alle vom westphälischen Stamme! Es ist nicht allein ein Kampf um unsere Freiheit und Gesittung;

63

The crushing defeat of the June uprising in Paris was a turning point in the train of revolutionary events in Europe. The reactionary forces, which had been compelled to retreat in the spring of 1848, were now regaining supremacy everywhere. They were taking the offensive.

Among the police reprisals against the *Neue Rheinische Zeitung* and the revolutionary movement as a whole, was the refusal to grant Marx Prussian citizenship. He was liable to be expelled from Germany.

With reaction stepping up its offensive, Marx and Engels, as true proletarian leaders, were in the thick of the people's struggle. They took a most active part in the activities of workers' and democratic organisations in Cologne.

64

Zeitung
des Arbeiter-Vereines zu Köln.

Freiheit, Brüderlichkeit, Arbeit.

Das Blatt erscheint am Sonntag und Donnerstag jeder Woche. Preis des Abonnements pro Vierteljahr 10 Sgr.; für auswärtige Abonnenten 12½ Sgr. Man abonnirt bei allen Postexpeditionen. Insertionsgebühren 6 Pf. per Petit-Zeile.

№ 40   Köln, Sonntag den 22. October.   1848

Comité Sitzung vom 16. Oktober 1848.

Der prov. Präs. B. Röser erklärte, daß Dr. Marx auf die Bitte der vom Vereine an Ihn abgesandten Deputation, sich an die Spitze unseres Vereines zu stellen, eingegangen, er ersuche Ihn daher seinen Platz einzunehmen.

Dr. Marx. Seine Stellung zu Köln sei prekär. Die Antwort, die er von dem Erminister Kühlwetter erhalten auf sein Renaturalsationsgesuch gleiche einem versteckten Ausweisungsbefehl. Er würde dagegen allerdings Protest bei der Nationalversammlung einlegen. Andererseits sei er eines angeblichen Preßvergehens wegen vor die Assisen verwiesen. Ueberdem sei er durch die einstweilige Zersprengung des Redaktionskomites der „Neuen Rheinischen Zeitung" mit Arbeiten überhäuft. Nichtsdestoweniger sei er bereit proisorisch bis zur Freilassung Dr. Gottschalks dem Wunsche der Arbeiter nachzukommen. Regierung und Bourgeoisie müßten sich überzeugen, daß sie trotz ihren Verfolgungen zum Trotz sich immer Leute fänden, bereit sich den Arbeitern zur Verfügung zu stellen.

Dr. Marx spricht dann ausführlicher über die revolutionäre Wirksamkeit der deutschen Arbeiter im Auslande und hebt schließlich die ausgezeichnete Rolle hervor, die sie in der neuesten Wiener Revolution spielen. Er schlägt daher eine Adresse an den Wiener Arbeiterverein vor. (Mit Acclamation angenommen.)

B. Röser stattete der Versammlung über die am 15. Oktober abgehaltene Volksversammlung Bericht ab. (Vergl.

darüber die vorige Nummer dieses Blattes.) Er stellte den Antrag, gegen das Gesetz, welches das Recht der Versammlung im Freien der Polizeiwillkühr preis giebt, zu protestiren.

Hierauf theilte er die Antwort auf die an den Generalprokurator gestellten Fragen mit, bezüglich Dr. Gottschalks, Annekes und Essers: ob, wann und wo dieselben vor die Assisen gestellt würden; warum Dr. Gottschalk und Anneke noch immer verweigert würde zu conferiren, da doch höheren Orts die Erlaubniß dazu ertheilt sei; ferner ob es der Frau Schapper nicht gestattet werden könne, ihren Mann zweimal wöchentlich zu besuchen.

In Bezug auf Dr. Gottschalk, Anneke und Esser antwortete der Herr Generalprokurator, daß dieselben vom Anklagesenat hier vor die Assisen verwiesen seien, und in Folge dessen eine außerordentliche Assisensitzung anberaumt sei, welche am 27. Nov. d. J. stattfinden solle; jedoch stände es dem öffentl. Ministerium frei, wenn es bei Verhandlung des Prozesses Unruhen befürchte, für diesen Fall an den Cassationshof in Berlin zu berichten, um die Verhandlungen vor einem anderweitigen Assisenhofe zu erwirken. Die Sache sei aber noch schwebend und wir sollten uns deshalb an den Oberprokurator verwenden, und beantragen daß der Prozeß hier zu Köln verhandelt würde, indem wir uns für die Ruhe und Ordnung verbürgten. (Welches am 18. d. geschehen ist.)

Daß Dr. Gottschalk und Anneke die Erlaubniß erhalten hätten zu conferiren, sei ihm nicht bekannt.

Schließlich bemerkte B. Röser: da der Verein bereits

65

66

64. *The house in Cologne where the Cologne Workers' Association held its meetings*

The Cologne Workers' Association was founded in April 1848 by members of the Communist League. It had a membership of some 7,000. At the workers' request, Marx became its president in October 1848. Accepting the post, Marx said: "The Government and the bourgeoisie ought to realise that, despite their acts of persecution, there were always persons to be found who would be ready to put themselves at the disposal of the workers."

65. *Minutes of the sitting of the Cologne Workers' Association Committee at which Marx was elected president, October 16, 1848*
Zeitung des Arbeiter-Vereines zu Köln, *October 22, 1848*

66. *A meeting of the Democratic Club in the summer of 1848*

In April 1848 a Democratic Society was founded in Cologne. Marx and Engels joined it.

Membership in democratic societies gave Communists access to the mass of the working people. It also enabled them to win petty-bourgeois democrats to their side. This was essential if there was to be a common front of struggle for victory of the bourgeois-democratic revolution.

In the summer of 1848, Marx and Engels were active in the Rhenish District Committee of Democrats, and saw to it that items publicising the activity of democratic organisations in various parts of Germany should appear regularly in the *Neue Rheinishe Zeitung.*

67

Late in August and early in September 1848 Marx visited Berlin and Vienna. The purpose of his visit was to tighten contacts with local democratic and workers' organisations, and to collect funds for the *Neue Rheinische Zeitung*.

Was 12 Millionen Menschen
von der
Wiener Reichsversammlung
verlangen.

Tag auf Tag vergeht, wo die Reichsversammlung über die Frage debattirt, ob der Bauer auch in der constitutionellen Zeit noch länger Robot und Zehent leisten soll, und ob er sich von der Herrschaft und Geistlichkeit loskaufen müsse oder nicht.

Diese Verhandlungen werden vielleicht noch einen Monat dauern, da 30 Deputirte über diesen Punkt lange Reden vortragen werden, bis man zu einem Resultate gelangen wird.

68

An die Arbeiter aller
Gewerbszweige.

Kameraden!

Wir haben einen Arbeiter-Verein gegründet, der seit dem 1. Juli d. J. in Wirksamkeit ist, und den Zweck hat, Interesse an Kunst, Wissenschaft und öffentlichem Leben durch leicht faßliche Vorträge bei den Arbeitern zu befördern und zu verbreiten, die Angelegenheiten derselben zu berathen, jedem Gelegenheit zu geben für das Gute und Wahre zu wirken, ihm einen Zufluchtsort zu bieten, wo er volle Anerkennung und würdigen Genuß findet. — Die Bedingungen sind: genaue Befolgung der selbstgegebenen Gesetze und der Beitrag von 20 kr. C. M. für den ersten Monat und 10 kr. für jeden folgenden. Einzelne Besuche werden gegen Erlegung von 4 kr. C. M. gestattet. — Die Versammlung findet regelmäßig Mittwoch und Samstag Abends 8 Uhr im Saale des Josephstädter Theater

69

70

Große
Arbeiter-
Revolution
im Prater.

Und wieder ist Blut geflossen, wieder kämpfte Bürger gegen Arbeiter. Es war ein gräßliches Schauspiel, diese halb todten und verstümmelten Menschen durch die Hauptstraßen schleppen zu sehen. Es war dieß wohl das fürchterlichste Blutbad Wiens seit den Märztagen, denn sein Gerücht erwähnt einiger Hundert Todte und Verwundete aus allen Ständen. — Jetzt kann die verteufelte Reaktion niederblicken auf die gemordeten Brüder, da Volkswehr und Arbeiter gegen einander kämpften, und somit das feste Freundschaftsband des 26. Mai auf immer zerrissen.

Der Hergang dieser blutigen Scenen ward mir von einigen Augenzeugen folgendermaßen erzählt: Die Arbeiter des Prater-Bezirkes, nachdem sie mit den Akkord-Arbeitern sich geraume Zeit stritten, und letztere von ihrer Thätigkeit abhalten wollten, machten aus Stroh einen Popanz, welchen sie bekleideten, den 5 kr. Dieb nannten, und nach feierlichem Umhertragen verbrennen oder beerdigen wollten. Da sie in dieser Prozession durch die ihnen sehr verhaßte Munizipal-Garde abgehalten wurden, so suchten sie sich mit ihren Krampen und Schaufeln mit Gewalt einen Weg gegen die Jägerzeile zu bahnen, um unter Absingung des Fuchsliedes ihren Gang fortzusetzen. Sie wurden durch die Munizipal-Cavallerie zerstreut, wobei schon einige Verwundungen vorfielen, und sie sich gegen den Feuerwerksplatz flüchten mußten.

Bei dieser Gelegenheit erbeutete die Sicherheitswache eine schwarze Fahne der Arbeiter, welche sie im Triumph unter Bivatgeschrei beim Bahngebäude vorbeitrugen. Die Arbeiter des Bahnhofes versammelten sich auf dem Damm, und gaben ihr Mißfallen an dem prahlenden Gepränge der

71

72

Die Constitution.

Tagblatt
für constitutionelles Volksleben und Belehrung

Verantwortlicher Redacteur:
F. Hafner.

Mit Redacteure
M. Grüner. F. Hauk

Motto: Freiheit und Arbeit!

№ 136.   Wien, Dinstag den 5. September   1848.

Arbeiter-Verein.

(Samstag, ben 2. Sept.) Vortrag von Schmit: Ueber das einige mächtige Oesterreich. Die Wirkungen der Reaction. Oesterreich unter Metternich. Ungarn und Croatien. Die Unterjochung Italiens.

Hr. Dr. Marles hält einen längeren Vortrag über Lohnarbeit und Capital. Er sagt in der Einleitung, alle Revolutionen sind sociale Revolutionen. Das Capital besteht nicht aus Geld, sondern aus Rohstoffen, Productionsinstrumenten und Lebensproducten, die Lohnarbeit macht das Capital den Erzeugnissen gegenüber. Die Behauptung, daß das Interesse des Capitalisten und des Lohnarbeiters dasselbe sei, ist falsch. Mit der Theilung der Arbeit wächst die Concurrenz unter den Arbeitern, es sinkt der Lohn; noch vielmehr aber durch das Maschinenwesen. Die Productioskosten bestimmen den Arbeitslohn. Die Civilisation vermehrt nicht das Wohlbefinden der Arbeiter, sondern bewirkt das Gegentheil. Es wachsen die Steuern und die Preise der Lebensbedürfnisse. Der Redner spricht noch über angewandte Heilmittel und deren Unzulänglichkeit, als z. B. Malte's Uebervölkerungstheorie. Die Armenhäuser

73

72. *Demonstration in Vienna on September 3, 1848, in commemoration of those killed in the workers' actions of August 23, 1848*

73. Die Constitution, *a daily newspaper, of September 5, 1848*

An account of Marx's report to a meeting of the Vienna Workers' Association, *Wage Labour and Capital*, on September 2, 1848, appeared in this issue.

74. *Uprising in Frankfurt. Guns fire on a barricade, September 18, 1848*

The moment word of the uprising in Frankfurt reached them, workers in Cologne came out in its support. A mass meeting was called on September 20, 1848, on Marx's initiative, which commended the bravery of the insurgents and started a collection of funds for them.

75. *Resolution of the mass meeting in Cologne on September 20, 1848, on the uprising in Frankfurt*

A leaflet

Dismayed by the scale and scope of the mass movement and the influence of the *Neue Rheinische Zeitung* on the working people, the Prussian government was priming for an assault on the revolutionary forces in Cologne.

76. *Announcement of the responsible publishers of the Neue Rheinische Zeitung on the paper's suspension, Cologne, September 28, 1848*

74

Beschluß der Volksversammlung.

Die auf Einladung des Sicherheits-Ausschusses, des Demokratischen- und des Arbeiter-Vereins am 20. September in Köln zu einer Volksversammlung zusammengetretenen Reichsbürger:

In Erwägung daß der Beschluß der Frankfurter Nationalversammlung vom 16. d. Mts. über die Genehmigung des ehrlosen Waffenstillstandes mit Dänemark ein Verrath an dem deutschen Volke und der Ehre der deutschen Waffen ist, erklären:

1) Die Mitglieder der Frankfurter Versammlung, mit Ausnahme derjenigen, welche sich dem Volke bereit erklärt haben auszutreten, sind Volksverräther;

2) Die Frankfurter Barricadenkämpfer haben sich um das Vaterland wohl verdient gemacht, und beschließen

3) daß diese Erklärung durch Zeitungen und durch Maueranschläge verbreitet werden soll.

"DURING THE STATE OF SIEGE IMPOSED ON COLOGNE, WHEN THE PEN HAS TO SUBMIT TO THE SABRE, THE *NEUE RHEINISCHE ZEITUNG* HAS BEEN FORBIDDEN TO APPEAR."

The far-flung campaign of protests against the state of siege and the suspension of the *Neue Rheinische Zeitung* compelled the government to beat a retreat: on October 12, 1848, the workers read the paper again. Editor-in-chief Karl Marx announced that the solid workers' support had made it possible to restart the paper.

An unsere geehrten Abonnenten

Durch den für Köln eingetretenen Belagerungszustand, wo die Feder dem Säbel untergeordnet sein muß, ist der

Neuen Rheinischen Zeitung

verboten zu erscheinen und kann dieselbe ihren Verpflichtungen, den geehrten Abonnenten gegenüber vorerst nicht nachkommen.

Wir dürfen indessen hoffen, daß der exceptionelle Zustand nur wenige Tage noch fortdauern wird, und werden wir dann im Laufe des Monats Oktober unser Blatt in vergrößertem Format von neuen kräftigen Mitteln unterstützt, unsern Abonnenten um so pünktlicher zugeben lassen können, da wir binnen Kurzem den Druck mittelst einer neuen Schnellpresse besorgen lassen werden.

Köln, den 28. September 1848.

Die Geranten

76

77

On October 6, 1848, after the Emperor had despatched the Vienna garrison to suppress the independence movement in Hungary, an uprising broke out in the Austrian capital.

At meetings of the Democratic Society, Marx called for aid to the insurgents. Stressing the international importance of the uprising, he warned that defeat of the revolution in Vienna would strengthen the hand of reactionaries in Berlin and the rest of Germany.

78

77. Storming the armoury in Vienna in the early morning hours of October 7, 1848

78. Farmers bringing food supplies to revolutionary Vienna

79. Barricades and street fighting in Vienna, October 1848

80. The uprising in Vienna suppressed, October 1848

79

80

81. *The execution of Robert Blum, a deputy of the Frankfurt National Assembly, who had taken part in the October uprising in Vienna*

"IN NOVEMBER 1848, AT A MEETING OF THE DEMOCRATIC SOCIETY, MARX ANNOUNCED THAT DEMOCRAT ROBERT BLUM HAD BEEN COURT-MARTIALLED AND EXECUTED BY A FIRING SQUAD IN VIENNA. A HUSH FELL OVER THE AUDITORIUM. MARX ASCENDED THE PLATFORM AND READ THE CABLE OF BLUM'S DEATH. AT FIRST, WE WERE PETRIFIED. THEN A REAL STORM BROKE OUT IN THE HALL."

FRIEDRICH LESSNER

82. Neue Rheinische Zeitung, November 7, 1848
    This issue contains Marx's article, "The Victory of the Counter-Revolution in Vienna"

"THE SECOND ACT OF THE DRAMA HAS JUST BEEN PERFORMED IN *VIENNA*, ITS FIRST ACT HAVING BEEN STAGED IN PARTS UNDER THE TITLE OF *THE JUNE DAYS*... WE SHALL SOON SEE THE THIRD ACT PERFORMED IN *BERLIN*."

KARL MARX

As Marx had predicted, the Prussian reactionaries lost no time to take action against the revolutionary forces. On the orders of King Frederick William IV, the authorities began preparations for dissolving the National Assembly in Berlin.

83. *A workers' demonstration in Berlin is fired upon on October 16, 1848*

84. *At the Prussian National Assembly deputies refuse to back the government's tax policy*

83

84

85

Extra-Blatt

zu Nr. 143 der Neuen Rheinischen Zeitung.

Mittwoch, den 15. November.

Das Ministerium ist in Anklage=zustand versetzt.

Die Stadt Brandenburg will nichts wissen von dem Ministerium Brandenburg und schickt eine Dank-Adresse an die Nationalversammlung.

Das ganze Land erkennt in seinen Adressen nur die Regierung der Nationalversammlung an.

Das Ministerium begeht neuen Hochverrath, indem es im Gegensatze zu dem Habeas-Corpus-Act ohne Genehmigung der Nationalversammlung den Belagerungszustand ausgesprochen und die Nationalversammlung selbst mit Bajonnetten aus dem Schützenhause vertrieben hat.

Die Nationalversammlung hat ihren Sitz im Volke, nicht in dem Umkreis dieser oder jener Steinhaufen. Vertreibt man sie aus Berlin, so wird sie in einem andern Orte tagen, in Breslau, Köln oder wo es ihr gutdünkt. Sie hat in ihrer Sitzung vom 13. diesen Beschluß gefaßt.

Die Berliner moquiren sich über den Belagerungszustand und lassen sich in keiner Weise durch denselben einschränken. Niemand liefert die Waffen ab.

85. *Dissolution of the Prussian National Assembly in Berlin on November 10, 1848*

In the *Neue Rheinische Zeitung* Karl Marx urged action to block the offensive of the counter-revolution. The paper called on the people to refuse to pay taxes and thereby deprive the German counter-revolutionaries of means to fight against the revolutionary movement.

86. *Karl Marx, "Impeachment of the Government"*
From an extra edition of the Neue Rheinische Zeitung *of November 15, 1848*

Keine Steuern mehr!!!

° **Köln**, 16. November.

Alle Zeitungen aus Berlin, mit Ausnahme des „Preußischen Staatsanzeigers", der „Vossischen Zeitung", und der „Neuen Preußischen Zeitung" sind ausgeblieben.

Die Entwaffnung der Bürgerwehr ist im Geheimerathsviertel vollzogen worden, aber nur im Geheimerathsviertel. Es ist dasselbe Bataillon, das am 21. Oktober die Maschinenbauer meuchelmordete. Seine Entwaffnung ist ein Gewinn für die Volkssache.

Die Nationalversammlung ist wiederum durch bewaffnete Macht aus dem Kölnischen Rathhause vertrieben worden. Sie begab sich dann in das Mylius Hotel, wo sie endlich einstimmig mit **226 Stimmen** den unten nachfolgenden Beschluß der Steuerverweigerung faßte.

„Das Ministerium Brandenburg ist nicht berechtigt, über Staatsgelder zu verfügen und Steuern zu erheben, so lange die Nationalversammlung nicht in Berlin ihre Sitzungen frei fortsetzen kann.

Dieser Beschluß tritt mit dem 17. November in Kraft.

Nationalversammlung vom 15. Novbr.

Von dem heutigen Tage an sind also die Steuern aufgehoben!!! Die Steuereinzahlung ist Hochverrath, die Steuerverweigerung erste Pflicht des Bürgers!

7

87. Karl Marx, "No More Taxes!!!"
From a special supplement to the Neue Rheinische Zeitung *of November 17, 1848*

"FROM TODAY TAXES ARE ABOLISHED!!! IT IS HIGH TREASON TO PAY TAXES. REFUSAL TO PAY TAXES IS THE PRIMARY DUTY OF THE CITIZEN!"

KARL MARX

88. Appeal of the Rhenish District Committee of Democrats calling on the people to form a militia and public safety committees to repulse the counter-revolution. Signed by Marx and other members of the Committee on November 18, 1848
From the Neue Rheinische Zeitung *of November 19, 1848*

Legal proceedings were started against Marx and other members of the Rhenish District Committee of Democrats in connection with this Appeal.

Deutschland.
Aufruf.

Köln, 18. Nov. Der Rheinische Kreisausschuß der Demokraten fordert alle demokratischen Vereine der Rheinprovinz auf, die Beschlußnahme und Durchführung folgender Maßregeln zu bewerkstelligen:

1) Nachdem die preußische Nationalversammlung selbst die Steuerverweigerung beschlossen hat, ist jihre gewaltsame Eintreibung überall durch jede Art des Widerstandes zurückzuweisen;

2) Der Landsturm zur Abwehr des Feindes ist überall zu organisiren. Für die Unbemittelten sind Waffen und Munition auf Gemeindekosten oder durch freiwillige Beiträge zu beschaffen.

3) Die Behörden sind überall aufzufordern, sich öffentlich darüber zu erklären, ob sie die Beschlüsse der Nationalversammlung anerkennen und ausführen wollen? Im Weigerungsfalle sind Sicherheitsausschüsse zu ernennen und zwar wo möglich im Einverständnisse mit den Gemeinderäthen. Der gesetzgebenden Versammlung widerstrebende Gemeinderäthe sind durch allgemeine Volkswahl zu erneuern.

Köln, den 18. November.

Im Namen des rheinischen Kreisausschusses der Demokraten.

Karl Marx. Karl Schapper. Schneider II.

88

89

89. *The Piazza del Popolo in Rome in the first few days of the Republic, 1849*

90. *"Proclamation of a Republic in Rome"*
Neue Rheinische Zeitung, *February 22, 1849*

"THE ITALIANS KNOW THAT THE UNITY OF A COUNTRY SPLIT INTO FEUDAL PRINCIPALITIES CAN ONLY BE ESTABLISHED BY ABOLISHING DYNASTIC RULE."

Neue Rheinische Zeitung.
Organ der Demokratie.

90

Belgien.

Brüssel, 18. Febr. Belgien begründet immer mehr die Ansicht, welche die „Neue Rheinische Zeitung" über den Musterstaat den Teutschen eröffnet hat. Freiheit und Fremdenschutz und demokratische Constitution sind Worte, womit unsere Hodys sich schmücken, um Unbefangene in die Polizeizellen zu liefern. Während man groß that vor Europa in den vergangenen Septemberfesten und den Artikel der Constitution unter die Lampen schrieb, während vor dem Ständehause die Inschrift prangte, Gastfreundschaft und Schutz für alle Fremde, beschlossen die Minister einstimmig, daß kein politischer Flüchtling in Belgien geduldet werde, es versteht sich von selbst, daß Windischgräz, Brandenburg und Jellachich ausgenommen sind und sich derselben Freundschaftlichkeit zu erfreuen gehabt hätten, welche die Minister Louis Philipps gefunden haben. Herr Guizot ist mehrmals mit einem falschen Passe hiergewiesen, die Journale haben davon gesprochen, die Polizei hat es nicht geläugnet; Demokraten aber dürfen sich dergleichen nicht einfallen lassen.

Italien.

Rom, 9. Febr. Diese Nacht um 2 Uhr verkündete das Geläute aller Glocken die wirklich erfolgte Einsetzung der Republik. Sie war nach einer langen, anfangs stürmischen Sitzung der Constituante durchgesetzt worden, welcher Maß nach der Niederlage des Ministeriums die Permanenz zu sichern gewußt hatte.

Florenz, 9. Febr. Der „Livorneser Courier" vom heutigen Tage meldet:

„Der Großherzog ist von St. Stefano in westlicher Richtung abgefahren auf einem großen Dampfboot mit englischer Flagge."

Die italienische Konstituante ist keine Frankfurter Nationalversammlung. Die Italiener wissen, daß die Einheit eines in feudale Fürstenthümer zersplitterten Landes nicht anders herzustellen ist als durch Abschaffung des Fürstenthums. Die Italiener haben 1848 den Reigen eröffnet, sie eröffnen ihn 1849. Aber welcher Fortschritt! In Italien kein Pius nonus mehr, wie in Frankreich kein Lamartine. Die phantastische Periode der europäischen Revolution, die Periode der Schwärmerei, des guten Willens und

91

Marx and Engels followed the rev-olutionary events in Hungary with deep sympathy. In the spring of 1849, when the Hungarians inflicted a few serious defeats on the Austrian troops, they hoped this would give fresh impulse to the revolutionary struggles in France, Germany and Italy. On Marx's request, Engels wrote several detailed reviews of the revolutionary developments in Hungary.

91. Hungarian revolutionary troops cap-ture the bastion in Buda on May 21, 1849

92. Frederick Engels, "The Magyar Struggle"
Neue Rheinische Zeitung, January 13, 1849

"FOR THE FIRST TIME IN THE REVOLUTIONARY MOVEMENT OF 1848, FOR THE FIRST TIME SINCE 1793, A NATION SURROUNDED BY SUPERIOR COUNTER-REVO-LUTIONARY FORCES DARES TO COUNTER THE COWARDLY COUN-TER-REVOLUTIONARY FURY BY REVOLUTIONARY PASSION."

FREDERICK ENGELS

Neue

Rheinische Zeitung

Organ der Demokratie.

№ 194.   **Köln,** Samstag den 13 Januar.   **1849.**

92

Zwei
politische Prozesse.

Verhandelt vor den Februar-Assisen in Köln.

I.
Der erste Preßprozeß der Neuen Rheinischen Zeitung.

II.
Prozeß des Kreis - Ausschusses der rheinischen Demokraten.

Köln, 1849.
Verlag der Expedition der Neuen Rheinischen Zeitung.

93

94

Seeing that attacks, threats and slanders did not unnerve Marx and Engels, the counter-revolutionaries started legal proceedings against them. On February 7 and 8, 1849, Marx was summoned into court on charges of breaching laws pertaining to the press and of incitement to mutiny.

93. Two Political Trials, *Cologne, 1849*
The title page

The pamphlet contains the speeches of Marx and Engels at the trials of the *Neue Rheinische Zeitung* and the Rhenish District Committee of Democrats in Cologne on February 7 and 8, 1849.

94. *Karl Marx's notes for the speech he made at the trial of the* Neue Rheinische Zeitung *on February 7, 1849*
A fragment

"MARX DID NOT DEFEND HIMSELF, HE ACCUSED THE MINISTRY," Friedrich Lessner recalled later. "HE SPOKE FOR ABOUT AN HOUR, HIS LEGAL ARGUMENTS RINGING CALM, DIGNIFIED AND ENERGETIC, ATTACKING WITH EVER-INCREASING FORCE THE STATE PROCURATOR, THE OLD BUREAUCRACY, THE OLD ARMY, THE OLD COURTS, THE OLD JUDGES WHO WERE BORN AND EDUCATED AND HAD GROWN OLD IN THE SERVICE OF ABSOLUTISM. 'THE FIRST DUTY OF THE PRESS,' MARX SAID, 'IS NOW TO UNDERMINE ALL THE FOUNDATIONS OF THE EXISTING POLITICAL SYSTEM.'"

The jury brought in a verdict of not guilty.

95

In the spring of 1849 Marx and
Engels parted ways with the petty-
bourgeois democrats by withdrawing
from the Rhenish District Committee of
Democratic Associations, and set about
forming an independent proletarian
party. A congress of workers' associations of Rhine Province and Westphalia was convened on their initiative on May 6, 1849. Aiming to set
up an all-German workers' association,
Marx and his followers travelled across
the country soliciting support. The
victory of the counter-revolution prevented them from carrying their plan
into effect.

In May 1849, armed uprisings broke
out in Southern and Western Germany
in defence of the Imperial Constitution
adopted by the Frankfurt National Assembly, which the mass of the people
saw as the only surviving gain of the
revolution. Engels took part in the
Elberfeld rising and in the campaign of
the Baden revolutionary army.

*95. The uprising in Dresden, May 3-8,
1849*

96

96. *Battle between the Baden revolutionary army and Prussian troops at Heidelberg, June 22, 1849*

After defeating the uprising on the Rhine, the counter-revolution set about settling scores with the *Neue Rheinische Zeitung* and its editors. Marx was ordered out of the country, and reprisals were launched against the paper's other editors. This made its further publication impossible.

The final issue of the paper, printed in red ink, appeared on May 19, 1849.

"WE HAD TO SURRENDER OUR FORTRESS," Engels wrote, "BUT WE WITHDREW WITH OUR ARMS AND BAGGAGE, WITH BAND PLAYING AND FLAG FLYING, THE FLAG OF THE LAST ISSUE, A RED ISSUE..."

97. *The last, May 19, 1849, issue of the* Neue Rheinische Zeitung

In their Address to the workers of Cologne, Marx and Engels wrote:

"IN BIDDING YOU FAREWELL THE EDITORS OF THE *NEUE RHEINISCHE ZEITUNG* THANK YOU FOR THE SYMPATHY YOU HAVE SHOWN THEM. THEIR LAST WORD EVERYWHERE AND ALWAYS WILL BE: *EMANCIPATION OF THE WORKING CLASS!*"

Neue

Rheinische Zeitung

Organ der Demokratie.

№ 301.   Köln, Samstag, den 19. Mai.   1849.

Abschiedswort der Neuen Rheinischen Zeitung.

Kein offner Hieb in offner Schlacht —
Es fällen die Rücken und Tücken
Es fällt mich die schleichende Niedertracht
Der schmutzigen West-Kalmücken!
Aus dem Dunkel flog der tödtend Schaft,
Aus dem Hinterhalt fielen die Stiche —
Und so lieg' ich nun da in meiner Kraft,
Eine stolze Rebellenleiche!

Auf der Lippe den Trotz und den zuckenden Hohn,
In der Hand den blitzenden Degen,
Noch im Sterben rufend: „Die Rebellion!"
So bin ich mit Ehren erlegen.
O gern wohl bestreuten mein Grab mit Sal,
Der Preuße zusammt dem Czare —
Doch es schicken die Ungarn, es schickt die Pfalz
Drei Salven mir über die Bahre!

Und der arme Mann im zerriß'nen Gewand,
Er wirft auf mein Haupt die Schollen;
Er wirft sie hinab mit der fleißigen Hand,
Mit der harten, der schwielenvollen.
Einen Kranz auch bringt er aus Blumen und
Mai'n,
Zu ruh'n auf meinen Wunden;
Den haben sein Weib und sein Töchterlein
Nach der Arbeit für mich gewunden.

Nun Ade, nun Ade, du kämpfende Welt,
Nun Ade, ihr ringenden Heere!
Nun Ade, u pulvergeschwärztes Feld,
Nun Ade, er Schwerter und Speere!
Nun Ade — doch nicht für immer Ade!
Denn sie töten den Geist nicht, ihr Brüder!
Bald richt' b mich rasselnd in die Höh',
Bald kehr' b reiniger wieder!

Wenn die letzte Krone wie Glas zerbricht,
In des Kampfes Wettern und Flammen.
Wenn das Volk sein letztes „Schuldig!" spricht,
Dann stehn wir wieder zusammen!
Mit dem Wort, mit dem Schwert, an der Do-
nau, am Rhein, —
Eine allzeit treue Gesellin
Wird dem Throne zerschmetternden Volke sein
Die Geächtete, die Rebellin!

F. FREILIGRATH.

An die Arbeiter Kölns.

Wir warnen Euch schließlich vor jem Putsch in Köln. Nach der militärischen Lage Kölns wäret ihr rettungslos verloren. Ihr habt in Elpersux gleichen, wie die Bourgeoisie Arbeiter ins Feuer schicke und sie hinterher aufs Niederträchtigste verrath. Der Belagerungszustand in Reih wurde die ganze Rheinprova demoralisiren und der Belagerungszustand ware die nothwendige Folge jeder Erhebung von Eurer Seite in diesem Augenblicke. Die Preußenhorden an Eurer Ruhe verzweifeln.

Die Redakteure der Neuen Rheinien Zeitung danken Euch beim Abschiede für die ihnen bewiesene Theilnahme. Ihr letztes Wort wird überall und immer sein: Emancipation der arbeitenden Klasse!   Die Redaktion der Neuen Rhein. Zeitung.

Deutschland.

* Köln, 18. Mai. Vor einiger Zeit wurde vonberlin aus ajneine hiesige Behörde die Forderung gestellt, alsbald den Belagerungszustand über Köln zu verhängen. Al bezweckte die standrechtliche Beseitigung der „Neuen Rheinisch Zeitung," obn man hieß auf unerwarteten Widerstand. Er wandte sich an die Kölnische Regierung an das hiesige Barkel, u demselben Zweck durch willkürliche Verhaftungen zu erreichen. Er scheiterte an den janischen Bedenken des Parteis, u scheiterte an dem gesunden Menschenverstand der rheinischen Geschworenen geschäftert war. Es blieb nichts andres rig, als zu

[...] einer Polizeihut seine Zuflucht zu nehmen und man hat für den Augenblick seinen Zweck erreicht. Die Neue Rheinische Zeitung hört einstweilen auf zu erscheinen. Am 16. Mal wurde ihrem Redacteur en chef Carl Marx folgender Regierungswisch mitgetheilt:

„In ihren neuesten Stücken (!) tritt die N. Rh. Z. mit der Aufreizung zur Verachtung der bestehenden Regierung, zum gewaltsamen Umsturz und der Einführung der socialen Republik immer entschiedener hervor. Es ist daher ihrem Redacteur en chef, dem Dr. Karl Marx, das Gastrecht (!), welches er so [...] schmählich verletzt, zu entziehen, und da derselbe eine Erlaubniß zum ferneren Aufenthalt in den hiesigen Staaten nicht erlangt hat, ihm aufzugeben, dieselben binnen 24 Stunden zu verlassen. Sollte er der an ihn ergehenden Aufforderung nicht freiwillig Genüge leisten, so ist derselbe zwangsweise über die Gränze zu bringen."

Köln, den 11. Mai 1849.
Königl. Regierung.
Moeller
An den Königl. Polizeidirektor Herrn Geiger hier.

Proklamation an die Frauen

Seit dem 1. Juni 1848, wo die »Neue Rheini Zeitung« wie ein fremder Wunderstern drohend und prächtig er zäubern und Herren heraufstieg und wo das Fräulkren wie humoristischer Kometenschweif hinterdrein kicherte, hat dieser Fetenschweif so unbeschreiblich viel gefressen, daß meine freundlich Leserinnen weinend ihre hohen Gesichter verhüllen werden, wo sie die schreckliche Kunde vernehmen, daß auch dieser Komschweif in der augenblicklichen Götterdämmerung der Neuen Rheinischen Zeitung, vom Auge profaner Sterblicher entrückt wird, u vielleicht erst später wieder dem Himmel u Erde kommen rustigZustand zu durchziehen.

„Und scheint die Sonne noch so schön,
Am Ende muß sie untergehn."

Ich habe mich von jeher für die Frauen gehalten ze Männer interesse ich mich selten.

1. Ich, ihr schönen Frauen, wende ich mich bahmit diesem Abschiedstraun, in dem ich alle Rosen und Disteln aner unerforschlichen Ziele zusammenbann. Die Rosen sind türlich für Euer, die Disteln für Eure allenfällige Männer.

Dieserlei habet ihr. Seit dem, was von uns euern Männern geworden ist! Aus jenen großen Staatsmänner mit denen man jetzt einmal mehr der Neiara Räuber bange m u auf jenen brauchtest. Gelernten, vor denen nicht einmal die tol Hunde die Wissenschaft bellten; aus jenen gefeierten Banksagern, die durch alle ihr patriotische Begeisterung nur zu einrochen Rase gelangten, u aus jenes falfen Schwärmern U-Deutschlands, die gleich melanpolischen Heidschauden, mit verdorbenen schwarzen, über die Leerentgerhebe der Gegenwart, der Sahar des Lebens entgegenbebeld.

Es thut mir leid, Frau Regierungsräthin, daß Sie sich in Ihrem Herrn Gemahl so geirrt haben. Sie hielten ihn für einen Solon und da kommt er auf der Berliner Nationalversammlung nach Hause zurück und es findet sich, daß er ein rechter Gimpel ist. Ich bedaure Sie, Frau Regierungsräthin. Trösten Sie Ihren Mann damit, daß er ein verbauntes Genie sei, aber vor allen Dingen: schaffen Sie sich diesen Menschen vom Halse — ja, ihr Frauen, gebt Euern Männern den Abschied, die sind keinen Schuß Pulver werth. — Wer möchte ein Kamesi umarmen!

Wunderliel haben uns die Familienväter in den Berliner und Frankfurter Nationalversammlungen mitgespielt. Wärt Ihr Frauen am Ruder gewesen, würde woold, Würd wäre anders geworden. Ihr bättet Eure ambrosischen Locken geschüttelt und nach kurzen Debatten hättet Ihr irgend einen Königi zum bunduten Kaiser gemacht und nach drei Tagen hättet Ihr ihn geköpft und aus seinem Blute wären blutrothe Rosen gewachsen, die Blumen der Liebe und der Republik!

Aber das ganze Unheil ist nur deshalb über Deut'land gekommen, weil man die deutsch Politik bisher für eine ernste, wichtige und nicht für eine Herzenssache hielt. Ihr Frauen seid dazu berufen, diesem Mißverhandniß ein für allemal abzuhelfen.

Fragt nicht nach dem: Wie? Ihr wißt es selbst am besten. Laßt eure alten Männer laufen, nehmt neue Männer, revolutionäre Männer — voila tout!

Wenn vor vierzig oder fünf und vierzig Jahren hieß: »die Franzosen kommen!« — da liefen alle jungen Mädchen und Frauen eilig aus'n Fenster und Kober die die Gardinen bei Seite und schauten in die Straße hinaus, bald lächer, bald verschämt, bei der Tambourmajor kam mit seinem großen Stock, und hinterherm die lustigen, kleinen Kerle, die ohne Weitere in die Stadt und in jedes Herz hineinmarschierten. — — Niemals hat es böslicher Kinder gegeben, als nach jenen gefürsteten Feldzügen!

Heute heißt es nicht mehr: »die Franzosen kommen!« nein, »die Ungarn kommen!« und diese Ungarn sollt Ihr freundlich empfangen. Dies ist die Herzenssache der deutschen Politik. Die Ungarn sind die Franzosen des neunzehnten Jahrhunderts!

Eruber lispelten die deutschen Mädchen im Momente des höchsten Gludes: »Du machst mich unglücklich!« Bald werden sie jubeln: »Du machst mich glücklich!« Denn die Ungarn werden sich in Deutsche verwandeln und die Deutschen in Ungarn und der Roß der glücklichen Lippen wird durch Berge und Wälder brennen, bis die Schneefelder Sibiriens aufthauen, und die Kosaken darin ersaufen von Don bis zum Dnieber.

Von Anbeginn seid Ihr Frauen gescheidter gewesen als alle Schriftgelehrten und Pharisäer, aber von Anbeginn wart ihr auch leidenschaftlicher als alle Schriftgelehrten und Pharisäer.

So fahrt denn heraus mit Eurer flammenden Leidenschaft und ergreift Eure zahmen Männer bei ihren liederlichen Zöpfen und hängt sie als Vogelscheuchen wohin Ihr wollt — nur fort mit ihnen!

Die Guillotine wird uns retten und die Leidenschaft der Weiber. Im Uebrigen empfehle ich mich Euch von ganzem Herzen. Die Nachtigallen singen in den Büschen, die Kugeln pfeifen und meine Proklamation ist zu Ende.

Georg Weerth

98

99

4

4. *The old Chelsea riverside in south-western London*

5. *The house at 4 Anderson Street, London, where the Marxes lived from the autumn of 1849 to April 1850*

Frederick Engels came to London in November 1849. For Marx and Engels Britain became a new, lifelong place of exile.

Many members of the Communist League were compelled to leave continental Europe.

5

8
9

Communist League members who emigrated to England

6. Karl Marx, London, 1861

7. Frederick Engels, Manchester, 1856

8. Konrad Schramm (c. 1822-1858), responsible editor of the Neue Rheinische Zeitung. Politisch-ökonomische Revue

9. Johann Georg Eccarius (1818-1889), German tailor, prominent figure in the Communist League in London

10. Wilhelm Wolff (1809-1864), an editor of the Neue Rheinische Zeitung

11. Wilhelm Liebknecht (1826-1900) took an active part in the 1848-49 revolution in Germany

12. August Willich (1810-1878) took part in the Baden-Palatinate uprising (1849); was expelled from the Communist League for disruptive activities

11

12

13. *Marx's list of names and addresses of members of the Communist League's Central Authority. Dates to August 1850*

A Committee of Support for German Refugees, consisting of members of the Communist League, was founded on Marx's initiative in London in September 1849.

14. *Appeal for Support for German Political Refugees signed by Karl Marx and others, dated September 20, 1849, in the* Neue Deutsche Zeitung, *September 26, 1849*

"THOUSANDS OF EMIGRANTS ARRIVED DAILY (IN LONDON—*ED.*). FEW OF THEM HAD ANY MEANS OF THEIR OWN, ALL WERE IN MORE OR LESS DIRE STRAITS, NEEDING AND LOOKING FOR HELP," Marx's wife Jenny recalled. "THIS WAS ONE OF THE MOST UNPLEASANT PERIODS OF OUR LIFE IN EXILE. EMIGRANT COMMITTEES WERE FOUNDED TO HELP THEM, MEETINGS WERE ARRANGED, APPEALS MADE, PROGRAMMES DRAWN UP AND GREAT DEMONSTRATIONS PREPARED."

14

15. Marx speaks at German Workers' Educational Society in London, an organisation closely associated with the Communist League

From November 1849 until the autumn of 1850 Marx delivered lectures at the Society on political economy and the *Manifesto of the Communist Party*.

An important part in the reorganisation of the Communist League was played by two addresses of its Central Authority written by Marx and Engels in March and June 1850. They outlined the action programme for League members.

16. Karl Marx and Frederick Engels, "Address of the Central Authority to the League, March 1850"

A fragment

"IT IS OUR INTEREST AND OUR TASK TO MAKE THE REVOLUTION PERMANENT... FOR US THE ISSUE CANNOT BE THE ALTERATION OF PRIVATE PROPERTY BUT ONLY ITS ANNIHILATION, NOT THE SMOOTHING OVER OF CLASS ANTAGONISMS BUT THE ABOLITION OF CLASSES, NOT THE IMPROVEMENT OF THE EXISTING SOCIETY BUT THE FOUNDATION OF A NEW ONE."

17. Karl Marx and Frederick Engels, "Address of the Central Authority to the League, June 1850"

A fragment

IX. Anhang.

1) Ansprache der Zentralbehörde an den Bund vom März 1850.

Die Zentralbehörde an den Bund.

„Brüder! In den beiden Revolutionsjahren 1848—49 hat sich der Bund in doppelter Weise bewährt; einmal dadurch, daß seine Mitglieder an allen Orten energisch in die Bewegung eingriffen, daß sie in der Presse, auf den Barrikaden und Schlachtfeldern voranstanden in den Reihen der allein entschieden revolutionären Klasse des Proletariats. Der Bund hat sich ferner dadurch bewährt, daß seine Auffassung der Bewegung, wie sie in den Rundschreiben der Kongresse und der Zentralbehörde von 1847 und im kommunistischen Manifeste niedergelegt war, als die einzig richtige sich erwiesen hat, daß die in jenen Aktenstücken ausgesprochenen Erwartungen sich vollständig erfüllten und die früher vom Bunde nur im Geheimen propagirte Auffassung der heutigen Gesellschaftszustände jetzt im Munde der Völker ist und auf den Märkten öffentlich geprebigt wird. Zu gleicher Zeit wurde die frühere feste Organisation des Bundes bedeutend gelockert. Ein großer Theil der Mitglieder, in der revolutionären Bewegung direkt betheiligt, glaubte die Zeit der geheimen Gesellschaften vorüber und das öffentliche Wirken allein hinreichend. Die einzelnen Kreise und Gemeinden ließen ihre Verbindungen mit der Zentralbehörde erschlaffen und allmälig einschläfern. Während also die demokratische Partei, die Partei der Kleinbürgerschaft, sich in Deutschland immer mehr organisirte, verlor die Arbeiterpartei ihren einzigen festen Halt, blieb höchstens in einzelnen Lokalitäten zu lokalen Zwecken organisirt und gerieth dadurch in der allgemeinen Bewegung vollständig unter die Herrschaft und Leitung der kleinbürgerlichen Demokraten. Diesem Zustande muß ein Ende gemacht, die Selbständigkeit der Arbeiter muß hergestellt werden. Die Zentralbehörde begriff diese Nothwendigkeit

2) Ansprache derselben Zentralbehörde an den Bund vom Juni 1850.

Die Zentralbehörde an den Bund.

Brüder!

Wir haben in unserem letzten Rundschreiben, das der Emissär des Bundes Euch überbrachte, die Stellung der Arbeiterpartei und speziell des Bundes, sowohl im gegenwärtigem Augenblick wie für den Fall einer Revolution, entwickelt.

Der Hauptzweck dieses Schreibens ist der Bericht über den Zustand des Bundes.

Die Niederlagen der revolutionären Partei im vorigen Sommer lösten die Organisation des Bundes für einen Augenblick fast vollständig auf. Die thätigsten Bundesmitglieder, bei den verschiebnen Bewegungen betheiligt, wurden versprengt, die Verbindungen hörten auf, die Abressen waren unbrauchbar geworden, die Korrespondenz wurde dadurch und durch die Gefahr der Brieferbrechung momentan unmöglich. Die Zentralbehörde war so bis gegen Ende des vorigen Jahres zur vollständigen Unthätigkeit verurtheilt.

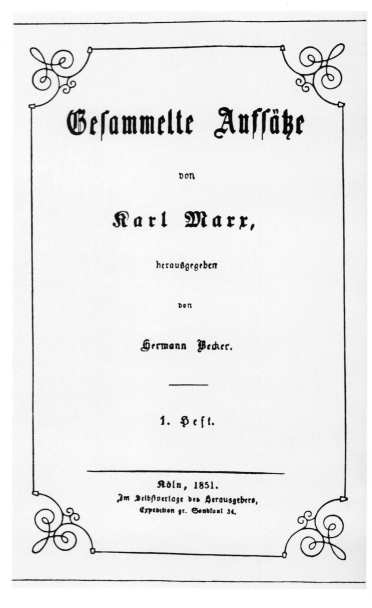

Unter der Preſſe befinden ſich:

Karl Marx's
geſammelte Aufſätze,

herausgegeben

von

Hermann Becker.

———

Marx's Arbeiten ſind theils in beſondern Flugſchriften, theils in periodiſchen Schriften erſchienen, jetzt aber meiſtens gar nicht mehr zu bekommen, wenigſtens im Buchhandel ganz vergriffen. Der Herausgeber glaubt deßhalb, dem Publikum einen Dienſt zu erweiſen, wenn er mit Bewilligung des Ver- faſſers dieſe Arbeiten, welche gerade ein Decennium umfaſſen, zuſammenſtellt und wieder zugänglich macht.

Der Plan iſt auf 2 Bände berechnet; der Band wird 25 Bogen umfaſſen. Dem zweiten Bande wird Marx's Portrait beigegeben. Die, welche bis zum 15 März 1851 auf dieſe Bände ſubſcribiren, erhalten ſolche in 10 Heften à 8 Sgr. Nach dieſem Termine tritt der Ladenpreis, 1 Thlr. 15 Sgr. per Band, ein.

Der erſte Band wird Marx's Beiträge zu den „Anekdota“ von Ruge, der (alten) „Rheiniſchen Zeitung“ (namentlich über Preßfreiheit, Holzdiebſtahlsgeſetz, Lage der Moſelbauern u. ſ. w.), den deutſch-franzöſiſchen Jahrbüchern, dem Weſtf. Dampfboote, dem Geſellſchaftsſpiegel u. ſ. w. und eine Reihe von Monogra- phien enthalten, die vor der Märzrevolution erſchienen, aber, wie Marx an Becker ſchreibt, „leider“ noch heute paſſen.

Beſtellungen nimmt an:

Geſammelte Aufſätze

von

Karl Marx,

herausgegeben

von

Hermann Becker.

———

1. Heft.

Köln, 1851.
Im Selbſtverlage des Herausgebers,
Expedition gr. Sandkaul 34.

---

18. *Front page of Hermann Becker's prospectus announcing the publication of Karl Marx's collected works in two volumes (1850)*

19. *Cover of the first part of Volume 1 of Marx's* Collected Works *published by Hermann Becker*

The publication was not completed. Soon after the first part of Volume 1 came off the press publisher Becker was arrested. It was on May 19, 1850.

Among the main tasks facing Marx and Engels at that time was to sum up the recent revolutionary events.

"A TIME OF APPARENT CALM SUCH AS THE PRESENT," wrote Marx and Engels, "MUST BE EM- PLOYED PRECISELY FOR THE PURPOSE OF ELUCIDATING THE PERIOD OF REVOLUTION JUST EXPERIENCED, THE CHARACTER OF THE CON- FLICTING PARTIES, AND THE SOCIAL CONDI- TIONS WHICH DETERMINE THE EXISTENCE AND THE STRUGGLE OF THESE PARTIES."

20. *Neue Rheinische Zeitung. Politisch-ökonomische Revue, January 1850. Altogether 6 issues of the review appeared*

"THE PERIODICAL BEARS THE TITLE OF THE NEWSPAPER OF WHICH IT IS TO BE CONSIDERED THE *CONTINUATION*. ONE OF ITS TASKS WILL CONSIST IN RETURNING IN RETROSPECT TO THE PERIOD WHICH HAS ELAPSED SINCE THE SUP- PRESSION OF THE *NEUE RHEINISCHE ZEITUNG...* IT PERMITS A COMPREHENSIVE AND SCIENTIFIC INVESTIGATION OF THE *ECONOMIC* CONDITIONS WHICH FORM THE FOUNDATION OF THE WHOLE POLITICAL MOVEMENT."

KARL MARX
and FREDERICK ENGELS

Neue

Rheinische Zeitung.

Politisch-ökonomische Revue,

redigirt von

Karl Marx.

———

Erstes Heft. — Januar 1850.

London,
C. Schramm, Gerant.

Hamburg & New-York.
In Commission bei Schuberth & Co.

1850.

Die

Klassenkämpfe in Frankreich

1848 bis 1850.

Von

Karl Marx.

Abdruck aus der „Neuen Rheinischen Zeitung"
Politisch=ökonomische Revue, Hamburg 1850.

———

Mit Einleitung

von

Friedrich Engels.

Berlin 1895

Verlag der Expedition des „Vorwärts", Berliner Volksblatt
(Th. Glocke).

21. Karl Marx, The Class Struggles in France, 1848 to 1850, *Berlin, 1895*
The title page

One of the principal works summing up the recent revolution. Here Marx elaborated his theory of revolution and the dictatorship of the proletariat, and also of the proletariat's allies in the struggle against the bourgeoisie.

The main part of this study appeared in the first three issues of the *Neue Rheinische Zeitung. Politisch-ökono-mische Revue* under the title, *From 1848 to 1849.* In 1895, Engels published it under separate cover, adding material about France that Marx had written a little later.

A counter-revolutionary coup occurred in France on December 2, 1851. Supporters of President Louis Bonaparte (Napoleon's nephew) dissolved the Legislative Assembly, and established a Bonapartist dictatorship. A year later, Louis Bonaparte declared himself Emperor Napoleon III.

22

22. The dissolution of the Legislative Assembly on December 2, 1851

23. A barricade in Faubourg Saint-Antoine on December 3, 1851

23

24

24. *Those arrested in the Quartier du Temple on December 5, 1851, are shot on the spot*

25. *Freedom of the press after the coup d'état*

26. *A cartoon of Napoleon III*

27. *Karl Marx*, The Eighteenth Brumaire of Louis Bonaparte, *first edition, 1852*

It was published in Die Revolution, *a weekly put out by Joseph Weydemeyer in New York in 1852*

Here Marx examines the reactionary Bonapartist coup as a result of the temporary defeat of the revolutionary forces, treachery of the bourgeoisie, and its alliance with the extreme reactionary wing.

Marx declares for the first time that the proletariat must tear down the bourgeois machinery of state. "All revolutions," he says, "perfected this machinery instead of breaking it."

"THE WORDS OF *THE EIGHTEENTH BRUMAIRE* ARE ARROWS AND JAVELINS, THEY ARE A STYLE THAT BRANDS AND KILLS. IF EVER HATE, SCORN AND ARDENT LOVE OF LIBERTY WERE EXPRESSED IN BURNING, DEVASTATING, LOFTY WORDS, IT IS IN *THE EIGHTEENTH BRUMAIRE,* WHICH COMBINES THE INDIGNANT SEVERITY OF A TACITUS WITH THE DEADLY SATIRE OF A JUVENAL AND THE HOLY WRATH OF A DANTE."

WILHELM LIEBKNECHT

25

26

Die Revolution,

Eine Zeitschrift in zwanglosen Heften.

Herausgegeben von

I. Weydemeyer.

Erstes Heft.

Der 18te Brumaire des Louis Napoleon

von

Karl Marx.

New-York.

Expedition: Deutsche Vereins-Buchhandlung von Schmidt und Helmich.
William-Street Nr. 191.

1852.

His Life
and
Work

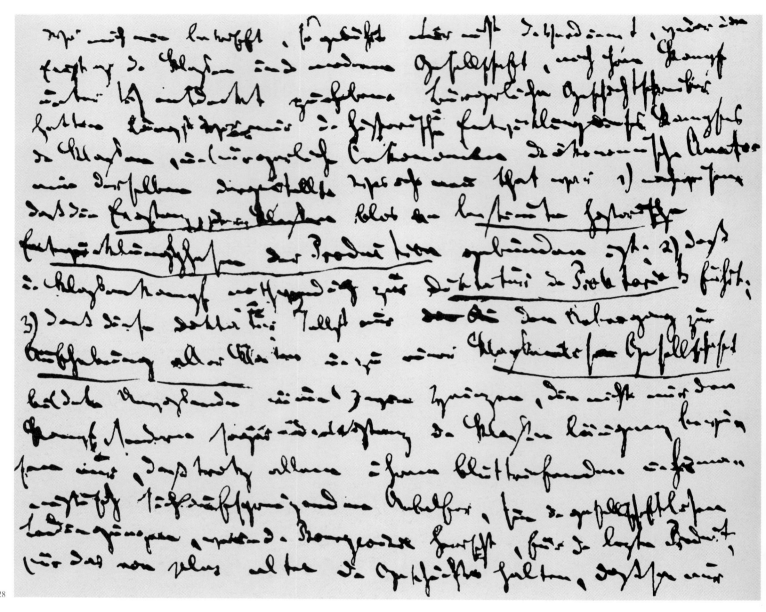

28

28. Marx's letter to Joseph Weydemeyer, March 5, 1852
A fragment

"MY OWN CONTRIBUTION WAS 1. TO SHOW THAT THE *EXISTENCE OF CLASSES* IS MERELY BOUND UP WITH *CERTAIN HISTORICAL PHASES IN THE DEVELOPMENT OF PRODUCTION*; 2. THAT THE CLASS STRUGGLE NECESSARILY LEADS TO THE *DICTATORSHIP OF THE PROLETARIAT*; 3. THAT THIS DICTATORSHIP ITSELF CONSTITUTES NO MORE THAN A TRANSITION TO THE *ABOLITION OF ALL CLASSES* AND TO A *CLASSLESS SOCIETY*."

KARL MARX

Most of the leaders of the Communist League in Germany were arrested in the summer of 1851. In a bid to discredit and destroy workers' and democratic organisations, the Prussian government put members of the Communist League on trial in Cologne on charges of high treason. Faking evidence, the police endeavoured to portray the League as a secret terrorist organisation.

The numerous evidence Marx collected of the vile fabrications of the Prussian police and judiciary were sent to Cologne for use at the trial, and then published in a pamphlet, *Revelations Concerning the Communist Trial in Cologne.*

29. A view of Cologne in the 1850s

30. In a Cologne court during the trial of Communists, October-November 1852

29

30

31
32

"THE DEFENDANTS, WHO RE-PRESENTED THE REVOLUTIO-NARY PROLETARIAT, STOOD DE-FENCELESS BEFORE THE RUL-ING CLASSES WHO WERE RE-PRESENTED BY THE JURY."

KARL MARX

The defendants at the Communist trial in Cologne

31. Peter Nothjung (c. 1823-1866), member of the Cologne Workers' Association and of the Communist League; sentenced to six years' imprisonment in a fortress

32. Roland Daniels (1819-1855), physician, prominent figure in the Communist League, was acquitted by the jury

33. Heinrich Bürgers (1820-1878), member of the Cologne community of the Communist League; member of the Central Authority of the Communist League in Cologne from 1850; sentenced to six years' imprisonment in a fortress

34

35
36

34. *Hermann Heinrich Becker (1820-1855), German journalist, member of the Communist League from 1850; sentenced to five years' imprisonment in a fortress*

35. *Ferdinand Freiligrath (1810-1876), German poet, member of the Communist League, was charged in absentia*

36. *Abraham Jacobi (b. 1832), physician, member of the Communist League; was acquitted by the jury*

37. *Friedrich Lessner (1825-1910), German tailor, member of the Communist League, sentenced to three years' imprisonment in a fortress*

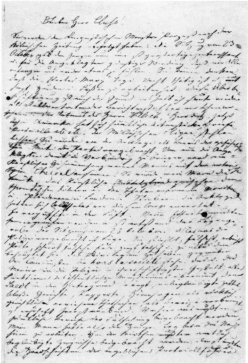
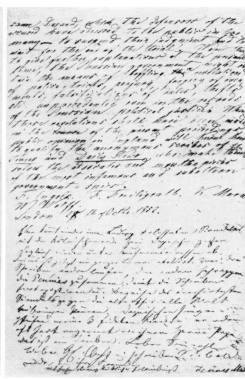

38

38. *Jenny Marx's letter of October 28, 1852 to Adolf Cluss, member of the Communist League, forced to emigrate to the United States after the defeat of the 1848-49 revolution*

"EVERYTHING ADDUCED BY THE POLICE IS UNTRUE," wrote Jenny. "THEY STEAL, FORGE, BREAK INTO DESKS, BEAR FALSE WITNESS AND, WITHAL, CLAIM THIS LICENCE *VIS-À-VIS* COMMUNISTS, WHO ARE OUTSIDE SOCIETY!... WE HERE (IN LONDON—*ED.*) HAD TO SUPPLY ALL PROOFS OF THE FORGERY. HENCE MY HUSBAND HAD TO WORK ALL DAY AND LATE INTO THE NIGHT."

39. *Jenny Marx with her daughter Jenny in the mid-1850s*

39

THE COLOGNE TRIALS.

(To the Editor of The "People's Paper.")

SIR,— The undersigned call your attention to the attitude of the Prussian Press, including even the most reactionary papers, such as the "Neue Preussische Zeitung" during the pending trial of the Communists at Cologne, and to the honourable discretion they observe, at a moment where scarcely a third part of the witnesses have been examined, when none of the produced documents have been verified, and not a word has fallen yet from the defence. While these papers, at the worst, represent the Cologne prisoners and the undersigned, their London friends, in accordance with the public accuser, as "dangerous conspirators who alone are responsible for the whole history of Europe of the latter four years, and for all the revolutionary commotions of 1848 and 1849" — there are in London two public organs, the "Times" and the "Daily News" which really have not hesitated to represent the Cologne prisoners and the undersigned as a "gang of sturdy beggars," swindlers, etc. The undersigned address to the English public the same demand which the defensors of the accused have addressed to the public in Germany—to suspend their judgment, and to wait for the end of the trials. Were they to give further explanations at the present time, the Prussian government might obtain the means of baffling a revelation of police-tricks, perjury, forgery of documents, falsification of documents, thefts, etc., unprecedented even in the records of Prussian political justice. When that revelation shall have been made in the course of the present proceedings, public opinion in England will know how to qualify the anonymous scribes of the "Times" and "Daily News," who constitute themselves the advocates and mouthpieces of the most infamous and subaltern government spies.

We are, Sir, yours fraternally,
F. ENGELS,
F. FREILIGRATH,
K. MARX.

London, October 28th.

40-41. Statement of Karl Marx and Frederick Engels on the Cologne Trial of Communists, dated October 28, 1852. It was published in a number of English newspapers

42. A police report on Karl Marx, Frederick Engels and the German refugees in London
A page of the manuscript

$$\mathfrak{Enthüllungen}$$

über den

$$\mathfrak{Kommunisten\text{-}Prozeß}$$

$$\mathfrak{zu\ Köln.}$$

Bafel,
Buchdruckerei von Chr. Kräfi.
1853.

43. Karl Marx, Revelations Concerning the Communist Trial in Cologne, *first edition, Basle, 1853*

Soon after the Cologne trial of Communists, Marx proposed at a meeting of the London branch of the Communist League to dissolve the local organisation and to declare the further existence of the League untimely.

44

Examining the specific features of the economic developments in Europe in the 1850s, Engels wrote that the economic revolution "has seized the whole of the Continent since 1848 and has caused big industry to take real root in France, Austria, Hungary, Poland and, recently, in Russia, while it has made Germany positively an industrial country of the first rank—all on a capitalist basis... The industrial revolution ... has everywhere produced clarity in class relations, ... has created a genuine bourgeoisie and a genuine large-scale industrial proletariat and has pushed them into the foreground of social development."

45

46

44. *A sugar refinery in Nantes, France*

45. *A foundry in Germany*

46. *Twisting machines in a British textile factory*

47

*47. Marx visited the First Great Exhibi-
tion at the Crystal Palace in London,
1851*

48. France at the time of the Second Empire. "In the liberal empire a gendarme is always at hand."

"SINCE 1849 COMMERCIAL AND INDUSTRIAL PROSPERITY HAS STRETCHED THE LOUNGE ON WHICH THE COUNTER-REVOLUTION HAS SLEPT IN SAFETY."

KARL MARX

49. "Go to Paris, my boy. Earn a livelihood…"

50. The Preston strike of 1853, England

Living in England, Marx continuous-ly assisted left-wing leaders of the Chartist movement. He exposed the half-baked democracy of bourgeois Britain, and the deceit and hypocrisy of the British parliamentary system.

The prime task of the British labour movement, Marx held, was to form an independent political party.

51. The Democratic Review, *London*

Published by Julian Harney, leader of the left-wing Chartists from June 1849 to September 1850. Marx and Engels were its frequent contributors.

THE

DEMOCRATIC REVIEW

OF

BRITISH AND FOREIGN

POLITICS, HISTORY, AND LITERATURE.

EDITED BY

G. JULIAN HARNEY.

VOL. II.

JUNE—SEPTEMBER, 1850.

LONDON:
J. WATSON, 3, QUEEN'S HEAD PASSAGE, PATERNOSTER ROW.
1850.

The People's Paper

THE CHAMPION OF
POLITICAL JUSTICE AND UNIVERSAL RIGHT.

[08] LONDON, SATURDAY, MARCH 18, 1864. [Price Fourpence.]

The Mass Movement.

THE LABOUR PARLIAMENT.

FRIDAY'S SITTING.

The house re-assembled at nine o'clock.

Mr. Clark Cropper in the chair.

The minutes having been read and confirmed, it was ordered that instead of 300 copies, 1,500 copies of the balance sheet should be printed.

Mr. E. Jones then read the following letter from Dr. Marx, of London:—

"28, Dean Street, Soho, London.
"9th March, 1854.

'I regret deeply to be unable, for the moment at least, to leave London, and thus to be prevented from expressing verbally my feelings of pride and gratitude on receiving the invitation to sit as Honorary Delegate at the Labour Parliament. The mere assembling of such a Parliament marks a new epoch in the history of the world. The news of this great fact will arouse the hopes of the working classes throughout Europe and America.

"Great Britain, of all other countries, has seen developed on the greatest scale, the despotism of Capital and the slavery of Labour. In no other country have the intermediate stations between the millionaire commanding whole industrial armies and the wages-slave living only from hand to mouth so gradually been swept away from the soil. There exist here no longer, as in continental countries, large classes of peasants and artisans almost equally dependent on their own property and their own labour. A complete divorce of property from labour has been effected in Great Britain. In no other country, therefore, the war between the two classes that constitute modern society has assumed so colossal dimensions and features so distinct and palpable.

But it is precisely from these facts that the working classes of Great Britain, before all others, are competent and called for to act as leaders in the great movement that must finally result in the absolute emancipation of Labour. Such they are from the conscious clearness of their position, the vast superiority of their numbers, the disastrous struggles of their past, and the moral strength of their present.

It is the working millions of Great Britain who first have laid down the real basis of a new society—modern industry, which transformed the destructive agencies of nature into the productive power of man. The English working classes, with invincible energies, by the sweat of their brows and brains, have called into life the material means of ennobling labour itself, and of multiplying its fruits to such a degree as to make general abundance possible.

By creating the inexhaustible productive powers of modern industry they have fulfilled the first condition of the emancipation of labour. They have now to realise its other condition. They have to free those wealth-producing powers from the infamous shackles of monopoly, and subject them to the joint control of the producers, who, till now, allowed the very products of their hands to turn against them and be transformed into as many instruments of their own subjugation.

The labouring classes have conquered nature; they have now to conquer men. To succeed in this attempt they do not want strength, but the organisation of their common strength, organisation of the labouring classes on a national scale—such, I suppose, is the great and glorious end aimed at by the Labour Parliament.

If the Labour Parliament proves true to the idea that called it into life, some future historian will have to record that there existed in the year 1854 two Parliaments in England, a Parliament at London, and a Parliament at Manchester—a Parliament of the rich, and a Parliament of the poor—but that men sat only in the Parliament of the men and not in the Parliament of the masters.

Yours truly,
KARL MARX.

52

---

52. Karl Marx, *"Letter to the Labour Parliament"*, The People's Paper

A Labour Parliament was convened on March 6, 1854 on the initiative of a revolutionary group of Chartists headed by Ernest Jones.

"ORGANISATION OF THE LABOURING CLASSES ON A NATIONAL SCALE—SUCH, I SUPPOSE, IS THE GREAT AND GLORIOUS END AIMED AT BY THE LABOUR PARLIAMENT," wrote Marx.

53. The file on Karl Marx and the file on Frederick Engels in the archives of the Prussian police, 1852-53

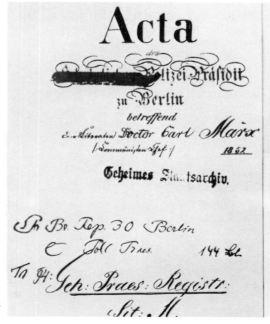

54. *Karl Marx*

55. *Announcement of the meeting to be held in London on February 27, 1855, to mark the anniversary of the French Revolution of 1848. Marx was among those invited*

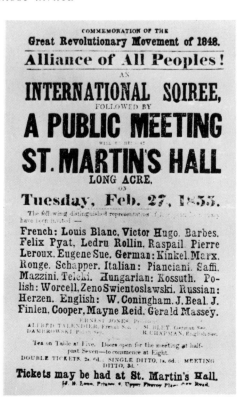

55

The first few years of life in London were especially trying for the Marx family. The want they lived in was compounded with painful bereavements. One-year-old Heinrich died of pneumonia on November 19, 1850, and little Franziska, born in March 1851, followed him to the grave 18 months later, on April 14, 1852. "Our beloved child's death," Jenny Marx recalled years later, "occurred at the time of the hardest privations, our German friends being unable to help us just then."

The most painful blow of all was the death of eight-year-old Edgar on April 6, 1855.

In all those years Frederick Engels's friendship and assistance were indispensable.

56. *Jenny Marx, wife of Karl Marx, in the early 1850s*

57. *The house at 28 Dean Street, Soho, London, where the Marxes lived from December 1850 to September 1856*

59

58. Jenny Marx, eldest daughter of the Marxes, in the early 1850s

59. Laura Marx, daughter of the Marxes, in the mid-1850s

60. Edgar's letter to his mother

61. Edgar Marx (Musch), son of the Marxes

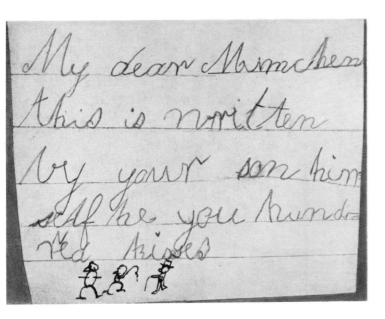

61

62. Frederick Engels, Brussels, 1862

63. Engels's home in Manchester

In November 1850 Frederick Engels was compelled to leave London for Manchester to devote himself to "filthy commerce" at the trading firm of Ermen & Engels. This enabled him to assist the Marxes financially.

Although the two friends lived in different cities, they were in constant and close communication with each other. Chiefly by mail. They sent each other letters almost every day, discussing crucial points of theory and practice. When Marx's girls grew up, they were frequent guests at Engels's home in Manchester. From time to time, Marx, too, would come to Manchester to relax or do a bit of work.

63

64

64. Marx, Engels and Marx's daughters (left to right) Laura, Eleanor, Jenny, London, 1864

The People's Paper,

THE CHAMPION OF
POLITICAL JUSTICE AND UNIVERSAL RIGHT.

Das Volk.

Expedition: 3, Litchfield Street, Soho.

Neue Oder-Zeitung.

New-York  Tribune.

Die Presse.

Abendblatt.

THE NEW
AMERICAN CYCLOPÆDIA:

66

In the summer of 1851, Marx accepted the offer to be correspondent of the *New-York Daily Tribune*, a progressive bourgeois paper. Marx enlisted Engels to help him out. In the subsequent ten years they contributed more than 500 articles on economy and international relations.

While a correspondent of the *New-York Daily Tribune*, Marx was also a frequent contributor to various other progressive publications, notably the workers' press in Britain and elsewhere.

65. Some of the periodicals to which Karl Marx contributed

66. A page from the noteboook of Marx's wife Jenny, showing when the articles of Karl Marx and Frederick Engels where posted to the New-York Daily Tribune *(some of the entries are in Marx's hand)*

Marx's articles for the *New-York Daily Tribune*, Engels wrote, "were not ordinary despatches but expositions of the political and economic situation in various European countries based on thorough study and often comprising a whole series of articles".

67

When a bourgeois revolution broke out in Spain in 1854, Marx set about studying the history of that country. "My principal study is now Spain," he wrote to Engels on September 2, 1854.

67. Revolution in Spain. The insurgents at the royal palace in Madrid on July 17, 1854

68. Karl Marx, Revolutionary Spain, *1854*
A page of the manuscript

Marx's studies of Spanish history culminated in a series of articles, *Revolutionary Spain*, which appeared in the *New-York Daily Tribune* from September to December 1854. They contained a searching examination of the Spanish people's struggles from the time of Napoleon's invasion to the bourgeois revolution of 1820-23.

A few of the articles were devoted to the Spanish bourgeois revolution of 1854.

Marx kept his finger on the pulse of events in Italy. In his articles, he showed that the country's liberation would involve a great revolutionary national insurrection. He called therefore for unity of the middle and petty bourgeoisie, the peasants, the progressive intelligentsia, and the then as yet numerically small working class. The aim of the insurrection would be the national liberation of Italy from Austrian and French rule, and the country's unification. The state that would emerge, he pointed out, should have a genuinely democratic basis, and should wipe out the remnants of feudalism.

"A SUCCESSFUL REVOLUTION IN ITALY," Marx wrote, "WILL BE THE SIGNAL FOR A GENERAL STRUGGLE ON THE PART OF ALL THE OPPRESSED NATIONALITIES TO RID THEMSELVES OF THEIR OPPRESSORS."

69

70

69. *The king's troops fire on insurgents in Palermo*

70. *Townsmen demonstrate for the incorporation of Naples in the Italian state*

71

71. *Garibaldi's 1,000 men on the march*

"IN GARIBALDI, ITALY HAD A HERO OF ANTIQUE DIGNITY, WHO WAS ABLE TO PERFORM WONDERS AND ACTUALLY DID. WITH A THOUSAND VOLUNTEERS, HE OVERTHREW THE ENTIRE KINGDOM OF NAPLES, IN FACT UNITED ITALY, AND TORE TO PIECES THE ARTIFICIAL WEB OF BONAPARTIST POLITICS. ITALY WAS FREE AND ESSENTIALLY UNITED—THOUGH NOT BY LOUIS NAPOLEON'S INTRIGUES, BUT BY THE REVOLUTION."

FREDERICK ENGELS

72
73

Democrats from Russia took part in the struggle for the liberation of Italy.

The Russian Garibaldians

72. Lev Mechnikov (1838-1888), geographer and public figure

73. Anna Toliverova-Jacobi (1842-1918), Russian writer

74. Vladimir Kovalevsky (1842-1883), palaeontologist, member of the revolutionary movement in Russia

75. The house at 1 Grafton Terrace, Maitland Park, Haverstock Hill (north-western part of London)

The Marxes lived here from 1856 to 1864. This was the time when Karl Marx defined the basic points of his economic theory.

"The money inherited after my mother's death," Jenny Marx recalled, "enabled us to move from Dean Street into a little house in romantic Hampstead at the foot of delightful Primrose Hill. When we first slept in our own beds, sat on our own chairs, and even had a drawing room of our own, with rococo furniture or, more precisely, with the old junk that we had bought by chance, it really seemed to us that we were in a magic castle and that trumpets and kettledrums were hailing our magnificence."

75

76. *Karl Marx, London, 1861*

77. *Marx's letter to his wife in Trier, where Jenny and her children stayed at her sick mother's, June 21, 1856*
A page of the manuscript

"My darling Sweetheart,
"I am writing to you again because I am alone and because it is irksome to converse with you all the time in my head without you knowing or hearing or being able to answer me. Bad as your portrait is, it serves its end well enough, and I now understand how it is that even the least flattering portraits of the mother of God, the 'Black Madonnas', could have their inveterate admirers—more admirers, indeed, than the good portraits."

78. Jenny Marx

79

79. Jenny and Laura, Marx's daughters

"They are both endowed with exceptionally warm hearts, are gifted and have becoming modesty and maidenly good manners. Little Jenny will be seventeen years old on the first of May (1861—*Ed.*). She is a girl of great charm and very attractive appearance, with her thick, shiny dark hair and equally dark, shining, gentle eyes and dark, Creole-like complexion, which has, however, acquired a genuine English bloom.

"Laura, who was fifteen years old last September (1860—*Ed.*), is perhaps prettier and has more regular features than her elder sister, whose very opposite she is. As tall, slender and finely built as little Jenny, she is in all other respects lighter, more radiant and transparent ... so lovely is her curly, wavy chestnut hair, so sweet the dear, greenish sparkling eyes, which flicker like eternal *feux de joie*, so noble and finely shaped is her forehead...

"At school they have always carried off the first prize. They are completely at home in English and know quite a lot of French. They can read Dante in

81

82

the Italian and also know a bit of Spanish...

"Little Jenny has a special talent for drawing and her pastels are the finest adornment of our rooms."

From Jenny Marx's letter to Louise Weydemeyer

84

80. Eleanor Marx, the youngest daughter of the Marxes, in the early 1860s

"The baby had only just been born when my poor, dear Edgar departed this life (in 1855—*Ed.*), and all the love we felt for the dear little boy, all the tenderness towards him, was transferred to his little sister, whom our elder daughters tended and nursed with almost maternal solicitude. Indeed, a more delightful child can hardly be imagined—pretty as a picture, guileless and with a whimsical sense of humour... She is a real pet of Karl's and dispels many a care with her laughter and chatter," Jenny Marx wrote to Louise Weydemeyer.

81. A copy of Rafael's "Madonna in the Armchair" by Marx's daughter Jenny. Jenny made a gift of it to Frederick Engels in 1859

82. A plate painted by Marx's daughter Jenny

83. A copy of Horace's portrait by Marx's daughter Jenny

84. A locket with a portrait of Karl Marx and a lock of Jenny Marx's hair. It belonged to the Marxes' eldest daughter, also Jenny

85. Marx's wallet

86. Marx's cigar-holder in a case

85

86

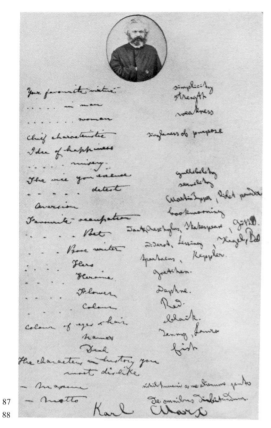

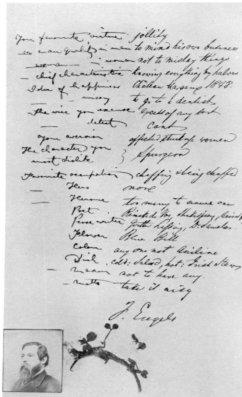

87
88

88. The "confession" of Frederick Engels

Your favourite virtue		jollity
" " in man		to mind his own business
" in woman		not to mislay things
Chief characteristic		knowing everything by halves
Idea of happiness		chateau margaux 1848 (a wine—Ed.)
" misery		to go to a dentist
The vice you excuse		excess of any sort
" detest		cant
Your aversion		affected stuckup women
The character you most dislike		Spurgeon (Baptist preacher—Ed.)
Favourite occupation		chaffing & being chaffed
" hero		none
" heroine		too many to name one
" poet		Reinecke Fox, Shakespeare, Ariosto, etc.
" prose writer		Goethe, Lessing, Dr. Samelson (oculist—Ed.)
" flower		Blue bell
" colour		any one not aniline
" dish		cold: salad, hot: Irish stew
" maxim		not to have any
" motto		take it easy

Marx's daughters were fond of a questions and answers game called Confessions popular in England in the mid-1860s.

Marx, all members of his family, Frederick Engels and other prominent personalities of the international working-class movement who happened to visit the Marxes, would take part in the game. Their answers are recorded in an album belonging to Marx's eldest daughter Jenny. Charles Longuet, Marx's great-grandson, made a gift of it to the Institute of Marxism-Leninism of the CC CPSU in 1960.

87. The "confession" of Karl Marx

Your favourite virtue		simplicity
" " in man		strength
" " woman		weakness
Chief characteristic		singleness of purpose
Idea of happiness		
" " misery		
The vice you excuse		gullibility
" detest		servility
Aversion		Martin Tupper, violet powder bookworming
Favourite occupation		
" poets		Dante, Aeschylus, Shakespeare, Goethe
" prose writers		Diderot, Lessing, Hegel, Balsac
" hero		Spartacus, Keppler
" heroine		Gretchen
" flower		Daphne
" colour		Red
colour of eyes & hair		Black
Names		Jenny, Laura
Dish		fish
The character in history you most dislike		
" maxim		nihil humani a me alienum puto
" motto		de omnibus dibitandum

89. The "confession" of Jenny, Marx's wife

Your favourite virtue	sincerity
" in man	perseverance
" " woman	affection
" chief characteristic	sensitiveness
" idea of happiness	health
" misery	dependence
The vice you excuse most	indecision
" detest most	ingratitude
Your aversion	debts
Favourite occupation	needlework
" poet	Goethe
" prose writer	Martin Luther
" hero	Coriolanus
" heroine	Florence Nightingale
Flower	rose
Colour	blue
Favourite maxim	Never mind
Motto	Nil desperandum

89

90

91

92

90. The "confession" of Marx's eldest daughter Jenny

91. The "confession" of Marx's daughter Laura

92. The "confession" of Marx's daughter Eleanor

93

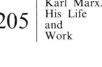

Die Presse.

№ 293. Wien, Freitag den 25. October 1861. 14. Jahrgang

From the day the Civil War began in the United States (1861-65), Marx's attention was riveted to that country.

He wrote more than forty articles about the Civil War in North America, most of them for *Die Presse*, a liberal Austrian paper, with which he was associated in 1861 and 1862. Showing the social and economic motives behind the Civil War, Marx observed that slavery in the South was incompatible with capitalist development and the policy of the industrial North.

Marx stressed that as long as the labour of Blacks was slave labour, the labour of Whites, too, could not be free. Struggle against the 300,000 American slaveowners, he pointed out, was a cause that concerned the entire international proletariat.

93. The Civil War in America. The battle at Front Royal, Virginia

94. Blacks volunteer to the Northern armies

95. Abraham Lincoln (1809-1865), President of the USA; in 1861-65 headed the struggle of the Northern States against slavery

"LINCOLN'S PLACE IN THE HISTORY OF THE UNITED STATES AND OF MANKIND WILL BE NEXT TO THAT OF WASHINGTON!"

KARL MARX

96. Karl Marx, "The North American Civil War"
  Die Presse

"THE PRESENT STRUGGLE BETWEEN THE SOUTH AND NORTH IS NOTHING BUT A STRUGGLE BETWEEN TWO SOCIAL SYSTEMS, THE SYSTEM OF SLAVERY AND THE SYSTEM OF FREE LABOUR."

KARL MARX

97

97. *An anti-slavery meeting in London*

98. *Marx's pocketbook with notes on Poland, 1863. Some of the notes are by Laura, who often helped her father*

99. *Encampment of Polish insurgents*

"THE ENGLISH WORKING CLASS HAS WON IMMORTAL HISTORICAL HONOUR FOR ITSELF BY THWARTING THE REPEATED ATTEMPTS OF THE RULING CLASSES TO INTERVENE ON BEHALF OF THE AMERICAN SLAVEHOLDERS BY ITS ENTHUSIASTIC MASS MEETINGS."

KARL MARX

Marx followed the liberation struggle of the people of Poland with close attention. He maintained that it could succeed only if the large mass of peasants became involved in it and it blended with the struggle for revolutionary democratic change.

100. Karl Marx and his daughter Jenny, Margate, 1866

101. Laura, Marx's daughter, London, 1864

102

During the Crimean War (1853-56)
fought by Great Britain, France, Tur-
key and Sardinia against Russia, Marx
and Engels followed all developments
and examined their substance in articles for the press.

103

102. Bombardment of Sebastopol by British, French and Turkish warships on October 3, 1854

103. A Russian battery on Malakhov Hill

104. Chart of the battle on the Chernaya river near Sebastopol. Drawn by Frederick Engels

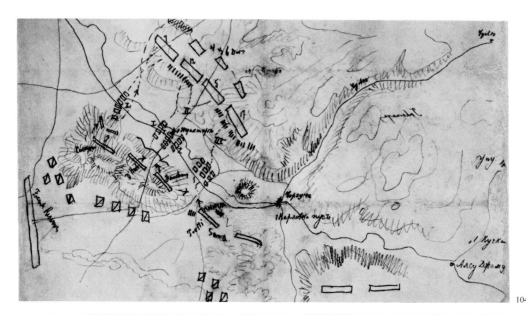

104

105

Following developments in Russia after its defeat in the Crimean War, Marx drew special attention to the movement for the abolition of serfdom. He contributed several articles on the subject to the *New-York Daily Tribune*, pointing out that "combustible matter" had accumulated and symptoms of "a servile war", a war of peasant serfs, were at hand.

105. Exaction of arrears

106. A peasant riot

106

107

"THE PRESENT COMMERCIAL CRISIS," wrote Marx to Ferdinand Lassalle, "HAS IMPELLED ME TO SET TO WORK SERIOUSLY ON MY OUTLINES OF POLITICAL ECONOMY, AND ALSO TO PREPARE SOMETHING ON THE PRESENT CRISIS."

107. *Karl Marx*

108. *Graphs by Marx containing figures related to the crisis*

A fragment

Reference material for articles that Marx wrote on the economic crisis of 1857-58

An economic crisis erupted in 1857—first in the United States, then also in European countries.

Writing about it, Marx showed its specificity from country to country, and drew important theoretical conclusions about the objective laws governing economic crises. He demonstrated their impact on the political situation and how they stimulated the working-class and democratic movement.

109

109. The Stock Exchange
110. The cotton famine in Britain.
People in Manchester line up for bread,
meat, milk and coal ration cards

110

111

The worldwide economic crisis of 1857 gave impulse to a fresh revolutionary surge in Europe and America.

111. A building workers' strike in London in 1859

112. A chart showing the movement of cotton prices as from January 1, 1857, which Engels drew at Marx's request

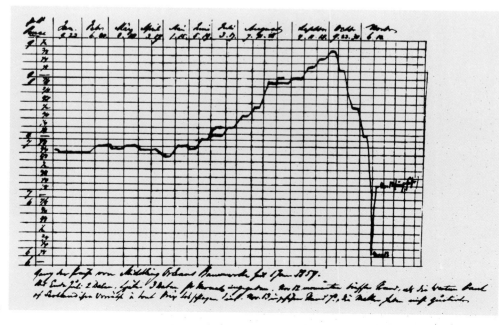

113

*113. Barricades being thrown up on
Montmartre Boulevard in Paris in 1860*

"I CONCLUDE," Marx wrote at the
time, "THAT NEITHER THE DE-
CLAMATION OF THE DEMA-
GOGUES, NOR THE TWADDLE OF
THE DIPLOMATS WILL DRIVE
MATTERS TO A CRISIS, BUT THAT
THERE ARE APPROACHING ECON-
OMICAL DISASTERS AND SOCIAL
CONVULSIONS WHICH MUST BE
THE SURE FORERUNNERS OF
EUROPEAN REVOLUTION."

114

115

In his articles on affairs in India, China, Persia, Algeria, Afghanistan, and Ireland, Marx set forth the basic theoretical principles that should govern the proletariat's nationalities and colonial policy.

Marx and Engels considered the national liberation movement in colonial countries an ally of the revolution in Europe.

116

114. *The revolt in India in 1857. The battle at the walls of Delhi*

115. *The battle of Meerut on May 10, 1857*

116. *Suppression of the revolt in India*

117. *Karl Marx, "The British Rule in India", New-York Daily Tribune, June 25, 1853*

"THE PROFOUND HYPOCRISY AND INHERENT BARBARISM OF BOURGEOIS CIVILISATION LIES UNVEILED BEFORE OUR EYES, TURNING FROM ITS HOME, WHERE IT ASSUMES RESPECT-ABLE FORMS, TO THE COLO-NIES, WHERE IT GOES NAKED."

KARL MARX

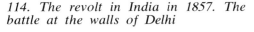

NEW-YORK DAILY TRIBUNE, SATURDAY, JUNE 25, 1853.

The British Rule in India.
Correspondence of The N. Y. Tribune.
LONDON, Friday, June 10, 1853.

Telegraphic dispatches from Vienna announce that the pacific solution of the Turkish, Sardinian and Swiss questions, is regarded there as a certainty.

Last night the debate on India was continued in the House of Commons, in the usual dull manner. Mr. Blackett charged the statements of Sir Charles Wood and Sir J. Hogg with bearing the stamp of optimist falsehood. A lot of Ministerial and Directorial advocates rebuked the charge as well as they could, and the inevitable Mr. Hume summed up by calling on Ministers to withdraw their bill. Debate adjourned.

Hindostan is an Italy of Asiatic dimensions, the Himalayas for the Alps, the Plains of Bengal for the Plains of Lombardy, the Deccan for the Appenines, and the Isle of Ceylon for the Island of Sicily. The same rich variety in the products of the soil, and the same dismemberment in the political configuration. Just as Italy has, from time to time, been compressed by the conqueror's sword into different national masses, so do we find Hindostan, when not under the pressure of the Mohammedan, or the Mogul, or the Briton, dissolved into as many independent and conflicting States as it numbered towns, er even villages. Yet, in a social point of view, Hindostan is not the Italy, but the Ireland of the East. And this strange combination of Italy and of Ireland, of a world of voluptuousness and of a world of woes, is anticipated in the ancient traditions of the religion of Hindostan. That religion is at once a religion of sensualist exuberance, and a religion of self-torturing asceticism ;a religion of the Lingam and of the Juggernaut; the religion of the Monk, and of the Bayadere.

I share not the opinion of those who believe in a golden age of Hindostan, without recurring, however, like Sir Charles Wood, for the confirmation of my view, to the authority of Khuli-Khan. But take, for example, the times of Aurung-Zebe; or the epoch, when the Mogul appeared in the North, and the Portuguese in the South; or the age of Mohammedan invasion, and of the Heptarchy in Southern India; or, if you will, go still more back to antiquity, take the mythological chronology of the Brahman himself, who places the commencement of Indian misery in an epoch even more remote than the Christian creation of the world.

There cannot, however, remain any doubt but that the misery inflicted by the British on Hindostan is of an essentially different and infinitely more intensive kind than all Hindostan had to suffer before. I do not allude to European despotism, planted upon Asiatic despotism, by the British East India Company, forming a more monstrous combination than any of the divine monsters startling us in the Temple of Salsette. This is no distinctive feature of British Colonial rule, but only an imitation of the Dutch, and so much so that in order to characterise the working of the British East India Company, it is sufficient to literally repeat what Sir Stamford Raffles, the *English* Governor of Java, said of the old Dutch East India Company:

"The Dutch Company, actuated solely by the spirit of gain, and viewing their subjects, with less regard or consideration than a West India planter formerly viewed a gang upon his estate, because the latter had paid the purchase money of human property, which the other had not, employed all the existing machinery of despotism to squeeze from the people their utmost mite of contribution, the last dregs of their labor, and thus aggravated the evils of a capricious and semi-barbarous Government, by working it with all the practised ingenuity of politicians, and all the monopolizing selfishness of traders."

117

New-York Daily Tribune.

VOL XIII......Nº 3,794.   NEW-YORK, TUESDAY, JUNE 14, 1853.   PRICE TWO CENTS.

REVOLUTION IN CHINA AND IN EUROPE.

A most profound yet fantastic speculator on the principles which govern the movements of Humanity, was wont to extol as one of the ruling secrets of nature, what he called the law of the contact of extremes. The homely proverb that "extremes meet" was, in his view, a grand and potent truth in every sphere of life; an axiom with which the philosopher could as little dispense as the astronomer with the laws of Kepler or the great discovery of Newton.

Whether the "contact of extremes" be such a universal principle or not, a striking illustration of it may be seen in the effect the Chinese revolution seems likely to exercise upon the civilized world.

118

118. Karl Marx, "Revolution in China and in Europe", New-York Daily Tribune, June 14, 1853

New-York Daily Tribune.

VOL XVI.......Nº 4,984.   NEW-YORK, FRIDAY, APRIL 10, 1857.   PRICE TWO CENTS.

A few years since, when the frightful system of torture in India was exposed in Parliament Sir James Hogg, one of the Directors of the Most Honorable East India Company, boldly asserted that the statements made were unfounded. Subsequent investigation however, proved them to be based upon facts which should have been well known to the Directors, and Sir James had left him to admit either "wilful ignorance" or "criminal knowledge" of the horrible charge laid at the Company's doors. Lord Palmerston, the present Premier of England, and the Earl of Clarendon, the Minister of Foreign Affairs, seem just now to be placed in a similar uncomfortable position. At the late Lord Mayor's banquet the Premier and, in his speech, while attempting to justify the atrocities committed upon the Chinese:

"If the Government had, in this case approved of their proceedings, they had undoubtedly followed a course which deserved to incur the censure of Parliament and of the country. We were persuaded, however, on the contrary, that these proceedings were necessary and vital. We felt that a great wrong had been inflicted on our country. We felt that our fellow countrymen in a distant part of the globe had been exposed to a series of insults, outrages and atrocities which could not be passed over in silence. [Cheers]. We felt that the treaty rights of this country had been broken, and that those legally charged with the defense of our interests in that quarter of the world were not only justified, but obliged to resent those outrages, so far as the power in their hands would enable them to do so. We felt that we should be betraying the trust which the citizens of the country had reposed in us if we had not approved of the proceedings which we thought to be right, and which we, if placed in the same circumstances, should have deemed it our duty to have pursued. [Cheers]."

Now, however much the people of England and the world at large may be deceived by such plausible statements, his Lordship himself certainly does not believe them to be true, or if he does, he has betrayed a wilful ignorance almost as unjustifiable as "criminal knowledge." Ever since the first report reached us of English hostilities in China, the Government journals of England and a portion of the American Press have been heaping wholesale denunciations upon the Chinese—sweeping charges of violation of treaty obligations—insults to the English flag—degradation of foreigners residing on their soil, and the like; yet not one single distinct charge has been made or a single fact instanced in support of these denunciations, save the case of the lorcha Arrow, and, with respect to this case, the

119

119. Karl Marx, "English Atrocities in China", New-York Daily Tribune, April 10, 1857

120

120. *British fleet firing on Chinese warjunks*

121. *Capture of Peking, October 12, 1860*

"WHATEVER BE THE SOCIAL CAUSES, AND
WHATEVER RELIGIOUS, DYNASTIC, OR NATIONAL
SHAPE THEY MAY ASSUME, THAT HAVE
BROUGHT ABOUT THE CHRONIC REBELLIONS
SUBSISTING IN CHINA FOR ABOUT TEN YEARS
PAST, AND NOW GATHERED TOGETHER IN ONE
FORMIDABLE REVOLUTION, THE OCCASION OF
THIS OUTBREAK HAS UNQUESTIONABLY BEEN
AFFORDED BY THE ENGLISH CANNON FORCING
UPON CHINA THAT SOPORIFIC DRUG CALLED
OPIUM."

KARL MARX

121

In 1857, Marx was invited to write for *The New American Cyclopaedia*. Engels produced a number of items on military subjects. Marx wrote a few biographical pieces, notably on Simon Bolivar, leader of national liberation movements in Latin America, and on Robert Blum, a participant in the 1848 revolution in Germany.

122. Frederick Engels, "Algeria"
From The New American Cyclopaedia, *Vol. I, 1858*

123. French troops fighting the insurgents at Ali-Mahdi, Algeria, 1859

ALGERIA, a division of northern Africa, formerly the Turkish pashalic of Algiers, but since 1830 included in the foreign dominions of France. It is bounded N. by the Mediterranean, E. by Tunis, W. by Morocco, S. by the Great Sahara. The extreme length is 500 miles from E. to W.; the extreme breadth 200 miles from N. to S. The Atlas ridge constitutes an important physical feature in the country, and divides the arable land of the sea-board from the desert. It also constitutes the northern and southern watershed of the province. The main ridge runs from east to west, but the whole province is intersected in all directions with spurs from the central range. The loftiest of the western mountains is Mount Wanashrees, the Mons Zalacus of Ptolemy; of the eastern the Jurjura and Aurep. These attain a height of nearly 7,000 feet. The principal river is the Shelliff. There are rivers of considerable size also, which flow from the south side of the Atlas, and lose themselves in the desert. None of these rivers are navigable. They are nearly dried up in the summer, but overflow a considerable extent of country in the spring and fertilize the soil.—The climate is not considered unhealthy by some travellers. Ophthalmia and cutaneous diseases are common. It is said there are no endemic fevers, but the great loss of the French troops by disease may perhaps lead to a different conclusion. The atmosphere is pure and bright, the summer very hot; and in the winter severe weather is occasionally experienced, especially in the hill country. On the limits of the desert the soil is arid and sandy, but between the mountain districts it is fertile, and especially so in the neighborhood of the streams. Grain crops of all kinds, fruits, European and tropical; flowers, and particularly roses, of remarkable beauty; and a species of sugar-cane, said to be the largest and most productive of any known species, grow in Algeria. The domestic animals of every variety are numerous. Horses, of course, are excellent; asses are of fine growth and much used for riding. The camel and dromedary of Algeria are very superior. The merino sheep is indigenous, and Spain was first supplied from Algeria. The Numidian lion, the panther and leopard, ostriches, serpents, scorpions, and other venomous reptiles, are abundant.—The Berbers, Kabyles, or Mazidh, for they are known by the three names, are believed to have been the aboriginal inhabitants. Of their history as a race little is known, further than that they once occupied the whole of north-western Africa, and are to be found also on the eastern coast. The Kabyles live in the mountain district. The other inhabitants are Arabs, the descendants of the Mussulman invaders. Moors, Turks, Kouloughs, Jews, and negroes, and lastly the French, are found in the country. The population in 1852 was 2,078,035, of which 134,115 were Europeans of all nations, beside a military force of 100,000 men. The Kabyles are an industrious race, living in regular villages, excellent cultivators, and working in mines, in metals, and in coarse woollen and cotton factories. They make gunpowder and soap, gather honey and wax, and supply the towns with poultry, fruit, and other provisions. The Arabs follow the habits of their ancestors, leading a nomadic life, and shifting their camps from place to place according as the necessities of pasturage or other circumstances compel them. The Moors are probably the least respectable of the inhabitants. Living in the towns, and more luxurious than either the Arabs or Kabyles, they are, from the constant oppression of their Turkish rulers, a

"FROM THE FIRST OCCUPATION OF ALGERIA BY THE FRENCH TO THE PRESENT TIME, THE UNHAPPY COUNTRY HAS BEEN THE ARENA OF UNCEASING BLOODSHED, RAPINE, AND VIOLENCE... THE ARAB AND KABYLE TRIBES, TO WHOM INDEPENDENCE IS PRECIOUS, AND HATRED OF FOREIGN DOMINATION A PRINCIPLE DEARER THAN LIFE ITSELF, HAVE BEEN CRUSHED AND BROKEN BY THE TERRIBLE RAZZIAS."

FREDERICK ENGELS

124. Frederick Engels, Barmen, 1861

125

125. *Simon Bolivar y Ponte (1783-1830), leader of the war of independence in the South American Spanish colonies; President of the Republic of Colombia (1819-30)*

BOLIVAR Y PONTE, SIMON, the "liberator" of Colombia, born at Caracas, July 24, 1783, died at San Pedro, near Santa Martha, Dec. 17, 1830. He was the son of one of the *familias Mantuanas*, which, at the time of the Spanish supremacy, constituted the creole nobility in Venezuela. In compliance with the custom of wealthy Americans of those times, at the early age of 14 he was sent to Europe. From Spain he passed to France, and resided for some years in Paris. In 1802 he married in Madrid, and returned to Venezuela, where his wife died suddenly of yellow fever. After this he visited Europe a second time, and was present at Napoleon's coronation as emperor, in 1804, and at his assumption of the iron crown of Lombardy, in 1805. In 1809 he returned home, and despite the importunities of Joseph Felix Ribas, his cousin, he declined to join in the revolution which broke out at Caracas, April 19, 1810; but, after the event, he accepted a mission to London to purchase arms and solicit the protection of the British government. Apparently well received by the marquis of Wellesley, then secretary for foreign affairs, he obtained nothing beyond the liberty to export arms for ready cash with the payment of heavy duties upon them. On his return from London, he again withdrew to private life, until, Sept. 1811, he was prevailed upon by Gen. Miranda, then commander-in-chief of the insurgent land and sea forces, to accept the rank of lieutenant-colonel in the staff, and the command of Puerto Cabello, the strongest fortress of Venezuela. The Spanish prisoners of war, whom Miranda used regularly to send to Puerto Cabello, to be confined in the citadel, having succeeded in overcoming their guards by surprise, and in seizing the citadel, Bolivar, although they were unarmed, while he had a numerous garrison and large magazines, embarked precipitately in the night, with 8 of his officers, without giving notice to his own troops, arrived at daybreak at La Guayra, and retired to his estate at San Mateo. On becoming aware of their commander's flight, the garrison retired in good order from the place, which was immediately occupied by the Spaniards under Monteverde. This event turned the scale in favor of Spain, and obliged Miranda, on the authority of the congress, to sign the treaty of Vittoria, July 26, 1812, which restored Venezuela to the Spanish rule. On July 30 Miranda arrived at La Guayra, where he intended to embark on board an English vessel. On his visit to the commander of the place, Col. Manuel Maria Casas, he met with a numerous company, among whom were Don Miguel Peña and Simon Bolivar, who persuaded him to stay, for one night at least, in Casas's house. At 2 o'clock in the morning, when Miranda was soundly sleeping, Casas, Peña, and Bolivar entered his room, with 4 armed soldiers, cautiously seized his sword and pistol, then awakened him, abruptly told him to rise and dress himself, put him into irons, and had him finally surrendered to Monteverde, who dispatched him to Cadiz, where, after some years' captivity, he died in irons. This act, committed on the pretext that Miranda had betrayed his country by the capitulation of Vittoria, procured for Bolivar Monteverde's peculiar favor, so that when he demanded his passport, Monteverde declared "Col. Bolivar's request should be complied with, as a reward for his having served the king of Spain by delivering up Miranda." He was thus allowed to sail for Curaçoa, where he spent 6 weeks, and proceeded, in company with his cousin Ribas, to the little republic of Carthagena. Previous to their arrival, a great number of soldiers

126. *Karl Marx, "Bolivar y Ponte"*
From The New American Cyclopaedia, *Vol. III, 1858*

127. *Karl Marx, "The War against Persia", January 1857*
A page of the rough draft

127

With the democratic movement on the upgrade, the bourgeoisie redoubled its attacks on Marx and Engels. Karl Vogt, a petty-bourgeois democrat and paid agent of Napoleon III, was to have played a central role in the campaign of slander that was unleashed after the Cologne trial. Marx exposed Vogt in a brilliant pamphlet, *Herr Vogt,* written in 1860.

The clash with Vogt is "crucial to the *historical vindication* of the party and its subsequent position in Germany," wrote Marx to Ferdinand Freiligrath in February 1860.

128. *Karl Marx,* Herr Vogt, *London, 1860*
The title page

Herr Vogt.

Von

Karl Marx.

London,
A. Petsch & Co., deutsche Buchhandlung,
78, FENCHURCH STREET, E.C

1860.

— 9 —

	Pensions.	Dons.
	fr.	fr.
ments égaux, c'est un don, peut-être une dot, de 25,000 francs	25,000	
Alexandrine figure encore, sur la liste des pensions en 1853, pour 6,000 francs mensuels; mais l'article qui la concerne est rayé au crayon.		
Viullet de Condrieu, membre de sociétés chorales et de secours mutuels dans l'Isère, a fait au Prince impérial un legs dont nous ignorons la valeur et que M. Anselme Petetin conseille de rendre public.		
Vieillard, ancien percepteur de Louis-Napoléon, sénateur, avait quelques menues dettes, payées en 1858; en tout, 10,000 francs. Cette somme ne paraît pas être une pension, car elle est soldée par parties inégales : 5,784 fr. 85 c. et fr. 4,215-15 . . .		10,000
Vignon (Claude). Pension de 6,000 francs, à partir de septembre 1862 .	6,000	
Villaume père (à Nancy). Pension de 1,500 fr. (1853).	1,500	
Vinet (Renan) En 1862 pension de 6,000 fr. .	6,000	
Vogt (?). Il lui est remis, en août 1859, 40,000 fr. . .		40,000

W

Waldor (Mme Mélanie) a reçu, en 1858, une somme de 5,000 francs		5,000
En décembre 1856, elle sollicite pour son cousin, M. Moret d'Aiguebelle, une sous-préfecture dans le Midi.		
Elle offre, en 1865, une cantate, *Paris au désert*, intercalée dans une pièce (*la circonstance* (Voyage de l'Empereur en Algérie).		
1.		2

129

"VOGT WAS MERELY ONE OF THE COUNTLESS MOUTHPIECES THROUGH WHOM THE GROTESQUE VENTRILOQUIST IN THE TUILERIES (NAPOLEON III—*ED.*) SPOKE IN FOREIGN TONGUES..."

KARL MARX

129. A page from the ledger showing payments out of Louis Bonaparte's secret budget

The ledger shows that in August 1859, Karl Vogt received 40,000 francs for his pro-Bonapartist activity in Germany and Switzerland.

130. A caricature of Karl Vogt

130

131

132

The International Industrial Exhibition in London opened in May 1862. It was attended by French workers' delegations from Paris, Lyons, and Amiens, and by workers from Germany. Their contacts with British trade union leaders helped establish more enduring ties between the proletariats of Britain, Germany, and France.

131. *The International Industrial Exhibition in London, 1862*

132. *Medal in commemoration of the Exhibition put out in 1862*

133. *Passport of Karl Marx, 1861*

In 1861, Marx went to Berlin to negotiate with Lassalle concerning the publication of a newspaper.

The General Association of German Workers was founded in Germany in 1863. It was the first mass organisation of German workers. While noting that the Association had good points, Marx and Engels chastised the opportunism that Ferdinand Lassalle, its initial president, had fostered there.

134. *A page from the Statutes of the General Association of German Workers, adopted on May 23, 1863*

135. *Ferdinand Lassalle (1825-1864)*

136. *Ferdinand Lassalle's letter to Bismarck, June 8, 1863*
A page of the manuscript

Engels had no idea that Lassalle was conniving with Bismarck, then president of the Prussian cabinet, when he wrote to Marx on June 11, 1863, that "the chap's now operating purely in the service of Bismarck".

137. *A caricature of Bismarck*

134

Politischer Eiertanz.

(Frankfurter Laterne, 30. Sept. 1863.)

137

CAPITAL

As long as there have been capitalists and workers on earth no book has appeared which is of as much importance for the workers...

Frederick Engels

1. Karl Marx, Hanover, end of April 1867

Here Marx worked out his theory of value and went on to formulate the theory of surplus value.

2. Page 19, Notebook III of the 1857-1858 manuscript where Marx first used, and explained, the term Mehrwert (surplus value)

"THE THEORY OF SURPLUS VALUE IS THE CORNERSTONE OF MARX'S ECONOMIC THEORY."

V. I. LENIN

3. Cover of Notebook M containing the "Introduction"

Before he began working on his manuscript, Marx produced the rough draft of an "Introduction" (August 23, 1857), setting forth more fully than anywhere else his understanding of the subject and method of political economy as a particular science.

4. A page from Marx's letter to Engels of April 2, 1858

The plan of Marx's contemplated economic, philosophic and socio-political study, as set forth in this letter, speaks of its immensity. It was to be divided into six books: 1) On Capital; 2) Landed Property; 3) Wage Labour; 4) The State; 5) International Trade; 6) The World Market.

5. An illustration for the first volume of Marx's Capital *by US artist Hugo Gellert*

At the height of the economic crisis of 1857, Marx set about collating his many years of economic research. The Marxian theory of revolution needed thorough economic grounding. "I am working like mad all night and every night collating my economic studies," Marx wrote Engels on December 8, 1857.

Between October 1857 and May 1858 Marx produced a manuscript of vast proportions, which he gave the title, *Outlines of the Critique of Political Economy.* This manuscript, indeed, was the first rough outline of *Capital.*

Making use of his economic manuscripts of 1857-58, Marx produced the original text of his *Contribution to the Critique of Political Economy* in August-November 1858, and made arrangements with Duncker, a Berlin publisher, to put it out in instalments. The book (Part One) came off the press on June 11, 1859 in 1,000 copies.

6. Karl Marx, A Contribution to the Critique of Political Economy, *Part One, Berlin, 1859*

The title page

This study contains the initial exposition of the Marxian theory of value. It shows the nature of commodities and labour in the setting of commodity production. The preface gives the classic definition of the materialist understanding of history.

"IN THE SOCIAL PRODUCTION OF THEIR EXISTENCE, MEN INEVITABLY ENTER INTO DEFINITE RELATIONS, WHICH ARE INDEPENDENT OF THEIR WILL, NAMELY RELATIONS OF PRODUCTION APPROPRIATE TO A GIVEN STAGE IN THE DEVELOPMENT OF THEIR MATERIAL FORCES OF PRODUCTION. THE TOTALITY OF THESE RELATIONS OF PRODUCTION CONSTITUTES THE ECONOMIC STRUCTURE OF SOCIETY, THE REAL FOUNDATION, ON WHICH ARISES A LEGAL AND POLITICAL SUPERSTRUCTURE AND TO WHICH CORRESPOND DEFINITE FORMS OF SOCIAL CONSCIOUSNESS. THE MODE OF PRODUCTION OF MATERIAL LIFE CONDITIONS THE GENERAL PROCESS OF SOCIAL, POLITICAL AND INTELLECTUAL LIFE. IT IS NOT THE CONSCIOUSNESS OF MEN THAT DETERMINES THEIR EXISTENCE, BUT THEIR SOCIAL EXISTENCE THAT DETERMINES THEIR CONSCIOUSNESS. AT A CERTAIN STAGE OF DEVELOPMENT, THE MATERIAL PRODUCTIVE FORCES OF SOCIETY COME INTO CONFLICT WITH THE EXISTING RELATIONS OF PRODUCTION OR—THIS MERELY EXPRESSES THE SAME THING IN LEGAL TERMS—WITH THE PROPERTY RELATIONS WITHIN THE FRAMEWORK OF WHICH THEY HAVE OPERATED HITHERTO. FROM FORMS OF DEVELOPMENT OF THE PRODUCTIVE FORCES THESE RELATIONS TURN INTO THEIR FETTERS. THEN BEGINS AN ERA OF SOCIAL REVOLUTION."

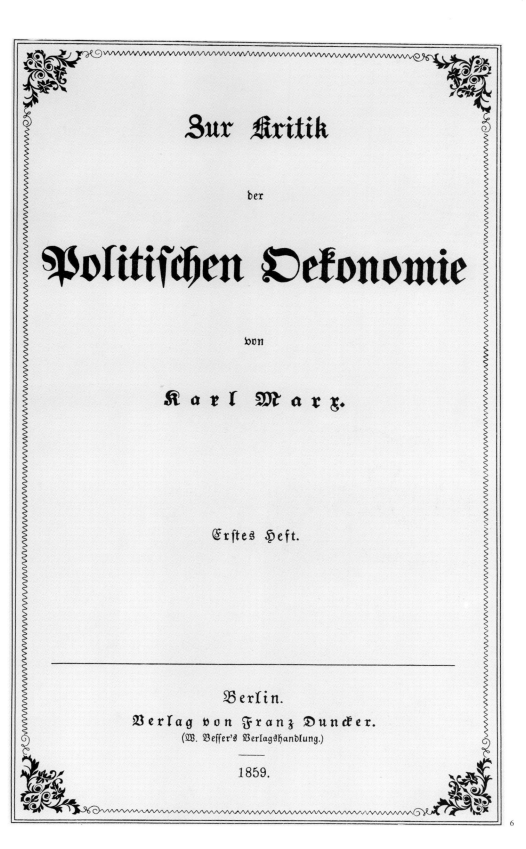

Zur Kritik

der

Politischen Oekonomie

von

Karl Marx.

Erstes Heft.

Berlin.
Verlag von Franz Duncker.
(W. Besser's Verlagshandlung.)

1859.

6

"THE ENORMOUS AMOUNT OF MATERIAL RELATING TO THE HISTORY OF POLITICAL ECONOMY ASSEMBLED IN THE BRITISH MUSEUM, THE FACT THAT LONDON IS A CONVENIENT VANTAGE POINT FOR THE OBSERVATION OF BOURGEOIS SOCIETY ... INDUCED ME TO START AGAIN FROM THE VERY BEGINNING AND TO WORK CAREFULLY THROUGH THE NEW MATERIAL."

KARL MARX

7. *The British Museum*

8. *In the British Museum's reading-room Marx usually occupied seat 7a*

9. *Karl Marx's address in the visitors' book of the British Museum's reading-room*

For many years, each day from nine in the morning until seven at night, Marx worked in one of the world's richest libraries, studying the prolific economic literature.

"I have been going to the Museum in the day-time and writing at night," Marx noted in one of his letters to Engels.

10. *The British Museum's reading-room after its reconstruction in the 1860s*

11

Outstanding classical English economists

11. William Petty (1623-1687)

12. Adam Smith (1723-1790)

13. David Ricardo (1772-1823)

13

From August 1861 to July 1863, Marx produced a new version of his economic study, setting forth his ideas in 23 notebooks totalling well over a thousand pages. The manuscript covers the main subjects that later went into the first, second and third volumes of *Capital*, and also contains the sole existing version of the fourth volume: *Theories of Surplus Value*.

While working on the manuscript, Marx decides on giving it the title of *Capital*, and to have the initial title, *A Critique of Political Economy*, as the sub-title.

The new manuscript of *Capital* as a whole was ready at the end of December 1865. On Engels's advice, Marx had only the first book printed for a start.

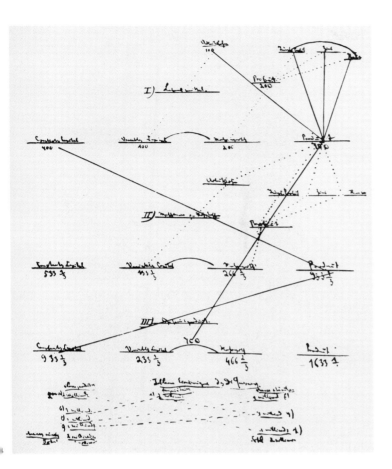

14. *Draft of a chart showing the process of reproduction elaborated upon subsequently in Volume II of* Capital
It was enclosed in Marx's letter to Engels of July 6, 1863

15. *A page from Marx's manuscript,* Theories of Surplus Value *(beginning of Notebook VI of the 1861-1863 Manuscript)*

16. *An illustration for the first volume of Marx's* Capital *by US artist Hugo Gellert*

"THERE CAN BE FEW BOOKS THAT HAVE BEEN WRITTEN IN MORE DIFFICULT CIRCUMSTANCES, AND I AM SURE I COULD WRITE A SECRET HISTORY OF IT WHICH WOULD TELL OF MANY, EXTREMELY MANY UNSPOKEN TROUBLES AND ANXIETIES AND TORMENTS. IF ONLY THE WORKERS HAD AN INKLING OF THE SACRIFICES THAT WERE NECESSARY TO COMPLETE THIS WORK, WHICH WAS WRITTEN ONLY FOR THEM AND FOR THEIR SAKE..."

JENNY MARX

17. *Engels's letter to Marx, April 4, 1867*

Here Engels voices his delight over the completion of Marx's *Capital* (Volume I)

18. *A view of the Harbour in Hamburg*

On April 12, 1867, Marx came to Hamburg to hand the manuscript to Otto Meissner. It had been decided to print *Capital* at Otto Wigand's printshop in Leipzig. The printer started on the book on April 29, 1867.

19. *The house in Leipzig where Volume I of Marx's* Capital *was printed*

From Hamburg, Marx went to see his friend Ludwig Kugelmann in Hanover. He stayed with the Kugelmanns for nearly a month. Here he received the first lot of proofs of his *Capital*.

20. *Ludwig Kugelmann (1830-1902), German physician, took part in the 1848-49 revolution; member of the International; friend of Marx and Engels*

In her *Reminiscences*, Kugelmann's daughter Franzisca wrote the following of Marx's visit:
"Instead of the morose revolutionary she had expected my mother was greeted by a smart, good-humoured gentleman whose warm Rhenish accent at once reminded her of home. Young dark eyes smiled at her from under a mane of grey hair, his movements and his conversation were full of youthful freshness."

17

18

19

The book came off the press on September 14, 1867, in 1,000 copies.

"IN THIS WORK I HAVE TO EXAMINE THE CAPITALIST MODE OF PRODUCTION, AND THE CONDITIONS OF PRODUCTION AND EXCHANGE CORRESPONDING TO THAT MODE...

"IT IS THE ULTIMATE AIM OF THIS WORK TO LAY BARE THE ECONOMIC LAW OF MOTION OF MODERN SOCIETY."

KARL MARX

20

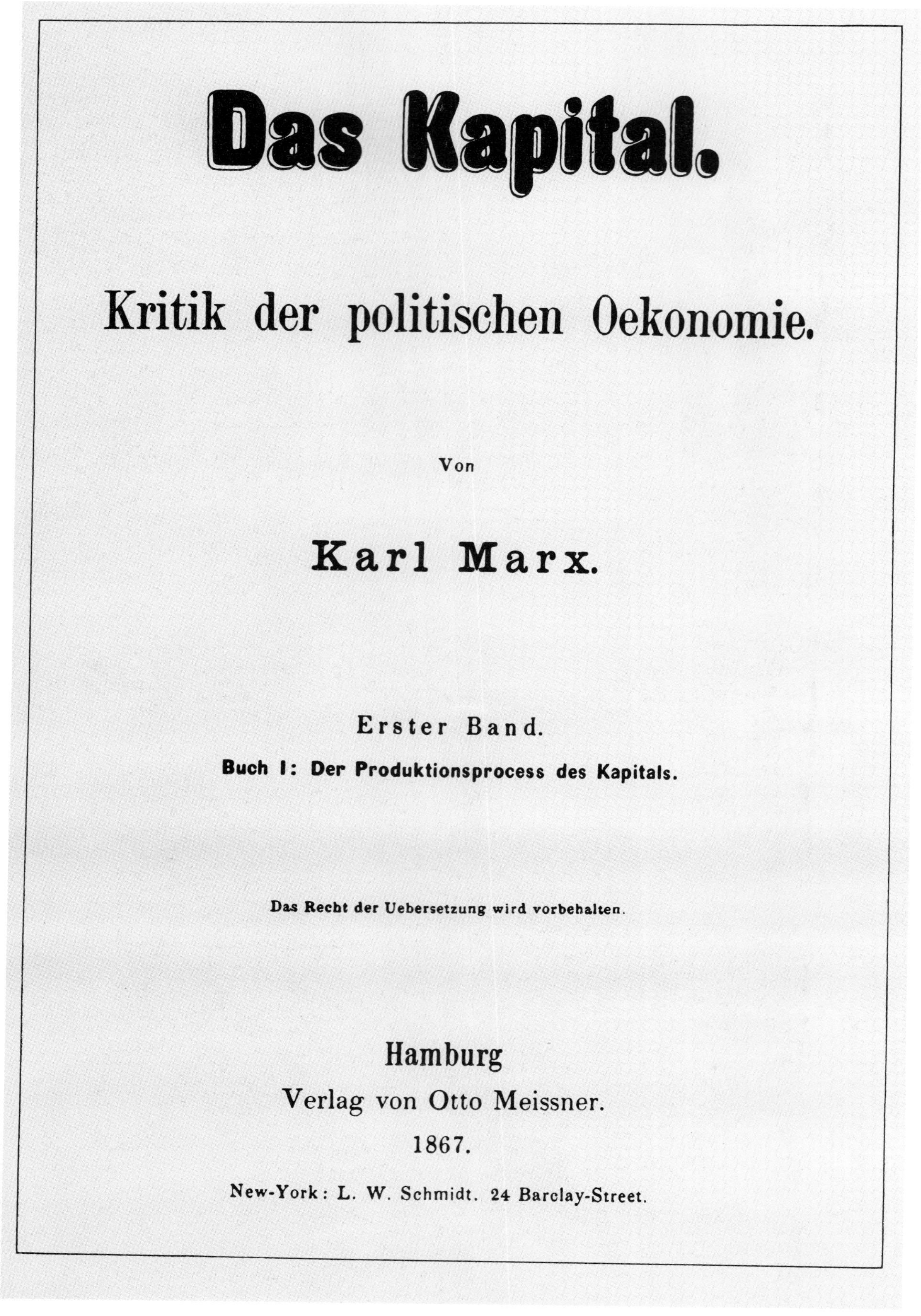

Das Kapital.

Kritik der politischen Oekonomie.

Von

Karl Marx.

Erster Band.

Buch I: Der Produktionsprocess des Kapitals.

Das Recht der Uebersetzung wird vorbehalten.

Hamburg

Verlag von Otto Meissner.

1867.

New-York: L. W. Schmidt. 24 Barclay-Street.

21. Karl Marx,
Capital, *Volume I,
Hamburg, 1867*

22. *Karl Marx*

23

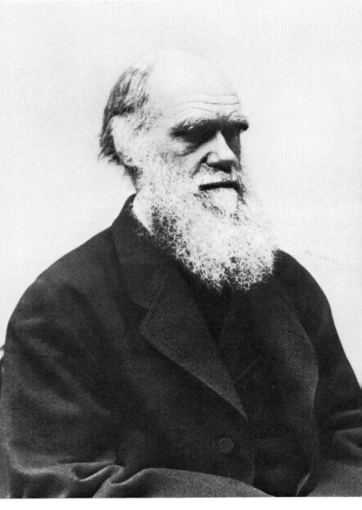

24. *Charles Darwin (1809-1882), English naturalist, founder of the scientific theory of evolution in biology*

25. *Darwin's letter to Marx of October 1, 1873, in which he thanks the latter for sending him a copy of* Capital

"THOUGH OUR STUDIES HAVE BEEN SO DIFFERENT, I BELIEVE THAT WE BOTH EARNESTLY DESIRE THE EXTENSION OF KNOWLEDGE AND THAT THIS IN THE LONG RUN IS SURE TO ADD TO THE HAPPINESS OF MANKIND."

CHARLES DARWIN

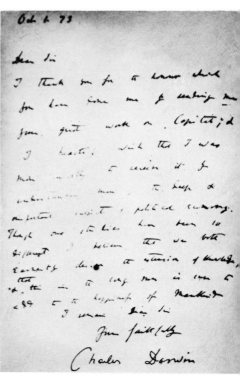

23. Wilhelm Wolff

Marx dedicated *Capital* to Wilhelm Wolff. The following was inscribed on the title page:

"*DEDICATED* TO MY UNFORGETTABLE FRIEND *WILHELM WOLFF*, INTREPID, FAITHFUL, NOBLE PROTAGONIST OF THE PROLETARIAT, BORN IN TARNAU ON JUNE 21, 1809, DIED IN EXILE IN MANCHESTER ON MAY 9, 1864."

"JUST AS DARWIN DISCOVERED THE LAW OF DEVELOPMENT OF ORGANIC NATURE, SO MARX DISCOVERED THE LAW OF DEVELOPMENT OF HUMAN HISTORY...

"BUT THAT IS NOT ALL. MARX ALSO DISCOVERED THE SPECIAL LAW OF MOTION GOVERNING THE PRESENT-DAY CAPITALIST MODE OF PRODUCTION AND THE BOURGEOIS SOCIETY THAT THIS MODE OF PRODUCTION HAS CREATED. THE DISCOVERY OF SURPLUS VALUE SUDDENLY THREW LIGHT ON THE PROBLEM...

"TWO SUCH DISCOVERIES WOULD BE ENOUGH FOR ONE LIFETIME. HAPPY THE MAN TO WHOM IT IS GRANTED TO MAKE EVEN ONE SUCH DISCOVERY."

FREDERICK ENGELS

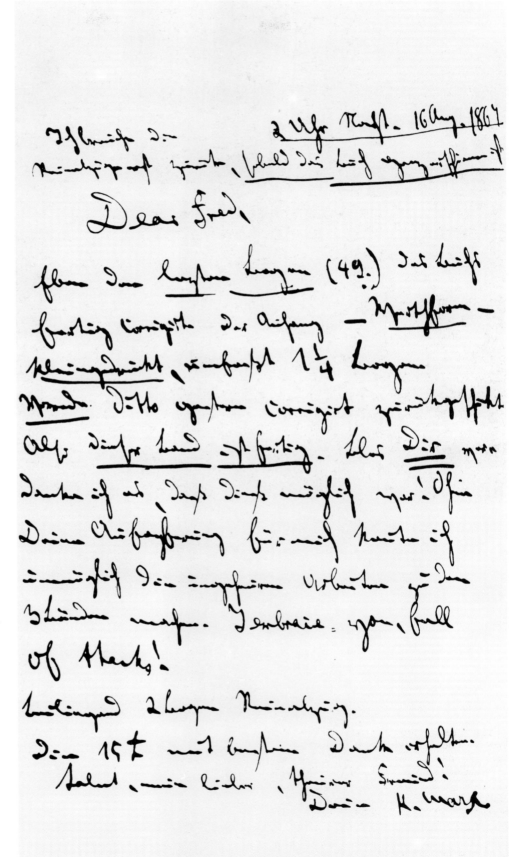

26. Marx's letter to Engels saying he has finished reading the proofs of Volume I of Capital.

"16 AUGUST 1867, 2.0 A.M.
"DEAR FRED,
"HAVE JUST FINISHED CORRECTING THE LAST SHEET (49th) OF THE BOOK... SO, THIS VOLUME IS FINISHED. I OWE IT TO YOU ALONE THAT IT WAS POSSIBLE! WITHOUT YOUR SELF-SACRIFICE FOR ME I COULD NOT POSSIBLY HAVE MANAGED THE IMMENSE LABOUR DEMANDED BY THE 3 VOLUMES. I EMBRACE YOU, FULL OF THANKS!...
"SALUT, MY DEAR, ESTEEMED FRIEND."

27

27. Marx's study in the house at
1 Maitland Park Road, where the
Marxes lived from 1864 to 1875 and
where Karl Marx completed Volume I
of Capital

A mock-up on display at the Marx
and Engels Museum in Moscow

28. Marx's desk chair

КАПИТАЛЪ.

КРИТИКА ПОЛИТИЧЕСКОЙ ЭКОНОМІИ.

СОЧИНЕНІЕ

КАРЛА МАРКСА.

ПЕРЕВОДЪ СЪ НѢМЕЦКАГО.

ТОМЪ ПЕРВЫЙ.

КНИГА I. ПРОЦЕССЪ ПРОИЗВОДСТВА КАПИТАЛА.

—◆—

С.-ПЕТЕРБУРГЪ.

ИЗДАНІЕ Н. П. ПОЛЯКОВА.

1872

Volume I of *Capital* in Russian, the first translation of the volume into a foreign language, appeared in St. Petersburg in 1872 in 3,000 copies.

29. *Karl Marx*, Capital. A Critique of Political Economy, *Volume I, St. Petersburg, 1872*

Cover

30. *Hermann Alexandrovich Lopatin (1845-1918), Russian revolutionary; friend of Karl Marx; translator of* Capital *into Russian*

31. *Nikolai Frantsevich Danielson (1844-1918), Russian economist; translator of* Capital *into Russian*

Marx commended the translation. "It is *masterly*," he wrote to Danielson on May 28, 1872.

PARIS

ÉDITEURS, MAURICE LACHATRE ET CIE

38, BOULEVARD DE SÉBASTOPOL, 38

Londres 18 Mars 1872

Au citoyen Maurice La Châtre.

Cher citoyen,

[handwritten letter in French]

Recevez, cher citoyen, l'assurance de mes sentiments dévoués.

Karl Marx.

34

The French translation of Volume I of *Capital* was first published in Paris in separate parts (instalments), the first coming out in 1872 and the last in 1875. Marx took part in preparing the edition.

32. Karl Marx, Capital
   Paris, Maurice Lachâtre Publishing House, 1872-75

Cover

33. Maurice La Châtre (1814-1900), progressive French journalist; took part in the Paris Commune; publisher of Volume I of Marx's Capital *in French*

34. Marx's letter to Maurice La Châtre, March 18, 1872

"I APPLAUD YOUR IDEA OF PUBLISHING THE TRANSLATION OF *DAS CAPITAL* AS A SERIAL. IN THIS FORM THE BOOK WILL BE MORE ACCESSIBLE TO THE WORKING CLASS, A CONSIDERATION WHICH TO ME OUTWEIGHS EVERYTHING ELSE."

35. Newspaper advertisement of the second German edition of Volume I of Capital in March 1872

36. Cover of the Berlin Polizeipräsidium's file concerning the second German edition of Volume I of Capital

"AFTER THE DEATH OF HIS FRIEND, ENGELS UNDERTOOK THE ONEROUS TASK OF PREPARING AND PUBLISHING THE SECOND AND THE THIRD VOLUMES OF *CAPITAL*. HE PUBLISHED VOLUME II IN 1885 AND VOLUME III IN 1894 (HIS DEATH PREVENTED THE PREPARATION OF VOLUME IV). THESE TWO VOLUMES ENTAILED A VAST AMOUNT OF LABOUR...

"BY PUBLISHING VOLUMES II AND III OF *CAPITAL* ENGELS ERECTED A MAJESTIC MONUMENT TO THE GENIUS WHO HAD BEEN HIS FRIEND, A MONUMENT ON WHICH, WITHOUT INTENDING IT, HE INDELIBLY CARVED HIS OWN NAME. INDEED THESE TWO VOLUMES OF *CAPITAL* ARE THE WORK OF TWO MEN: MARX AND ENGELS."

V. I. LENIN

37. *Frederick Engels, London, summer of 1888*

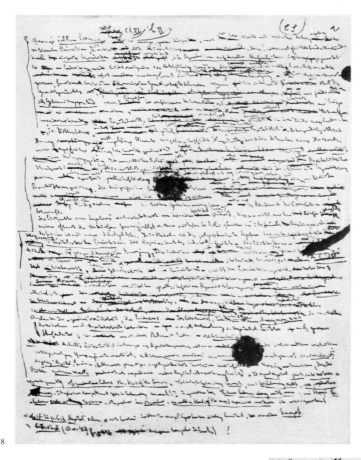

38

"AH, THAT SECOND VOLUME! IF YOU ONLY KNEW, MY OLD FRIEND, IN WHAT A HURRY I AM TO COMPLETE IT... I AM WORRIED BECAUSE I AM *THE ONLY ONE ALIVE* WHO CAN DECIPHER THIS HANDWRITING AND THE ABBREVIATIONS OF WORDS AND OF ENTIRE PHRASES."

ENGELS TO P. L. LAVROV

38. *A page of Marx's manuscript related to* Volume II *of* Capital

39. *The same page as dictated by Engels to a scribe, with his subsequent changes*

40. *Karl Marx,* Capital. A Critique of Political Economy, *Volume II, Hamburg, 1885*

The title page

Das Kapital.

Kritik der politischen Oekonomie.

Von

Karl Marx.

Zweiter Band.

Buch II: Der Cirkulationsprocess des Kapitals.

Herausgegeben von Friedrich Engels.

———

Das Recht der Uebersetzung ist vorbehalten.

———

Hamburg
Verlag von Otto Meissner.
1885.

42. *Karl Marx*, Capital. A Critique of Political Economy, *Volume III, Hamburg, 1894*

The title page

41

41. *Jenny, Karl Marx's wife*

"THE SECOND AND THIRD BOOKS OF *CAPITAL* WERE TO BE DEDICATED, AS MARX HAD STATED REPEATEDLY, TO HIS WIFE."

FREDERICK ENGELS

"*DAS KAPITAL* IS OFTEN CALLED, ON THE CONTINENT, 'THE BIBLE OF THE WORKING-CLASS'. THAT THE CONCLUSIONS ARRIVED AT IN THIS WORK ARE DAILY MORE AND MORE BECOMING THE FUNDAMENTAL PRINCIPLES OF THE GREAT WORKING-CLASS MOVEMENT, NOT ONLY IN GERMANY AND SWITZERLAND, BUT IN FRANCE, IN HOLLAND AND BELGIUM, IN AMERICA, AND EVEN IN ITALY AND SPAIN, THAT EVERYWHERE THE WORKING-CLASS MORE AND MORE RECOGNISES, IN THESE CONCLUSIONS, THE MOST ADEQUATE EXPRESSION OF ITS CONDITION AND OF ITS ASPIRATIONS, NOBODY ACQUAINTED WITH THAT MOVEMENT WILL DENY."

FREDERICK ENGELS

Das Kapital.

Kritik der politischen Oekonomie.

Von

Karl Marx.

Dritter Band, zweiter Theil.

Buch III:
Der Gesammtprocess der kapitalistischen Produktion.
Kapitel XXIX bis LII.

Herausgegeben von Friedrich Engels.

Hamburg
Verlag von Otto Meissner.
1894.

CAPITAL:

A CRITICAL ANALYSIS OF CAPITALIST PRODUCTION

By KARL MARX

*TRANSLATED FROM THE THIRD GERMAN EDITION, BY
SAMUEL MOORE AND EDWARD AVELING*

AND EDITED BY

FREDERICK ENGELS

VOL. I.

ARDVA·QVÆ·PVLCRA

LONDON:

SWAN SONNENSCHEIN, LOWREY, & CO.,

PATERNOSTER SQUARE.

1887.

45

43. The title page of the first English edition of Capital

44. Eleanor Aveling (1855-1898), Karl Marx's youngest daughter, wife of Edward Aveling. Took part in translating Volume I of Capital *into English*

45. Edward Aveling (1851-1898), English socialist; a translator of Volume I of Capital *into English*

46. Samuel Moore (c. 1830-1912), English lawyer, friend of Marx and Engels. Translated Volume I of Capital *into English*

"IN ENGLAND, TOO, THE THEORIES OF MARX, EVEN AT THIS MOMENT, EXERCISE A POWERFUL INFLUENCE UPON THE SOCIALIST MOVEMENT WHICH IS SPREADING IN THE RANKS OF 'CUL-TURED' PEOPLE NO LESS THAN IN THOSE OF THE WORKING-CLASS."

FREDERICK ENGELS

46

THE FIRST INTERNATIONAL

Let us bear in mind this fundamental principle of the International: solidarity! It is by establishing this life-giving principle on a reliable base among all the workers in all countries that we shall achieve the great aim which we pursue.

Karl Marx

1. The International Working Men's Association, commonly known as the First International, was founded at an international meeting at St. Martin's Hall, London, on September 28, 1864

"PAST EXPERIENCE HAS SHOWN HOW DISREGARD OF THAT BOND OF BROTHERHOOD WHICH OUGHT TO EXIST BETWEEN THE WORKMEN OF DIFFERENT COUNTRIES, AND INCITE THEM TO STAND FIRMLY BY EACH OTHER IN ALL THEIR STRUGGLES FOR EMANCIPATION, WILL BE CHASTISED BY THE COMMON DISCOMFITURE OF THEIR INCOHERENT EFFORTS. THIS THOUGHT PROMPTED THE WORKING MEN OF DIFFERENT COUNTRIES ASSEMBLED ON SEPTEMBER 28, 1864, IN PUBLIC MEETING AT ST. MARTIN'S HALL, TO FOUND THE INTERNATIONAL ASSOCIATION."

KARL MARX

2. Karl Marx, London, 1872

3. Frederick Engels, Manchester, 1864

2

BEE-HIVE NEWSPAPER.

A JOURNAL OF GENERAL INTELLIGENCE, ADVOCATING INDUSTRIAL INTERESTS

No. 156. [REGISTERED FOR TRANSMISSION ABROAD] LONDON, SATURDAY, OCTOBER 8, 1864. Price Twopence

THE INTERNATIONAL MEETING AT ST. MARTIN'S HALL.—The committee appointed at the meeting above referred to assembled at 18, Greek street, Soho, on Wednesday evening, Mr. Odgers in the chair. There was a very full attendance, about 40 being present. Several French and Italian friends were added to the committee, which now represents nearly all the Nationalities of Europe.

4. St. Martin's Hall, London

*5. Report about the first meeting of
the International's General Council*
Bee-Hive Newspaper, *October 8,
1864*

Marx was the heart and soul, the
true organiser and leader, of the
International, and, in fact, the head
of its General Council, the writer of
its programme documents, of its
many addresses, appeals, reports,
and resolutions. "To describe
Marx's activity in the International,"
Engels once said, "is to write the
history of this Association."

*6. Marx's letter to Engels in Man-
chester, November 4, 1864*
A page of the manuscript

"AT THE MEETING, WHICH
WAS *CHOCK-FULL* (FOR THERE
IS NOW EVIDENTLY A REVIVAL
OF THE WORKING CLASSES TAK-
ING PLACE) ... IT WAS RESOLVED
TO FOUND A WORKINGMEN'S IN-
TERNATIONAL ASSOCIATION,
WHOSE GENERAL COUNCIL IS TO
HAVE ITS SEAT IN LONDON AND
IS TO 'INTERMEDIATE' BETWEEN
THE WORKERS' SOCIETIES IN
GERMANY, ITALY, FRANCE, AND
ENGLAND."

"BUT IT IS GOOD," Engels
wrote in his reply of November 7,
1864, "THAT WE ARE AGAIN
MAKING CONTACT WITH
PEOPLE WHO DO AT LEAST
REPRESENT THEIR CLASS,
WHICH IS WHAT REALLY MAT-
TERS ULTIMATELY."

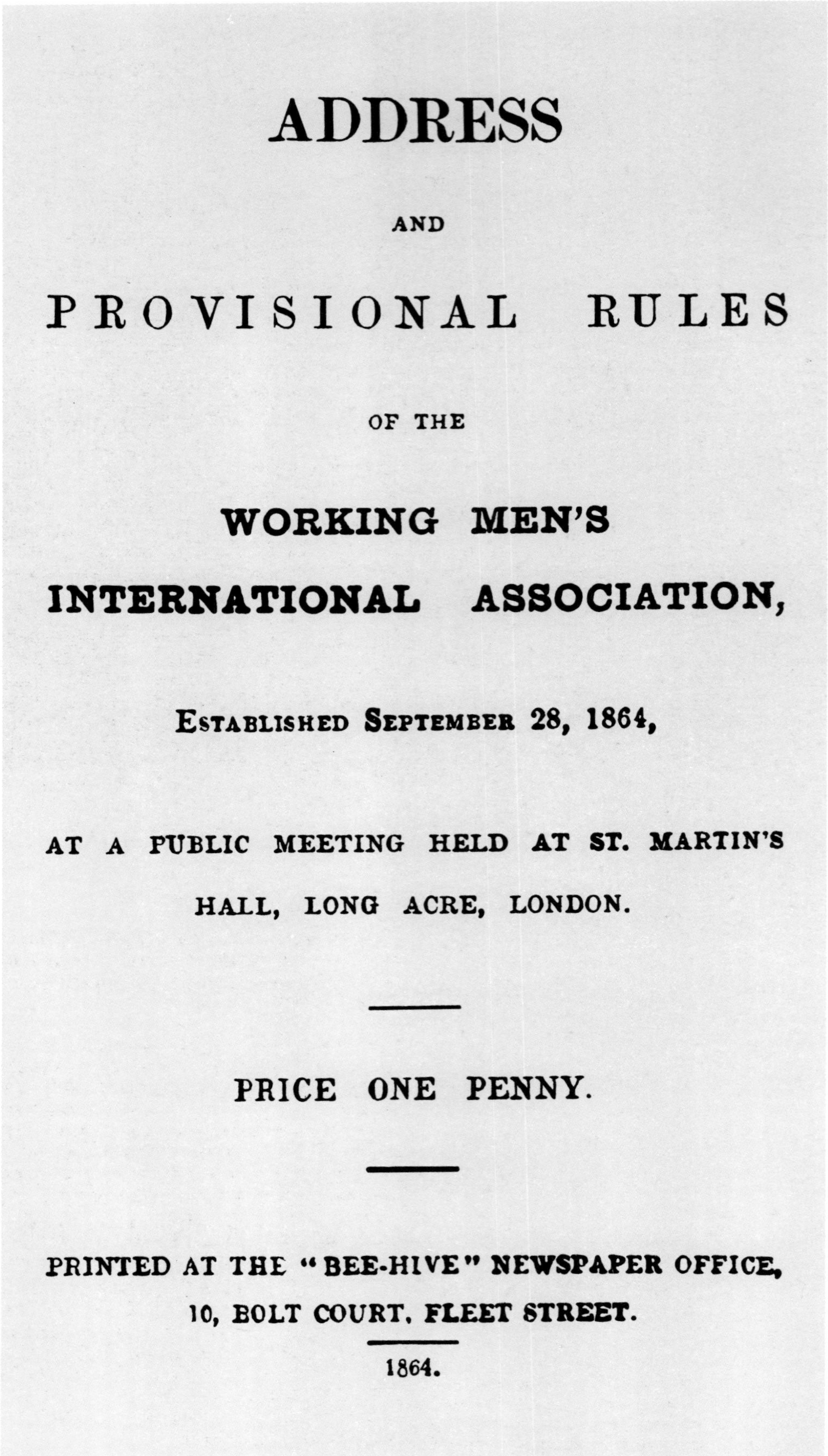

ADDRESS

AND

PROVISIONAL RULES

OF THE

WORKING MEN'S

INTERNATIONAL ASSOCIATION,

Established September 28, 1864,

AT A PUBLIC MEETING HELD AT ST. MARTIN'S
HALL, LONG ACRE, LONDON.

———

PRICE ONE PENNY.

———

PRINTED AT THE "BEE-HIVE" NEWSPAPER OFFICE,
10, BOLT COURT, FLEET STREET.
———
1864.

7. Inaugural Address and Provisional Rules of the International Working Men's Association, London, 1864
The title page

The Inaugural Address and the Provisional Rules, which were the International's initial programme documents, were written by Marx and unanimously adopted by the General Council. They defined the aims and methods of the liberation struggle of the working class, and asserted the principles of proletarian internationalism.

9. The house at 256 High Holborn, London, where the General Council of the International held its meetings in 1868 to 1872

"THE MEETINGS IN HIGH HOLBORN, WHERE THE GENERAL COUNCIL USED TO GATHER AT THAT TIME, WERE AS DISTURBING AND TIRING AS ANYONE COULD IMAGINE. THE BABBLE OF DIFFERENT LANGUAGES, THE TREMENDOUS DIFFERENCES IN TEMPERAMENT, AND THE VARIETY OF VIEWS—IT WAS ENORMOUSLY DIFFICULT TO COPE WITH ALL THAT. AND THOSE WHO ACCUSED MARX OF INTOLERANCE SHOULD HAVE SEEN AT LEAST ONCE HOW HE MANAGED TO GRASP THE THOUGHTS OF OTHER PEOPLE IN FLIGHT AND PROVE THEIR CONCLUSIONS INCORRECT."

FRIEDRICH LESSNER

8. The house at 18 Greek Street, London, where the General Council of the International held its meetings in 1864 to 1866

The General Council held weekly meetings to discuss the crucial issues of the working-class movement—mutual aid, joint action, propagation of the revolutionary doctrine, and so on.

10

Members of the General Council
of the First International

10. Karl Marx, Hanover, 1867

11. Eugène Dupont (c. 1831-1881)

12. Friedrich Lessner (1825-1910)

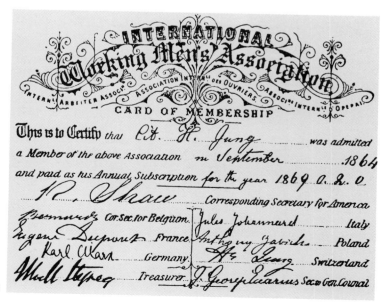

13. Hermann Jung (1830-1901)

14. Johann Georg Eccarius (1818-1889)

15. Hermann Alexandrovich Lopatin (1845-1918)

16. The International's card of membership issued to Hermann Jung

26

23. *Card of membership in the IWA section of tapestry makers (Paris)*

24. *The document certifying that the London Operative Bricklayers' Society had been admitted to the International*

25. *Karl Marx,* The Inaugural Address and the Rules of the International Working Men's Association *published in different countries*

26. *Meeting in a workers' quarter*

Another economic crisis erupted in European countries in 1866. Unemployment, the high cost of living owing to a crop failure, and the famine that resulted from it, built up tensions. A powerful wave of strikes rolled across the continent.

With Marx at its head, the General Council conducted campaigns of solidarity with strikers in Britain, France, Germany, Switzerland, and other countries.

27. Karl Marx, Wages, Price and Profit
A fragment

Marx's lecture read at the General Council meetings of June 20 and 27, 1865

The lecture refuted the mistaken views of Owenite John Weston, who maintained that the struggles of workers and trade unions for wage rises and economic benefits were "futile". Marx set forth the surplus value theory in popular form.

In its further dealings, the General Council adhered to the theoretical and tactical ideas set out by Marx.

28. A workers' meeting before a strike

29. A page from the minutes of the General Council's meeting on January 24, 1865 with the record of Marx's speech

Marx spoke against the penetration of bourgeois elements into the General Council.

30. Karl Marx, "On Proudhon"
Der Social-Demokrat, *February 1, 1865*

Here Marx chastises Proudhon for his petty-bourgeois views, and at the same time criticises Lassalle's opportunism.

31. Subscription list issued by the General Council to raise funds for striking Belgian workers

32

THE BELGIAN MASSACRES.

To the Workmen of Europe and the United States.

There passes hardly a week in England without strikes—and strikes upon a grand scale. If, on such occasions, the Government was to let its soldiers loose upon the Working Class, this land of strikes would become a land of massacres, but not for many a week. After a few such physical force experiments, the powers that be would be nowhere. In the United States, too, the number and scale of strikes have continued to increase during the last few years, and even sometimes assumed a riotous character. But no blood was spilt. In some of the great military states of continental Europe, the era of strikes may be dated from the end of the American civil war. But here, again, no blood was spilt. There exists but one country in the civilised world where every strike is eagerly and joyously turned into a pretext for the official massacre of the Working Class. That country of single blessedness is *Belgium*! the model state of continental constitutionalism, the snug, well-hedged, little paradise of the landlord, the capitalist, and the priest. The earth performs not more surely its yearly revolution than the Belgian Government its yearly Working Men's massacre. The massacre of this year does not differ from last year's massacre, but by the ghastlier number of its victims, the more hideous ferocity of an otherwise ridiculous army, the noisier jubilation of the clerical and capitalist press, and the intensified frivolity of the pretexts put forward by the Governmental butchers.

It is now proved, even by the involuntary evidence of the capitalist press, that the quite legitimate strike of the puddlers in the Cockerill Ironworks, at Seraing, was only converted into a riot by a strong posse of cavalry and gendarmerie suddenly launched upon that place in order to provoke the people. From the 9th to the 12th of April these stout warriors not only recklessly charged with sabre and bayonet the unarmed workmen, they indiscriminately killed and wounded harmless passers by, forcibly broke into private houses, and even amused themselves with repeated furious onslaughts on the travellers pent up in the Seraing Railway Station. When these days of horror had passed away, it became bruited about that Mr. *Kamp*, the mayor of Seraing, was an agent of the Cockerill Joint Stock Company, that the Belgian Home Minister, a certain Mr. *Pirmez*, was the largest shareholder in a neighbouring colliery also on strike, and that His Royal Highness the Prince of Flanders, had invested 1,500,000 francs in the Cockerill concern. Hence people jump to the truly strange conclusion that the Seraing massacre was a sort of joint stock company *coup d'etat*, quietly plotted between the firm Cockerill and the Belgian Home Minister, for the simple purpose of striking terror unto their disaffected subjects. This calumny, however, was soon after victoriously refuted by the later events occurring in Le Borinage, a colliery district where the Belgian Home Minister, the said Mr. *Pirmez*, seems not to be a leading capitalist. An almost general strike having broken out amongst the miners of that district, numerous troops were concentrated, who

33

32. *Rioting Belgian miners at Charleroi in 1868*

"IN BELGIUM THE INTERNATIONAL ASSOCIATION HAS MADE IMMENSE STRIDES. THE COAL LORDS OF THE BASIN OF CHARLEROI, HAVING DRIVEN THEIR MINERS TO RIOTS BY INCESSANT EXACTIONS, LET LOOSE UPON THOSE UNARMED MEN THE ARMED FORCE WHICH MASSACRED MANY OF THEM. IT WAS IN [THE] MIDST OF THE PANIC THUS CREATED THAT OUR BELGIAN BRANCH TOOK UP THE CAUSE OF THE MINERS, DISCLOSED THEIR MISERABLE ECONOMICAL CONDITION, RUSHED TO THE RESCUE OF THE FAMILIES OF THE DEAD AND WOUNDED, AND PROCURED LEGAL COUNSEL FOR THE PRISONERS."

KARL MARX

34

33. Karl Marx, "The Belgian Massacres"
 A leaflet Marx wrote on instructions of the International's General Council on May 4, 1869

The leaflet tells of the bloody massacre that the Belgian authorities visited upon striking metal workers and miners in Seraing and Borinage.

34. Strikers assaulted by police in Britain

35

36

35. A meeting of English workers in Hyde Park, London, demanding universal suffrage, 1866

A centre for parliamentary reform, extending the franchise, was formed in Britain on the initiative and under the guidance of Marx and the International's General Council. It was called the Reform League, which, under Marx's influence, demanded universal manhood suffrage. The working class took a conspicuous part in the reform movement.

36. Membership card of the Land and Labour League issued to Karl Marx

The Land and Labour League founded in London in 1869 with the assistance of the IWA General Council and Karl Marx, had general democratic demands in its programme, namely: nationalisation of land, reduction of the working-day, and so on. Marx held that the League would facilitate the propagation of revolutionary ideas and that it would help organise the British working class.

37. Strike at a sugar refinery in Paris

"THE GROWING POWER OF THE INTERNATIONAL ... MANIFESTED ITSELF IN THE STRIKES OF ROUBAIX, AMIENS, PARIS, GENEVA, AND SO ON."

KARL MARX

38. A strikers' meeting in Paris, 1869

37

38

39

39. *Strike at a cigar factory in Berlin in the 1860s*

40. *Iron and steel works in Freiburg, a centre of the German working-class movement*

41. *Karl Marx, "To the Striking Miners of the Ruhr Valley"*
  Der Volksstaat, *July 27, 1872*
  Written on the instructions of the General Council of the International

42. *Karl Marx,* A Warning. *An Appeal to the German Workers*
        A page of the manuscript

It was written on the instructions of the International's General Council on May 4, 1866, to warn German and Danish workers that they were being recruited by British industrialists for use as strikebreakers.

"IT IS A POINT OF HONOUR WITH THE GERMAN WORKERS TO PROVE TO OTHER COUNTRIES THAT THEY, LIKE THEIR BROTH-

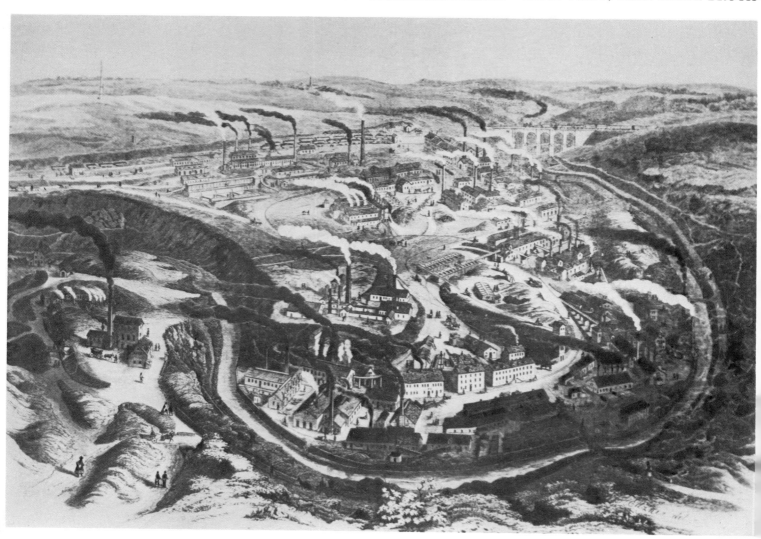

40

Der Volksstaat

No. 60 — Sonnabend, 27. Juli — 1872

Der Volksstaat

Organ der sozial-demokratischen Arbeiterpartei und der Internationalen Gewerksgenossenschaften.

An die streikenden Bergarbeiter im Ruhrthal.

Die deutsche Kapitalistenpresse verlangt von Euch, Ihr sollt Eure Forderungen achtstündiger Schicht und 25 Prozent Lohnerhöhung fallen lassen und die Arbeit wieder aufnehmen, damit nicht die deutsche Industrie gezwungen werde, ihre Kohlen aus England kommen zu lassen und so das deutsche Geld ins Ausland gehe, statt deutsche Arbeit zu bezahlen.

Es ist dies das ewige Jammergeschrei der Bourgeois, sobald die Arbeiter sich auf ihre eigenen Füße stellen und irgend welche Forderung zu ertrotzen versuchen. In England, wo diese alte Leier nun schon an die vierzig Jahre gespielt worden ist, achtet kein Mensch mehr darauf. In dem vorliegenden Falle aber ist es der Mühe werth, nachzuweisen, daß die Kapitalistenpresse Euch absichtlich täuschen will, wenn sie Euch erzählt, die Hüttenbesitzer und Fabrikanten brauchten blos nach England zu schreiben, um so viel Kohlen zu bekommen, wie sie nur wollen.

In England hat der Kohlenverbrauch seit 1869 in bisher unerhörter Weise zugenommen, durch den allgemeinen Aufschwung der englischen Industrie, der seitdem eingetreten, die Zunahme der Fabriken, den vermehrten Konsum der Eisenbahnen, die reißende Vermehrung der See-Dampfschifffahrt — hauptsächlich jedoch durch die kolossale Ausdehnung der Eisenindustrie, die in den letzten drei Jahren alle früheren Perioden der Prosperität weit übertroffen hat. Die „Daily News", ein liberales Kapitalistenblatt (Nummer vom 12. Juli d. J.) sagt hierüber: „Eine der Hauptursachen der gegenwärtigen Kohlentheuerung ist ohne Zweifel der plötzliche und beispiellose Aufschwung der Eisenindustrie. Der Norden von England liefert ungefähr den vierten Theil aller im Lande gewonnenen Kohlen. Ein großer Theil derselben geht nach London und dem Süden und Osten von England; sehr viel wird auch für Dampfschiffe gebraucht; aber neuerdings hat die Entwicklung der Eisenhütten in Cleveland (ganz in der Nähe der Zechen) eine plötzliche Lokalnachfrage nach Kohlen geschaffen. Dies Wachsthum eines Geschäftszweigs, der jetzt wohl nicht unter fünf bis sechs Millionen Tons jährlich verbraucht, gab der Kohlengewinnung selbststrebend eine gewaltige Hebung. Dazu kam der rasche Aufschwung im Hämatiteisenerz-Bezirk an der Westküste. Die Hochöfen von Cumberland und Lancashire beziehen ihren Brennstoff fast ausschließlich aus dem Kohlenbecken von Durham, und brauchen, nach mäßiger Schätzung, anderthalb Millionen Tons im Jahr. Die im Bau begriffenen neuen Hochöfen, in Nordengland allein, werden jährlich drei Viertel Million Tons nöthig haben. Dazu kommen neue Walzwerke und neue Hochöfen an der Westküste. Es ist daher nicht befremdlich, daß die Brennstoff-Frage im ganzen Norden von England bald eine Lebensfrage wurde, und es verstand sich, daß die Kohlenpreise rasch stiegen. In Süd-Staffordshire, Schottland, Süd-Wales, Derbyshire, West-Yorkshire und anderen Gegenden brachten dieselben Ursachen steigende Kohlenpreise zu Wege."

Unter diesen Umständen machten es die englischen Bergarbeiter wie Ihr; sie verlangten höheren Lohn und kürzere Arbeitszeit. Die englischen Bergwerksbesitzer, wie immer ihren deutschen Konkurrenten an Einsicht und Welterfahrung weit überlegen, widersetzten sich nicht ernstlich, sondern bewilligten alle Forderungen. Hört, was die „Daily News" weiter erzählt: „Von Zeit zu Zeit wurde der Lohn erhöht . . . Die Bergarbeiter verlangten ferner eine systematische Verkürzung der Arbeitszeit. Es wird nun von Fachleuten behauptet, daß ein Arbeiter jetzt nur ³/₄ von dem Kohlenquantum gewinnt, das er früher, bei flauem Geschäft und niedrigerem Lohn gewann.

Dafür könnte man mehr Arbeiter anstellen; aber diese sind eben nicht im Augenblick zu haben. Allerdings hat man manche aus den Ackerbaubezirken kommen lassen; aber Häuer haben eine lange Lehrzeit nöthig und die Abhülfe kann hier also nur langsam und allmählich eintreten. Augenblicklich haben die Arbeiter in einigen Gegenden die Beschränkung der Arbeitszeit auf acht Stunden täglich durchgesetzt, während überall Lohnerhöhungen so rasch auf einander folgen, daß kein Ausweg übrig scheint, als höhere Kohlenpreise."

Dazu kommt noch ein anderer Umstand. Die obersten Kohlenflöze sind in fast ganz England erschöpft und es muß immer tiefer gebaut werden. Hört wieder den Artikel der „Daily News": „Die besten Lagen dieser werthvollen Kohlenflöze in Süd-Staffordshire sind ihres Inhalts beraubt. In vielen Gegenden dieses einst kohlenreichen Strichs sind die Zechen erschöpft und die Halden werden immer mehr wieder in Acker- und Weideland verwandelt, obwohl noch Tausende von Morgen (Halden) öde liegen. Indeß sind die Hülfsquellen des Bezirks noch nicht erschöpft. Tiefere Schächte rings um das alte Kohlengebiet werden angelegt. . . . Aber, wie die Dinge liegen, wird es, selbst mit den neuesten Hülfsmitteln, immer kostspieliger, die Kohlen zu heben, wozu noch kommt, daß die Zechen weiter von den Hüttenwerken abliegen. Was wir von Süd-Staffordshire gesagt haben, gilt von vielen anderen Gegenden. Die Kohlen müssen aus größerer Tiefe geholt und auf weiten Entfernungen bis zu ihrem Bestimmungsort transportirt werden."

Die Folge davon ist, daß die Kohlenpreise sich, für Abnahme an der Zeche, wie „Daily News" sagt, „verdoppelt haben" und daß eine wahre Kohlennoth eingetreten ist, die die Aufmerksamkeit des ganzen Landes in Anspruch nimmt. Ein anderes Blatt, das ökonomische Hauptblatt der englischen Kapitalisten, der „Oekonomist" vom 20. Juli sagt:

„Seit Anfang dieses Jahres sind die Kohlen unaufhörlich im Preis gestiegen, bis sie jetzt zwischen 60 und 100 Prozent theurer sind als vor einem Jahr, ... ehe noch ein oder zwei Wochen vergehen, kann der Aufschlag weit mehr als 100 Prozent betragen, ohne daß irgend ein ernstliches Zeichen da wäre, daß er nicht noch weiter gehen werde. Die Kohlenausfuhr im Juni d. J. war 1,108,000 Tons, oder 4 Prozent mehr als im Juni v. J., aber ihr Werth war 758,000 Pfd. Sterling, oder 53 Prozent mehr. Dies Jahr war der Werth der im Juni ausgeführten Kohlen durchschnittlich 13 Schilling 9 Pence (oder 4 Thaler 17½ Gr.) pro Ton; voriges Jahr 9 Schilling 4 Pence (oder 3 Thlr. 3½ Gr.)". Der „Spectator", ein drittes Kapitalistenblatt, (20. Juli) führt ebenfalls an, daß in London gute Hauskohlen von 23 Schilling oder 7 Thlr. 20 Gr. auf 35 Schilling oder 11 Thlr. 20 Gr. gestiegen sind.

Aus diesen Thatsachen könnt Ihr ersehen, was es auf sich hat mit den Drohungen der Hüttenbesitzer und Fabrikanten, ihre Kohlen aus England zu beziehen. Herr Alfred Krupp mag so viel Ukase erlassen wie er will, die englischen Kohlen wird er theurer bezahlen müssen als Ruhrkohlen, und es ist sehr die Frage, ob er sie überhaupt bekommt.

In meiner Stellung als Sekretair des Generalraths der Internationalen Arbeiter-Assoziation für Deutschland habe ich es für meine Schuldigkeit gehalten, diese Thatsachen zu Eurer Kenntniß zu bringen.

London, 21. Juli 1871.

Karl Marx.

42

THE LOCK-OUT OF THE BUILDING TRADES AT GENEVA.

The General Council of the International Working Men's Association

TO THE

WORKING MEN and WOMEN of EUROPE and the UNITED STATES

Fellow Workers—

By order of the Council,

B. LUCRAFT, Chairman.
JOHN WESTON, Treasurer.
GEORGE ECCARIUS, Gen. Sec.

256, High Holborn, London W.C. July 5th, 1870.

43

ERS IN FRANCE, BELGIUM AND SWITZERLAND, KNOW HOW TO DEFEND THE COMMON INTERESTS OF THEIR CLASS AND WILL NOT BECOME *OBEDIENT MERCENARIES OF CAPITAL* IN ITS STRUGGLE AGAINST LABOUR."

KARL MARX

43. This leaflet was written by Marx on July 5, 1870 on the instructions of the General Council of the International

"THE GENERAL COUNCIL OF THE INTERNATIONAL WORKING MEN'S ASSOCIATION ... CALLS

UPON ALL HONEST WORKING MEN AND WOMEN, THROUGHOUT THE CIVILISED WORLD, TO ASSIST BOTH BY MORAL AND MATERIAL MEANS THE GENEVA BUILDING TRADES IN THEIR JUST STRUGGLE AGAINST CAPITALIST DESPOTISM."

KARL MARX

44

44. A view of Geneva in the 1860s

Marx did a tremendous amount of work in preparation of the International's congresses and conferences. He worked out their agendas, drafted resolutions, and planned the activity of General Council congress delegations.

During the International's period of activity in Europe (1864-72) it held two conferences, both in London, and five congresses. Marx took a direct part in the London Conferences (1865 and 1871), and the Hague Congress (1872).

45

The International's First Congress was held in Geneva from September 3 to 8, 1866. It was attended by 60 delegates from IWA sections in Britain, France, Germany, and Switzerland. Marx was highly active in organising the congress.

45. Delegates to the Geneva Congress of the First International

"IT IS ONE OF THE GREAT PURPOSES OF THE ASSOCIATION TO MAKE THE WORKMEN OF DIFFERENT COUNTRIES NOT ONLY *FEEL* BUT *ACT* AS BRETHREN AND COMRADES IN THE ARMY OF EMANCIPATION."

KARL MARX

46

Supplément au journal le Peuple Belge. — Jeudi 24 septembre 1868.

TROISIÈME CONGRÈS
DE
L'ASSOCIATION INTERNATIONALE DES TRAVAILLEURS.
COMPTE RENDU OFFICIEL.

47

46. A view of Brussels in the mid-19th century

The Third Congress of the International was held in Brussels from September 6 to 13, 1868. A hundred delegates attended from IWA sections in Britain, Belgium, France, Italy, Germany, Switzerland, and Spain.

The main resolutions and the General Council report were drafted by Marx.

47. Resolutions of the International's Brussels Congress

The resolutions contained an appeal to combat wars, and demanded that arable land, woods, quarries, coalmines, railways and roads, canals, posts and the telegraph should be made public property.

The congress inflicted a serious defeat on the Proudhonists and reduced their influence.

48. *An illustration for the first volume of Marx's* Capital *by US artist Hugo Gellert*

49. *The International's Brussels Congress resolution in which workers of all countries are advised to study Marx's* Capital
Supplement to Le Peuple Belge, *Brussels, 1868*

APPENDICE.
Séances administratives.

Les séances de la matinée, de 9 à 1 heure, ont été consacrées au réglement des comptes du Conseil général de Londres et des diverses sections, aux modifications à apporter aux statuts, aux élections, à la fixation du siége du Conseil général et du prochain Congrès, au vote sur les résolutions présentées dans les séances publiques, etc, en un mot à toutes les propositions relatives aux affaires et à l'administration de l'Association internationale.

Voici cependant quelques résolutions prises dans ces séances et destinées à être publiées :

Dans la séance de mercredi matin, le délégué de la branche française de Londres a donné lecture d'un long mémoire émanant de ses commettants. Outre plusieurs propositions de l'ordre administratif, ce mémoire donne une longue série de questions économiques à étudier et à résoudre par l'Internationale. L'Association prendra ces questions en considération pour composer les ordres du jour des Congrès des années subséquentes.

Dans la séance de vendredi, les délégués allemands recommandent à tous les travailleurs la lecture et la traduction du grand ouvrage de Karl Marx, intitulé : «Das Capital, Kritik der politischen Œconomie.» C'est le plus beau plaidoyer scientifique en faveur de l'affranchissement du prolétariat, que l'école socialiste allemande ait produit jusqu'à ce jour.

Voici cette résolution : « Nous allemands délégués au Congrès international des ouvriers, recommandons aux hommes de toutes les nationalités l'ouvrage de Marx « le Capital » et les engageons à faire leur possible pour que cet ouvrage important soit traduit dans les langues dans lesquelles il ne l'est pas encore, et déclarons que Karl Marx a l'estimable mérite d'être le premier économiste qui a scientifiquement analysé le capital et qui l'a réduit à ses éléments primordiaux. »

Une résolution semblable a été passée aux Congrès des ouvriers allemands, tenues à Hamburg et à Nuremberg ; — un des membres les plus actifs du Congrès de Nuremberg, Lieblnecht, membre de la diète de l'Allemagne du Nord, rédacteur en chef du « Démocrate-hebdomadaire », un des principaux organes de la classe ouvrière, a dénoncé publiquement et directement les économistes bourgeois de vouloir faire la conspiration du silence autour de cet ouvrage, qu'il leur est impossible de réfuter.

Il a été voté également dans la séance de vendredi :

1° Que la décision prise par les Congrès de Genève et de Lausanne, concernant les cotisations à payer au Conseil général s it mise en exécution;

2° Que pour pouvoir participer et avoir le droit de prendre part aux conclusions des Congrès à venir par l'intermédiaire de leurs délégués respectifs, les sections doivent se conformer à la résolution des Congrès de Genève et de Lausanne;

3° Que tous les Comités centraux des différents groupes de sections soient tenus d'envoyer chaque trimestre au Conseil général, un rapport touchant l'Administration et l'état financier des sections situées dans leur ressort.

Dans la séance de samedi matin, le Congrès a décidé, à l'unanimité des membres présents, de protester contre certaines insinuations malveillantes, contenues dans un article du journal la Cigale, à l'adresse de la délégation parisienne et des délégués qui, au Congrès, avaient traité la question de la guerre exclusivement au point de vue de l'économie sociale.

Quant aux séances de l'après-midi, de 3 à 6 heures, elles ont été tenues au local du Cygne et consacrées aux réunions des diverses commissions d'étude nommées pour élaborer des rapports et rédiger des résolutions sur les neuf questions à l'ordre du jour.

50

51

50. A view of Basle in the 1860s

The Fourth Congress of the International was held in Basle from September 6 to 11, 1869. It was attended by 78 delegates from IWA sections in Britain, France, Germany, Austria, Switzerland, Belgium, Italy, Spain, and the United States.

The General Council's report to the congress compiled by Marx was wholeheartedly approved by the delegates. Like the Brussels Congress, the forum in Basle called for the abolition of private landownership, thus reaffirming the socialist platform of the IWA.

51. Delegates to the International's Basle Congress

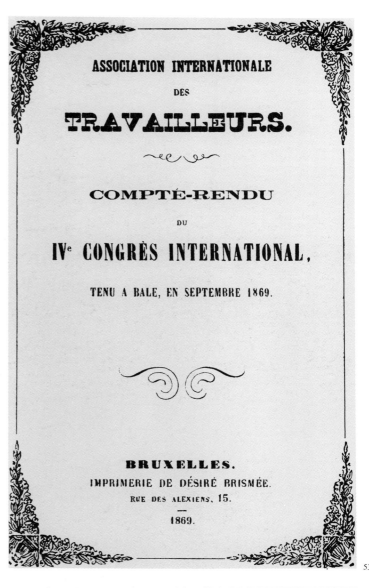

52. A pass to Basle Congress sittings issued to Wilhelm Liebknecht

53. Proceedings of the Basle Congress, Brussels, 1869
The title page

Bakunin and his followers, who urged abstention from political struggle, suffered ignominious defeat. "Bakunin displayed his antipathy for political action. However, Liebknecht, Rittinghausen and others gave him a good drubbing; even after the meeting he roared like a wild lion. Most of the French came out against him," Lessner wrote to Marx.

54. The standard of the International's Basle section

55

56

57

55. Frederick Engels, Hamburg, 1862

Though Engels was an active member of the International Working Men's Association, he was not on its General Council until he moved from Manchester to London in 1870. Marx kept him informed of the General Council's activity by mail and took counsel with him on crucial issues related to the International. During his years in Manchester, Engels wrote dozens of articles on the strategy and tactics of the labour movement.

56. The International's card of membership issued to Frederick Engels

58

59

57. *Frederick Engels*, The Prussian Military Question and the German Workers' Party, *Hamburg, 1865*
The title page of the first edition

Here Engels takes the Lassalleans to task for their conciliatory line. He says the main objective of the German proletariat should be forming a truly independent workers' party.

"THE WORKERS' PARTY WILL NOT PLAY THE PART OF A MERE APPENDAGE TO THE BOURGEOISIE BUT OF AN INDEPENDENT PARTY QUITE DISTINCT FROM IT. IT WILL REMIND THE BOURGEOISIE AT EVERY OPPORTUNITY THAT THE CLASS INTERESTS OF THE WORKERS ARE DIRECTLY OPPOSED TO THOSE OF THE CAPITALISTS AND THAT THE WORKERS ARE AWARE OF THIS. IT WILL RETAIN CONTROL OF AND FUTHER DEVELOP ITS OWN ORGANISATION AS DISTINCT FROM THE PARTY ORGANISATION OF THE BOURGEOISIE, AND WILL ONLY NEGOTIATE WITH THE LATTER AS ONE POWER WITH ANOTHER. IN THIS WAY IT WILL SECURE FOR ITSELF A POSITION COMMANDING RESPECT, EDUCATE THE INDIVIDUAL WORKERS ABOUT THEIR CLASS INTERESTS AND WHEN THE NEXT REVOLUTIONARY STORM COMES ... IT WILL BE READY TO ACT."

FREDERICK ENGELS

58. *Lizzie Burns, Frederick Engels's wife, in the 1870s*

59. *The house in Manchester where Frederick Engels lived*

60

In the 1860s Marx and Engels again devoted themselves mostly to the workers' movement in Germany. They thought it most important and urgent to disprove Lassalleanism and to see to the revival of revolutionary traditions among the German workers.

Marx was corresponding secretary for Germany in the International's General Council and had close contacts with Wilhelm Liebknecht and August Bebel, those two outstanding German labour leaders, and the foremost German workers.

60. Wilhelm Liebknecht (1826-1900)

61. August Bebel (1840-1913)

The election of Bebel and Liebknecht, those two leaders of the social-democratic movement in Germany, to the North-German Reichstag in 1867, was a big success for labour.

62. A meeting of the Union of German Workers' Educational Associations, 1868

In July 1868, the Union formally recognised the principles set forth in the programme documents of the International worked out by Karl Marx.

62

63. A view of Eisenach in the 1860s

64. The house in Eisenach where the Social-Democratic Workers' Party of Germany was founded at the congress held August 7 to 9, 1869

For the first time an essentially Marxist programme was adopted as a guide to action by a mass workers' party.

Marx and Engels called the Eisenach party "our party", and helped its leaders energetically in every way they could.

63

65. Der Volksstaat, *April 2, 1870*

The newspaper of the Social-Democratic Workers' Party of Germany. A medium propagating revolutionary ideas, it printed articles by Marx and Engels, and documents of the International.

65

Januar. **Erſter Jahrgang.** N° 1.

Der Vorbote.

Organ
der Internationalen Arbeiter-Aſſociation.

Monatsſchrift
redigirt von Joh. Ph. Becker.

Der Preis à 6 Monate für Genf mit Poſtlohn 80 Cent., für die übrige Schweiz 90 Cent., für Deutſchland 36 Kreuz. oder 10 Sgr., für Frankreich und Italien Fr. 1 20, für England 1½ Schl. Der Preis für 12 Monate iſt der doppelte und für einzelne Nummern 10 Cent.

Man abonnirt auf allen Poſtämtern, oder auch direkt auf dem Büreau der Redaltion und Expedition **PRÉ L'ÉVÊQUE** 33, Genf. Agentur für Frankreich: G. A. Alexander, Straßburg, 5, **RUE BRULÉE**; Paris 2, **COUR DU COMMERCE, SAINT-ANDRÉ-DES-ARTS.** Agenturen für England und überſeeische Länder, 8, **LITTLE NEW PORT-STREET, LEICESTER-SQUARE W. C.,** London. Auch kann der „Vorbote" jederzeit auf dem Wege des Buchhandels bezogen werden.

Was wir wollen und ſollen.

Geſtützt auf das Recht der Selbſtbeſtimmung, wollen wir für alle Völker in Beſeitigung jedweden Reſtes mittelalterlicher Einrichtungen und moderner Klaſſenherrſchaft, die Herſtellung des einen freien Volksſtaates anſtreben.

Wir werden nie eine andere Sonveränität und Majeſtät als die Volksſonveränität und Volksmajeſtät anerkennen.

Als unumgängliches Mittel zum Zwecke wollen wir die Solidarität (Geſammtverbindlichkeit) aller Völker verwirklichen helfen.

Wir werden nur ſolchen Nationalitätsbeſtrebungen Vorſchub leiſten, welche auf ganze Freiheit, Selbſtſtändigkeit und Gleichberechtigung Aller hinzielen um jedes Volk in Ebenbürtigkeit, als organiſches Glied der großen Kette des Menschenthums dem freien Bunde allgemeiner Eidgenoſſenſchaft einverleiben zu können.

Wie wir nach Außen die Racenabneigungen und den Kriegsgeiſt,

67

66. Der Vorbote, No. 1, 1870

Published as an organ of the International in Switzerland. Its editor was Johann Philipp Becker

67. *Johann Philipp Becker (1809-1886), friend and associate of Karl Marx and Frederick Engels, organised German sections of the International in Switzerland*

66

68. *Karl Marx, "Concerning the Persecution of the Members of the French Sections"*
A page of the manuscript pasted into the General Council's Minute Book

In a bid to prevent the spread of revolutionary ideas in France, the government of Napoleon III started court proceedings against the local sections of the International on the ludicrous charge of conspiracy. Marx tore the charges to bits in his articles and public utterances.

"THE VERY NATURE OF AN ASSOCIATION WHICH IDENTIFIES ITSELF WITH THE WORKING CLASSES, WOULD EXCLUDE FROM IT EVERY FORM OF SECRET SOCIETY. IF THE WORKING CLASSES, WHO FORM THE GREAT BULK OF ALL NATIONS, WHO PRODUCE ALL THEIR WEALTH, AND IN THE NAME OF WHOM EVEN THE USURPING POWERS ALWAYS PRETEND TO RULE, CONSPIRE, THEY CONSPIRE PUBLICLY, AS THE SUN CONSPIRES AGAINST DARKNESS, IN THE FULL CONSCIOUSNESS THAT WITHOUT THEIR PALE THERE EXISTS NO LEGITIMATE POWER."

KARL MARX

69. *The trial of members of the Paris section of the International*

68

69

70

70. *A view of New York in the 1870s*

71. *A street in New York*

72. *Friedrich Adolph Sorge (1828-1906), friend and associate of Karl Marx, organised sections of the International in the USA*

73. *Membership card of the North American section of the International*

71

RECEIPT.

	Stamp, a. c.	Stamp, a. c.
Month	**1873**	**1874**
January	... ...	
February	... ...	
March	... ...	
April	... ...	
May	... ...	
June	... ...	
July	... ...	
August	... ...	
September	... ...	
October	... ...	
November	... ...	... ...
December	... ...	... ...

...74. The Address was written by Karl Marx on May 12, 1869

"IN THE STATES THEMSELVES, AN INDEPENDENT WORKING-CLASS MOVEMENT, LOOKED UPON WITH AN EVIL EYE BY YOUR OLD PARTIES AND THEIR PROFESSIONAL POLITICIANS, HAS ... SPRUNG INTO LIFE. TO FRUCTIFY IT WANTS YEARS OF PEACE...

"A SECOND WAR, NOT HALLOWED BY A SUBLIME PURPOSE AND A GREAT SOCIAL NECESSITY, BUT OF THE OLD WORLD'S TYPE, WOULD FORGE CHAINS FOR THE FREE LABOURER INSTEAD OF TEARING ASUNDER THOSE OF THE SLAVE. THE ACCUMULATED MISERY LEFT IN ITS TRACK WOULD AFFORD YOUR CAPITALISTS AT ONCE THE MOTIVE AND THE MEANS TO DIVORCE THE WORKING CLASS FROM ITS BOLD AND JUST ASPIRATIONS BY THE SOULLESS SWORD OF A STANDING ARMY."

KARL MARX

INTERNATIONAL WORKING MEN'S ASSOCIATION.

Address to the National Labour Union of the United States.

FELLLOW-WORKMEN,

In the initiatory programme of our Association we stated :—"It was not the wisdom of the ruling classes, but the heroic resistance to their criminal folly by the working classes of England, that saved the West of Europe from plunging headlong into an infamous crusade for the perpetuation and propagation of slavery on the other side of the Atlantic." Your turn hâs now come to stop a war, the clearest result of which would be, for an indefinite period, to hurl back the ascendant movement of the working class on both sides of the Atlantic.

We need hardly tell you that there exist European powers anxiously bent upon hurrying the United States into a war with England. A glance at commercial statistics will show that the Russian export of raw produce, and Russia has nothing else to export, was rapidly giving way before American competition, when the civil war suddenly turned the scales. To convert the American ploughshares into swords would just now rescue from impending bankruptcy that despotic power which your republican statesmen have, in their wisdom, chosen for their confidential adviser. But quite apart from the particular interests of this or that government, is it not the general interest of our common oppressors to turn our fast-growing international co-operation into an internecine war?

In a congratulatory address to Mr. Lincoln on his re-election as president, we expressed our conviction that the American civil war would prove of as great import to the advancement of the working class as the American war of independence had proved to that of the middle class. And, in point of fact, the victorious termination of the anti-slavery war has opened a new epoch in the annals of the working class. In the States themselves, an independent working class movement, looked upon with an evil eye by your old parties and their professional politicians, has since that date sprung into life. To fructify it wants years of peace. To crush it, a war between the United States and England is wanted.

The next palpable effect of the civil war was, of course, to deteriorate the position of the American workman. In the United States, as in Europe, the monster incubus of a national debt was shifted from hand to hand, to settle down on the shoulders of the working class. The prices of necessaries, says one of your statesmen, have since 1860 risen 78 per cent., while the wages of unskilled labour rose 50 per cent., those of skilled labour 60 per cent. only. "Pauperism," he complains, "grows now in America faster than population." Moreover, the sufferings of the working classes set off as a foil the new-fangled luxury of financial aristocrats, shoddy aristocrats, and similar vermin bred by wars. Yet for all this the civil war did compensate by freeing the slave, and the consequent moral impetus it gave to your own class movement. A second war, not hallowed by a sublime purpose and a great social necessity, but of the old world's type, would forge chains for the free labourer instead of tearing asunder those of the slave. The accumulated misery left in its track would afford your capitalists at once the motive and the means to divorce the working class from its bold and just aspirations by the soulless sword of a standing army.

On you, then, depends the glorious task to prove to the world that now at last the working classes are bestriding the scene of history no longer as servile retainers, but as independent actors, conscious of their own responsibility, and able to command peace where their would-be masters shout war.

In the name of the General Council of the International Working Men's Association, British nationality : R. Applegarth, carpenter ; M. J. Boon, engineer ; J. Backley, painter ; J. Hales, elastic webb weaver ; Harriet Law, B. Lucraft, chairmaker ; J. Milner, tailor ; G. Odger, shoemaker, J. Ross, bootcloser ; B. Shaw, painter ; Cowell Stepney ; J. Warren, trunkmaker ; J. Weston, hand-railmaker. French nationality : E. Dupont, instrument maker ; Jules Johannard, lithographer ; Paul Lafarque. German nationality : G. Eccarius, tailor ; F. Lessner, tailor ; W. Limbury, shoemaker ; Marx Karl. Swiss nationality : H. Jung, watchmaker ; A. Muller, watchmaker. Belgian nationality : P. Bernard, painter. Danish nationality : J. Cohn, cigar maker. Polish nationality : Zabicki, compositor.

B. LUCRAFT, *Chairman.*

COWELL STEPNEY, *Treasurer.*

J. GEORGE ECCARIUS, *General Secretary.*

London, May 12th, 1869.

74

A Russian section of the International was founded in Geneva in March 1870. It consisted of Russian émigrés, followers of the great Russian revolutionary democrat Nikolai Chernyshevsky.

75. Narodnoye Delo, *No. 6-7, 1870*

The newspaper was published in Geneva in 1868 to 1870 by a group of Russian revolutionary émigrés. From April 1870 on it became the organ of the Russian section of the International.

75

 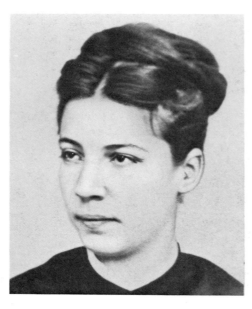 

78
79

Members of the Russian section of the First International

76. *Nikolai Isaakovich Utin (1841-1883)*

77. *Victor Ivanovich Bartenev (1838-1918)*

78. *Elizaveta Lukinichna Dmitrieva-Tomanovskaya (1851-after 1917)*

79. *Anna Vasilievna Korvin-Krukovskaya (1843-1887)*

80. *The Russian section's letter to Marx of March 12, 1870, asking him to represent it in the General Council*

"THE RUSSIAN DEMOCRATIC YOUTH HAS NOW WON THE OPPORTUNITY TO EXPRESS ITS DEEP GRATITUDE TO YOU THROUGH ITS EXILED BROTHERS FOR THE HELP YOU HAVE GIVEN OUR CAUSE WITH YOUR THEORETICAL AND PRACTICAL PROPAGANDA..."

81. *Marx's letter to members of the Committee of the International's Russian section in Geneva, of March 24, 1870. It was published in* Narodnoye Delo *on April 15, 1870*

A fragment

ГЛАВНЫЙ СОВѢТЪ МЕЖДУНАРОДНАГО ТОВАРИЩЕСТВА РАБОЧИХЪ

Членамъ Комитета Русской Секціи въ Женевѣ.

Граждане,

Въ своемъ засѣданіи 22-го Марта Главный Совѣтъ объявилъ, единодушнымъ вотомъ, что ваша программа и статутъ согласны съ общими статутами Международнаго Товарищества Рабочихъ. Онъ поспѣшилъ принять вашу вѣтвь въ составъ Интернаціонала. Я съ удовольствіемъ принимаю почетную обязанность, которую Вы мнѣ предлагаете, быть вашимъ представителемъ при Главномъ Совѣтѣ.

81

LA EMANCIPACION.

PERIODICO SOCIALISTA.

SE PUBLICA TODOS LOS SABADOS.

LA TRIBUNE DU PEUPLE

ABONNEMENT :
POUR TOUTE LA BELGIQUE

UN AN . . . FR. 5 00
SIX MOIS . . » 2 75

JOURNAL DE LA SOCIÉTÉ : LE PEUPLE,

Organe de l'Association internationale des Travailleurs.

ON S'ABONNE

CHEZ L'IMPRIMEUR
RUE DES ALEXIENS 13.
A BRUXELLES

BEE-HIVE NEWSPAPER.

A JOURNAL OF GENERAL INTELLIGENCE, ADVOCATING INDUSTRIAL INTERESTS

L'INTERNATIONALE

ORGANE DES SECTIONS BELGES

DE L'ASSOCIATION INTERNATIONALE DES TRAVAILLEURS.

The International

UNITY IS STRENGTH

HERALD.

Der Vorbote.

Organ

der Internationalen Arbeiter-Association.

82. The press media of the International

"OUR ASSOCIATION HAS MADE GREAT PROGRESS. IT ALREADY HAS 3 OFFICIAL ORGANS, ONE IN LONDON, *THE WORKMAN'S ADVOCATE*, ONE IN BRUSSELS, *LA TRIBUNE DU PEUPLE*, ONE PUT OUT BY THE FRENCH SECTION IN SWITZERLAND, *JOURNAL DE L'ASSOCIATION INTERNATIONALE DES TRAVAILLEURS, SECTION DE LA SUISSE ROMANDE* (GENEVA), AND IN A FEW DAYS TIME A JOURNAL IS TO BE PUT OUT BY THE GERMAN-SWISS SECTION, *DER VORBOTE*, UNDER THE EDITORSHIP OF J. P. BECKER."

MARX TO LUDWIG KUGELMANN

Marx and the International's General Council never failed to back democratic and liberation movements.

The Irish national liberation movement was in a period of drive and animation in 1867 when, examining the developments on the island, Marx concluded that the workers' struggle in the metropolitan country, England, should align itself with the Irish national liberation movement.

83

83. Karl Marx and his eldest daughter Jenny, 1869

In commemoration of the Polish uprising of 1863, Jenny wore a Polish insurgents' cross. After the execution of the Irish Fenians in 1867, she wore it on an emerald ribbon, emerald being the colour symbolising Ireland's struggle for liberation.

84. La Marseillaise of March 19, 1870, printed Jenny Marx's article on the Irish problem. She wrote the article jointly with her father

N.89. — Samedi 19 Mars 1870.   Le Numéro : PARIS, 15 centimes; DÉPARTEMENTS ET ÉTRANGER 20 centimes   Samedi 19 Mars 1870. 3e N° 89.

LA MARSEILLAISE

Rédacteur en chef
HENRI ROCHEFORT

J. MILLIÈRE

PARIS. — Un mois 5 francs. — Trois mois, 13 fr. 50 — Six mois, 22 francs — Un an, 54 francs.   DÉPARTEMENTS - Un mois et francs. — Trois mois, 16 francs. — Six mois, 22 francs — Un an, 64 francs.

Londres, le 16 mars 1870.

La lettre de O'Donovan Rossa, que je vous avais communiquée dans ma dernière correspondance, a été l'événement de la semaine passée.

Le *Times* a reproduit la lettre sans commentaire, le *Daily News* a publié

un commentaire sans la lettre. « Comme on s'y devait attendre, » dit-il, « M. O'Donovan Rossa prend pour son thème les règles de prison auxquelles il est *assujetti pour quelque temps* (for a while) » Que c'est atroce, ce a *pour quelque times*, » en parlant d'un homme déjà emprisonné depuis cinq ans et con-

84

The Fenian Prisoners at Manchester and the International Working men's Association.

At a special meeting of the General Council of the I. W. A. held at the office 16 Castle Street West W. on Wednesday evening the following memorial was adopted:

"Memorial of the General Council of the International Workingmen's Association.

"To the Right Hon. Gathorne Hardy Her Majesty Secretary of State.

"The memorial of the undersigned, representing Workingmen's Associations in all parts of Europe sheweth — That the execution of the Irish prisoners condemned to death at Manchester will greatly impair the moral influence of England upon the European continent. The execution of the four prisoners resting upon the same evidence and the same verdict which by the free pardon of Maguire have been officially declared, the one false, the other erroneous, will bear the stamp not of a judicial act, but of political revenge. But even if the verdict of the Manchester jury and the evidence it rests upon had not been tainted by the British government itself, the latter would now have to choose between the blood handed practices of old Europe and the magnanimous humanity of the young Transatlantic Republic.

The commutation of the sentence for which we pray will be an act not only of justice, but of political wisdom.

By order of the General C. of the I. W. A.

John Weston Chairman

H. Shaw, Secretary for America

Eugene Dupont " " France,

85. *Karl Marx,* The Fenian Prisoners at Manchester and the International Workingmen's Association
A page of the manuscript Transcribed by Marx's wife Jenny

The memorial was written on the instructions of the General Council in November 1867. It exposes the British government's brutality in suppressing the liberation movement of the Irish.

86. *An attempt to free the imprisoned Fenians in Manchester, 1867.*

87. *British troops suppress Irish Fenians, 1871*

"ON THE IRISH QUESTION, TOO, MARX AND ENGELS PURSUED A CONSISTENTLY PROLETARIAN POLICY, WHICH REALLY EDUCATED THE MASSES IN A SPIRIT OF DEMOCRACY AND SOCIALISM. ...THE POLICY OF MARX AND ENGELS ON THE IRISH QUESTION SERVES AS A SPLENDID EXAMPLE OF THE ATTITUDE THE PROLETARIAT OF THE OPPRESSOR NATIONS SHOULD ADOPT TOWARDS NATIONAL MOVEMENTS, AN EXAMPLE WHICH HAS LOST NONE OF ITS IMMENSE *PRACTICAL* IMPORTANCE."

V. I. LENIN

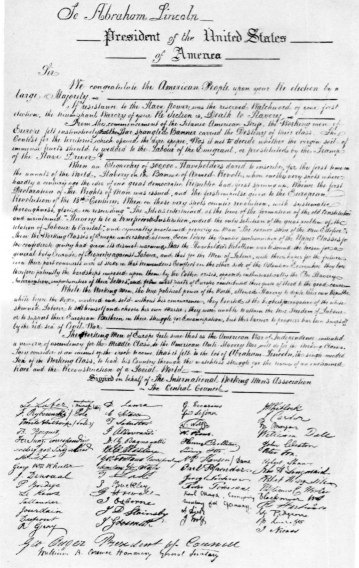

88

88. *Karl Marx, "To Abraham Lincoln, President of the United States of America"*

Written in November 1864 when Abraham Lincoln was re-elected President of the United States for a second term.

"WE CONGRATULATE THE AMERICAN PEOPLE UPON YOUR RE-ELECTION BY A LARGE MAJORITY.

"IF RESISTANCE TO THE SLAVE POWER WAS THE RESERVED WATCHWORD OF YOUR FIRST ELECTION, THE TRIUMPHANT WARCRY OF YOUR RE-ELECTION IS, DEATH TO SLAVERY."

KARL MARX

89. *Abraham Lincoln and the Northern army commanders at a field headquarters in 1865*

89

90

90. *Volunteers cheer Garibaldi in Florence, 1866*

Commending the great Italian patriot Garibaldi for his part in the liberation of Italy, Marx exposed the Bakuninists' attempt to belittle his role.

91. *The credentials issued to Giuseppe Boriani, a member of the Italian workers' movement of the 1870s. Drawn up by Frederick Engels, corresponding secretary of the General Council for Italy*

"Citizen Giuseppe Boriani," the credentials said, "is accepted member of the International Working Men's Association and is authorised to admit new members and form new sections, on condition that he, and the members and sections newly admitted, recognise as obligatory the official documents of the Association..."

Frederick Engels

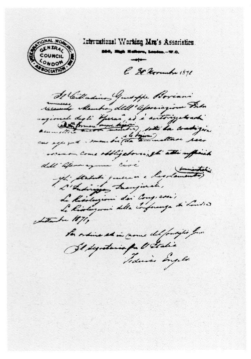

91

93

*Genral Council of the International Workingmens
Association
Mandate.*

*Frederick Engels, of Nᵒ 122 Regents Park Road,
London, is appointed provisionally representative of the
General Council of the International Workingmens Association
for Italy. He is authorized and directed to act in
the name of the General Council according to the instruction
he will receive from time to time.*

*By order & in the name of the General Council
New York, Jan 25ᵗʰ 1873.   The general secretary
                                                    F. A. Sorge*

94

93. *The house at 122 Regent's Park
Road, London, where Engels lived from
September 1870 to 1894*

94. *The mandate issued to Frederick
Engels as corresponding secretary of
the International's General Council for
Italy*

On moving to London on September 20, 1870, Engels joined in the work of the General Council, and was made corresponding secretary for Belgium, Italy, Spain, Portugal, and Denmark.

THE PARIS COMMUNE. 1871

Working men's Paris, with its Commune, will be for ever celebrated as the glorious harbinger of a new society.

Karl Marx

1. Karl Marx

THE GENERAL COUNCIL

OF THE

Jnternational Workingmen's Association

ON THE WAR.

TO THE MEMBERS OF THE INTERNATIONAL WORKING-MEN'S ASSOCIATION

IN EUROPE AND THE UNITED STATES.

In the inaugural Address of the INTERNATIONAL WORKINGMEN'S ASSOCIATION, of November, 1864, we said:—"If the emancipation of the working classes requires their fraternal concurrence, how are they to fulfil that great mission with a foreign policy in pursuit of criminal designs, playing upon national prejudices and squandering in piratical wars the people's blood and treasure?" We defined the foreign policy aimed at by the International in these words:— "Vindicate the simple laws of morals and justice, which ought to govern the relations of private individuals, as the laws paramount of the intercourse of nations."

No wonder that Louis Bonaparte, who usurped his power by exploiting the war of classes in France, and perpetuated it by periodical wars abroad, should from the first have treated the International as a dangerous foe. On the eve of the plebiscite he ordered a raid on the members of the Administrative Committees of the International Workingmen's Association throughout France, at Paris, Lyons, Rouen, Marseilles, Brest, &c, on the pretext that the International was a secret society dabbling in a complot for his

2

The Franco-Prussian War began on July 19, 1870. On the same day the General Council gathered to draw up an address to members of the International. It was essential to show the character of the war, to define the tactics of the working class, to call upon it to resist the policy of annexations, militarism, and chauvinism. The address was drawn up by Karl Marx on the instructions of the General Council.

3

2. "First Address of the General Council of the International Working Men's Association on the Franco-Prussian War"
Written by Karl Marx on July 19-23, 1870
A fragment of the front page of the leaflet

Marx praised the anti-war actions of the foremost French and German workers, and the sections of the International. He wrote:

"THE VERY FACT THAT WHILE OFFICIAL FRANCE AND GERMANY ARE RUSHING INTO A FRATRICIDAL FEUD, THE WORKMEN OF FRANCE AND GERMANY SEND EACH OTHER MESSAGES OF PEACE AND GOODWILL; THIS GREAT FACT, UNPARALLELED IN THE HISTORY OF THE PAST, OPENS THE VISTA OF A BRIGHTER FUTURE. IT PROVES THAT IN CONTRAST TO OLD SOCIETY, WITH ITS ECONOMICAL MISERIES AND ITS POLITICAL DELIRIUM, A NEW SOCIETY IS SPRINGING UP, WHOSE INTERNATIONAL RULE WILL BE *PEACE*, BECAUSE ITS NATIONAL RULER WILL BE EVERYWHERE THE SAME—*LABOUR!*"

LA MARSEILLAISE

Henri ROCHEFORT Rédacteur en chef

Protestation contre la guerre

Commune de Neuilly-sur-Seine

La guerre est-elle juste? — Non.
La guerre est-elle nationale? — Non.
Elle est dynastique.

Au nom de l'humanité, de la démocratie et des véritables intérêts de la France, nous adhérons complétement et énergiqnement à la protestation de l'*Internationale* contre la guerre.

Guérin, tisseur, Quedy, Normandin, Meslier, Brousse, Valet, Lelmaire, Marchandisse, Laforge, Danez, Labbé Caron, Bouzy, Girard, Bonjour, Bony, Boisse, Langlois, Laplace, Legrey, Marsalot, Michel, Decamp, Viton fils, Theveult, Frach, Blandin, Hennequin, Delair, Amand, Lefevre, Trainé, Chrétien, Bouëts, Pérot, Froment. Prevost, Guille, fils, Decamps père, Guille père, Four, Obry, Deveille, Brumant, Rigault fils, Roger, Boursier, Martin, Binet, Rigaud, Leclercq, Viton père, Laplace, Davoust, Mercier (Achille), Houssay, Brignolet. A. Bernadot, J. Carré, Rochard, J. Bonin, Bressier, E. Delalande, Bonneville, Puligny; Emile Leroy, Dumont, G. Seylier, Thomas, O. Bacquoy, Nicolas, Marielle, Cevallois père. Charlet. Colombier, Malardier.

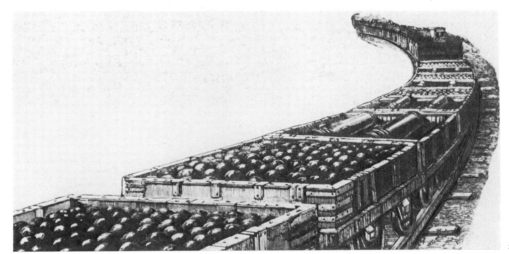

3. *Dispersal of an anti-war demonstration in Paris in August 1870*

4. *The protest of the Neuilly-sur-Seine section of the International against the war*
    La Marseillaise, *July 22, 1870*

"IN THE NAME OF HUMANITY, OF DEMOCRACY, AND THE TRUE INTERESTS OF FRANCE, WE ADHERE COMPLETELY AND ENERGETICALLY TO THE PROTESTATION OF THE INTERNATIONAL AGAINST THE WAR."

5. *Conveyance of shells*

6. *German soldiers departing for the frontlines*

7

8

7. Defeat of the French army at Sedan

The disaster at Sedan on September 2 completed the chain of Napoleon's defeats. It showed that the Second Empire was in a deep crisis.

"THE FRENCH CATASTROPHE OF 1870 STANDS UNPARALLELED IN THE HISTORY OF THE MODERN WORLD," wrote Marx. "IT SHEWED OFFICIAL FRANCE, THE FRANCE OF LOUIS BONAPARTE, THE FRANCE OF THE RULING CLASSES AND THEIR STATE PARASITES—A PUTRESCENT CADAVER."

"THE VERY MOMENT THAT THE UTTER ROTTENNESS OF THE IMPERIALIST ARMS BECAME EVIDENT, THE PRUSSIAN MILITARY *CAMARILLA* HAD RESOLVED UPON CONQUEST."

KARL MARX

8. A caricature of Napoleon III and Wilhelm

9

9. France is proclaimed a republic, September 4, 1870

10. Demonstration in Paris hailing the overthrow of the monarchy and the proclamation of a republic, September 1870

On September 4, when word of the defeat at Sedan reached Paris, a revolution broke out there.

Bowing to the demands of the people, the Corps législatif deposed Napoleon III, and a republic was proclaimed in France.

The head of the government, which declared itself a government of national defence, was General Louis Trochu, a reactionary and a follower of the Duc d'Orléans. The vice-president and foreign minister was a right-wing republican, Jules Favre.

10

SECOND ADDRESS.

In our first manifesto of the 23rd of July we said :—

"The death-knell of the Second Empire has already sounded at Paris. It will end, as it began, by a parody. But let us not forget that it is the Governments and the ruling classes of Europe who enabled Louis Napoleon to play during eighteen years the ferocious farce of the *Restored Empire*."

Thus, even before war operations had actually set in, we treated the Bonapartist bubble as a thing of the past.

If we were not mistaken as to the vitality of the Second Empire, we were not wrong in our apprehension lest the German war should " lose its strictly defensive character and degenerate into a war against the French people." The war of defence ended, in point of fact, with the surrender of Louis Bonaparte, the Sedan capitulation, and the proclamation of the Republic at Paris. But long before these events, the very moment that the utter rottenness of the Imperialist arms became evident, the Prussian military camarilla had resolved upon conquest. There lay an ugly obstacle in their way—*King William's own proclamations at the commencement of the war*. In his speech from the throne to the North German Diet, he had solemnly declared to make war upon the Emperor of the French, and not upon the French people. On the 11th of August he had issued a manifesto to the French nation, where he said : " The Emperor Napoleon having made, by land and sea, an attack on the German nation which desired and still desires to live in peace with the French people, I have assumed the command of the German armies to *repel his aggression*, and I have been led by *military events to cross the frontiers of France*." Not content to assert the defensive character of the war by the statement that he only assumed the command of the German armies " to repel aggression," he added that he was only " led by military events" to cross the frontiers of France. A defensive war does, of course, not exclude offensive operations, dictated by " military events."

Thus this pious king stood pledged before France and the world to a strictly defensive war. How to release him from his solemn pledge ? The stage-managers had to exhibit him as reluctantly yielding to the irresistible behest of the German nation. They at once gave the cue to the liberal German middle class, with its professors, its capitalists, its aldermen, and its penmen. That middle class, which in its struggles for civil liberty had, from 1846 to 1870, been exhibiting an unexampled spectacle of irresolution, incapacity, and cowardice, felt, of course, highly delighted to bestride the European scene as the roaring lion of German patriotism. It re-vindicated its civic independence by affecting to force upon the Prussian Government the secret designs of that same Government. It does penance for its long-continued and almost religious faith in Louis Bonaparte's infallibility, by shouting for the dismemberment of the French Republic. Let us for a moment listen to the special pleadings of those stout-hearted patriots !

They dare not pretend that the people of Alsace and Lorraine pant for the German embrace : quite the contrary. To punish their French patriotism, Strasburg, a town with an independent citadel commanding it, has for six days been wantonly and fiendishly bombarded by " German " explosive shells, setting it on fire, and killing great numbers of its defenceless inhabitants ! Yet, the soil of those provinces once upon a time belonged to the whilom German Empire. Hence, it seems, the soil and the human beings grown on it must be confiscated as imprescriptible German property. If the map of Europe is to be remade in the antiquary's vein, let us by no means forget that the Elector of Brandenburg, for his Prussian dominions, was the vassal of the Polish Republic.

The more knowing patriots, however, require Alsace and the German-speaking part of Lorraine as a " material guarantee " against French aggression. As this contemptible plea has bewildered many weak-minded people, we are bound to enter more fully upon it.

11

11. "Second Address of the General Council of the International Working Men's Association on the Franco-Prussian War"
    Written by Karl Marx on September 9, 1870
        The first page of the leaflet

The Second Address exposed the annexationist plans of Bismarck's government, which wanted to seize Alsace-Lorraine. Marx called on the sections of the International to come out against the partitioning of France and for the recognition of the French Republic proclaimed after the downfall of the Second Empire.

Marx also warned workers against over-rating the bourgeois provisional government of France.

12. "Undersized" was the title of the cartoon of the government of the French Republic

13. "Me, I don't want a king…"

"PARIS ARMED WAS THE REVOLUTION ARMED. A VICTORY OF PARIS OVER THE PRUSSIAN AGGRESSOR WOULD HAVE BEEN A VICTORY OF THE FRENCH WORKMAN OVER THE FRENCH CAPITALIST AND HIS STATE PARASITES. IN THIS CONFLICT BETWEEN NATIONAL DUTY AND CLASS INTEREST, THE GOVERNMENT OF NATIONAL DEFENCE DID NOT HESITATE ONE MOMENT TO TURN INTO A GOVERNMENT OF NATIONAL DEFECTION."

KARL MARX

J EN VEUX PAS DE ROI, MOI...

14. May the Nations Follow Our Example

15. The francs-tireurs in action at Rouen, October 6, 1870

RÉPUBLIQUE. FRANÇAISE

The mass of the people resisted the German invaders. The war turned gradually into a people's war. Yet that was what the ruling clique and the propertied classes of France dreaded most. At first secretly, then overtly, they conspired with Bismarck, obtaining his consent to help suppress the revolutionary movement in France.

16

16. The uprising of October 31, 1870
National Guardsmen, carrying a red banner inscribed, "Long Live the Commune!", tender their demands to the Trochu government

17. The uprising of October 31, 1870
Gustave Flourens speaks in the conference hall of the National Defence Government

18. *A group of Paris workers who had taken part in revolutionary actions*

In response to the treacherous policy of the National Defence Government— its capitulation of Metz and its surrender negotiations with the Prussians— the workers of Paris rose up on October 31, 1870. They captured the Hôtel de Ville, and arrested some members of the government. Owing to its poor organisation, the workers' uprising was defeated.

17

18

19

The bombardment of encircled Paris began at the end of December. Hunger and disease carried away thousands of lives. Frightened by the prospect of fresh revolutionary upheavals, the government was counting on its compact with the Prussians.

19. A view of Paris bombarded by German guns

20

20. A cartoon of Bismarck being given the key to Paris

21. The surrender of Jules Favre and Trochu

"TROCHU'S PLAN, FROM THE VERY DAY OF THE PROCLAMATION OF THE REPUBLIC, WAS *THE CAPITULATION OF PARIS AND OF FRANCE...* IN A LETTER TO GAMBETTA, JULES FAVRE HIMSELF CONFESSED SO MUCH THAT THE ENEMY TO BE PUT DOWN, WAS NOT THE PRUSSIAN SOLDIER, BUT THE PARIS 'DEMAGOGUE REVOLUTIONIST'... THE ATTEMPTS OF THE PARIS WORKMEN ON THE 5TH OF OCTOBER, THE 31ST OF OCTOBER ETC., TO SUPPLANT THESE TRAITORS BY THE COMMUNE, WERE PUT DOWN AS CONSPIRACIES WITH THE PRUSSIANS!"

KARL MARX

22. Vinoy, Thiers and Favre pilloried

The National Assembly in Versailles ratified the humiliating treaty of peace with the Bismarck government.
Under the terms of that predaceous treaty, France lost Alsace-Lorraine and undertook to pay the enormous indemnity of 5 billion gold francs, the burden of which the government intended to shift to the shoulders of the people.

23. Thiers and Favre separate Alsace and Lorraine from France

"HISTORY WILL MEASURE ITS RETRIBUTION, NOT BY THE EXTENT OF THE SQUARE MILES CONQUERED FROM FRANCE, BUT BY THE INTENSITY OF THE CRIME OF REVIVING, IN THE SECOND HALF OF THE 19TH CENTURY, *THE POLICY OF CONQUEST!*"

KARL MARX

Juvena. 22

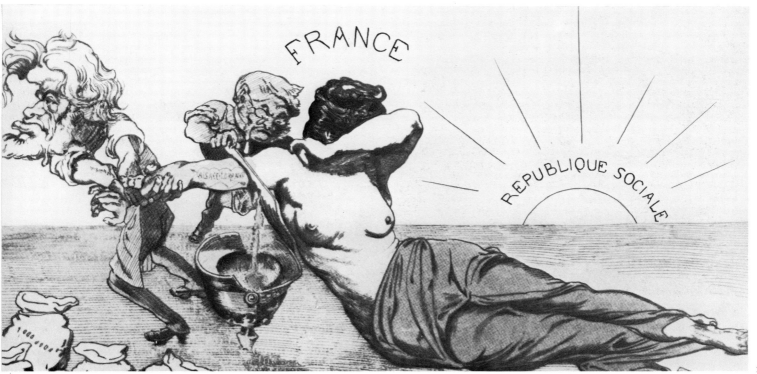

23

24

25

*24. Guns of the National Guard outside
the Hôtel de Ville*

*25. Up in the heights of Montmartre on
the eve of the uprising*

"THIERS OPENED THE CIVIL WAR BY SENDING VINOY, AT THE HEAD OF A MULTITUDE OF *SERGENTS-DE-VILLE* AND SOME REGIMENTS OF THE LINE, UPON A NOCTURNAL EXPEDITION AGAINST MONTMARTRE, THERE TO SEIZE, BY SURPRISE, THE ARTILLERY OF THE NATIONAL GUARD. IT IS WELL KNOWN HOW THIS ATTEMPT BROKE DOWN BEFORE THE RESISTANCE OF THE NATIONAL GUARD AND THE FRATERNISATION OF THE LINE WITH THE PEOPLE."

KARL MARX

26. *"Daylight frightens them"*

27. *National Guard headquarters in the Hôtel de Ville, March 18, 1871*

26

27

28

In the revolution of March 18, 1871, it was the Central Committee of the National Guard that took power first. It was then taken over by the Paris Commune, the world's first worker government, elected by the people of the city.

RÉPUBLIQUE FRANÇAISE.

LIBERTÉ, ÉGALITÉ, FRATERNITÉ.

AU PEUPLE.

Citoyens,

Le Peuple de Paris a secoué le joug qu'on essayait de lui imposer.

Calme, impassible dans sa force, il a attendu sans crainte comme sans provocation les fous éhontés qui voulaient toucher à la République.

Cette fois, nos frères de l'armée n'ont pas voulu porter la main sur l'arche sainte de nos libertés. Merci à tous; et que Paris et la France jettent ensemble les bases d'une République acclamée avec toutes ses conséquences, le seul Gouvernement qui fermera pour toujours l'ère des invasions et des guerres civiles.

L'état de siége est levé

Le Peuple de Paris est convoqué dans ses sections pour faire ses Élections communales.

La sûreté de tous les citoyens est assurée par le concours de la Garde nationale.

Hôtel-de-Ville. Paris, le 19 mars 1871.

29

30

REPUBLIQUE FRANÇAISE

Liberté. — Égalité. — Fraternité

Association Internationale

DES TRAVAILLEURS

CONSEIL FÉDÉRAL DES SECTIONS PARISIENNES

Chambre Fédérale des Sociétés ouvrières

29. *Manifesto of the National Guard on the victory of the revolution in Paris, March 19, 1871*

A poster

"CITIZENS, THE PEOPLE OF PARIS HAVE THROWN OFF THE YOKE WHICH WAS BEING IMPOSED ON THEM... PARIS AND FRANCE WILL JOINTLY LAY THE FOUNDATIONS OF A REPUBLIC, TO BE ACCLAIMED WITH ALL THE CONSEQUENCES THAT MAY ENSUE, THE ONLY GOVERNMENT THAT WILL FOREVER END THE ERA OF INVASIONS AND CIVIL WARS."

30. *"Citizens, the carnival is over. I'm sweeping out the masks"*

31. *Place de Corderie 6, where the Bureau of the International's Paris sections had its offices*

After the March 18 revolution, the International's sections in France invigorated their activities.

32. *Address of the Federal Council of the International's Paris sections to the working people of the French capital, calling on them to back the Commune at the elections on March 26, 1871*

A poster

33

33. The Paris Commune is festively proclaimed in the square outside the Hôtel de Ville

34. The red flag on the July Column

"THE RED FLAG, HOISTED BY THE PARIS COMMUNE, CROWNS IN REALITY ONLY THE GOVERNMENT OF WORKMEN FOR PARIS!"

KARL MARX

35. The Paris Commune addresses the people, March 29, 1871

"YOU ARE THE MASTERS OF YOUR DESTINY. DRAWING STRENGTH FROM YOUR SUPPORT, THE REPRESENTATIVES YOU HAVE JUST CHOSEN WILL REPAIR THE DISASTERS CAUSED BY THE DEPOSED AUTHORITIES; THE DISLOCATED INDUSTRIES, THE SUSPENDED WORK, THE PARALYSED COMMERCIAL TRANSACTIONS, WILL RECEIVE POWERFUL IMPULSE."

"WHAT FLEXIBILITY, WHAT HISTORICAL INITIATIVE, WHAT A CAPACITY FOR SACRIFICE IN THESE PARISIANS! AFTER SIX MONTHS OF HUNGER AND RUIN, CAUSED BY INTERNAL TREACHERY EVEN MORE THAN BY THE EXTERNAL ENEMY, THEY RISE, IN THE FACE OF THE PRUSSIAN BAYONETS, AS IF THERE HAD NEVER BEEN A WAR BETWEEN FRANCE AND GERMANY AND THE ENEMY WERE NOT STANDING AT THE GATES OF PARIS! HISTORY HAS NO COMPARABLE EXAMPLE OF SIMILAR GREATNESS!"

KARL MARX

36. The National Guard in the square outside the Hôtel de Ville on March 28, 1871, hails the inauguration of the Paris Commune

RÉPUBLIQUE FRANÇAISE

N° 44   LIBERTÉ — ÉGALITÉ — FRATERNITÉ   N° 44

COMMUNE DE PARIS

Citoyens,

Votre Commune est constituée.

Le vote du 26 mars a sanctionné la Révolution victorieuse.

Un pouvoir lâchement agresseur vous avait pris à la gorge : vous avez, dans votre légitime défense, repoussé de vos murs ce gouvernement qui voulait vous déshonorer en vous imposant un roi.

Aujourd'hui, les criminels que vous n'avez même pas voulu poursuivre abusent de votre magnanimité pour organiser aux portes même de la cité un foyer de conspiration monarchique. Ils invoquent la guerre civile ; ils mettent en œuvre toutes les corruptions ; ils acceptent toutes les complicités ; ils ont osé mendier jusqu'à l'appui de l'étranger.

Nous en appelons de ces menées exécrables au jugement de la France et du monde.

Citoyens,

Vous venez de vous donner des institutions qui défient toutes les tentatives.

Vous êtes maîtres de vos destinées. Forte de votre appui, la représentation que vous venez d'établir va réparer les désastres causés par le pouvoir déchu : l'industrie compromise, le travail suspendu, les transactions commerciales paralysées, vont recevoir une impulsion vigoureuse.

Dès aujourd'hui, la décision attendue sur les loyers ;

Demain, celle des échéances ;

Tous les services publics rétablis et simplifiés ;

35

36

37

37. *Karl Marx, Margate, 1866*

Marx and Engels, who were in London, lost no time marshalling aid for the Paris Commune. Whatever the Commune did, and all the developments in revolutionary Paris, were closely followed by the International's General Council.

Marx was in close communication with the Paris Communards, members of the International's sections in Paris, helping them with his advice and criticising their mistakes.

8. Léo Frankel

9. Louis Eugène Varlin

In a letter to the Communards Frankel and Varlin, Marx warned of the French reactionaries' conspiring with the Prussians to suppress the Commune. Prominent Commune functionary, elected to the Commission of Labour and Exchange, Léo Frankel wrote Marx, asking for his opinion of the reforms that were to have laid the foundation for a social republic.

38
39

40. Paul Lafargue

In a letter to Marx dated April 8, 1871, Lafargue wrote: "I've been in Paris since two days ago. I saw the leaders of the Commune, who, like the rest of Paris, are full of enthusiasm. They still hope to capture Versailles and are acting to that effect. Vaillant has told me there was no lack in people, though leaders were scarce. Perhaps Engels could come here and apply his talents in the service of the revolution? I'll write in greater detail later..."

40

41
42

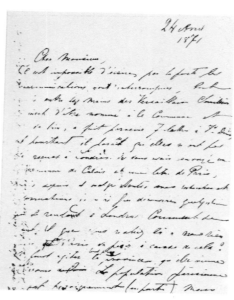

41. *Elizaveta Lukinichna Dmitrieva-Tomanovskaya*

42. *Dmitrieva-Tomanovskaya's letter to Hermann Jung in London, of April 24, 1871 (letters to Marx were also sent care of Jung, who was a member of the International's General Council)*

Dmitrieva left for Paris on March 28, 1871, the day the Commune was constituted, to take part in the struggle of the Paris workers. In letters meant for Marx and the General Council, she referred to the need for agitation in the provinces and among peasants, and wrote of her own part in the activities of the Union of Women in Defence of Paris and in Aid of the Wounded.

"I call public meetings," she wrote. "We have constituted women's committees in all districts and in the town halls, and, besides, a central committee... I speak every evening, and write a lot... If the Commune wins, our organisation will turn from a political into a social body, and we will set up sections of the International. This idea is highly popular..."

43. *A meeting of women Communards*

An active role in marshalling the mass of the people at the time of the Commune was played by the revolutionary Paris clubs.

44

45

44. *A revolutionary club at the Folies-Bergère*

45. *A list of Paris Commune functionaries drawn up by Marx in July 1871*

From the very start, Marx followed the progress of the Paris revolution, and took detailed notes on what the papers reported about the Communards and their activity, and their heroic resistance to the onslaught of the Versailles reactionaries.

46
47

Prominent personalities of the Paris Commune

46. *Adolphe Alphonse Assi (1840-1886), mechanic, member of the International; member of the General Security Commission of the Commune*

47. *Edouard Vaillant (1840-1915), journalist, member of the International; member of the Executive Commission of the Commune*

48. *Eugène Varlin (1839-1871), worker, a leader of the Paris sections of the International; member of the Finance Commission and Food Commission of the Commune; shot by the Versailles people*

49. *Auguste Vermorel (1841-1871), journalist and historian; member of the Paris Commune*

50. *Walery Wróblewsky (1836-1908), Polish revolutionary democrat; member of the International; general of the Commune*

51. *Pascal Grousset (1845-1909), journalist, Blanquist; Chairman of the Foreign Relations Committee of the Commune*

52. *Charles Delescluze (1809-1871), journalist, member of the Military Commission of the Commune; killed on the barricades in Paris*

53. *Simon Dereure (1838-1900), member of the International; Blanquist; member of the Paris Commune*

54. *Jaroslaw Dombrowski (1836-1871), Polish revolutionary democrat; general of the Commune; in May 1871 became Commander-in-Chief of its Armed Forces, was killed on the barricades*

55. *Jules Paul Johannard (1843-1892), member of the General Council of the International; member of the Foreign Relations Committee of the Commune*

56. *François Jourde (1843-1893), a leader of the uprising of March 18, Chairman of the Finance Commission of the Commune*

53
54

50
51

57. *Zéphyrin Camélinat (1840-1932), member of the International; active member of the Paris Commune; organised minting of coins of the revolution*

58. *Anna Vasilievna Korvin-Krukovskaya (married Jaclard), (1843-1887), Russian revolutionary; member of the Commune; writer; corresponded with Marx*

52

57
58

59
60

61

59. Gustave Courbet (1819-1877), realist painter; member of the Educational Commission of the Commune

60. Frédéric Cournet (1839-1885), journalist, Blanquist; member of the General Security Commission of the Commune

61. Pyotr Lavrovich Lavrov (1823-1900), Russian sociologist and journalist; an ideologist of Narodism; member of the International; took part in the Paris Commune

62. Paul Lafargue (1842-1911), member of the General Council of the International; took part in the Paris Commune, husband of Karl Marx's daughter Laura

63. Gustave Lefrançais (1826-1901), member of the International; member of the Commune's Executive Commission, Labour and Exchange Commission, and Finance Commission

64. Prosper Olivier Lissagaray (1838-1901), journalist; though he held no official posts, he promoted the Commune in his newspapers

65. Charles Longuet (1839-1903), socialist, active member of the International; editor-in-chief of the Commune's Journal Officiel de la République Française; *in 1872 married Karl Marx's eldest daughter Jenny*

66. Benoît Malon (1841-1893), Left Proudhonist; member of the International and the Paris Commune

67. Jean Baptiste Millière (1817-1871), lawyer and journalist; member of the editorial board of the socialist newspaper Commune; *arrested by the Versailles people and shot without trial*

68. Louise Michel (1830-1905), active member of the Paris Commune; teacher and writer

69. Jean Louis Pindy (1840-1917), worker, member of the International and the Paris Commune; Proudhonist

66
67

107

On May 21, the Versailles troops thrust into Paris. By that time they held an 8:1 advantage in numbers over the National Guard defending the city. The "bloody week" of May began, highlighted by the heroism of the Communards and the brutality of their antagonists.

107. Fighting outside the Palais de l'Élysée

108. Battle standard of the 67th Battalion of the Paris Commune, under the command of Assi, a member of the International

REPUBLIQUE FRANÇAISE

67.ᵐᵉ BATAILLON.

COMMUNE de PARIS

108

109

110

109. *The battle at Neuilly*

110. *The fighting at the Père Lachaise Cemetery*

111. *Execution of Communards at the wall of the Père Lachaise Cemetery*

112. *The last man on the barricade*

111

"EVEN THE ATROCITIES OF THE BOURGEOIS IN JUNE, 1848, VANISH BEFORE THE INEFFABLE INFAMY OF 1871. THE SELF-SACRIFICING HEROISM WITH WHICH THE POPULATION OF PARIS—MEN, WOMEN, AND CHILDREN—FOUGHT FOR EIGHT DAYS AFTER THE ENTRANCE OF THE VERSAILLESE, REFLECTS AS MUCH THE GRANDEUR OF THEIR CAUSE, AS THE INFERNAL DEEDS OF THE SOLDIERY RE-FLECT THE INNATE SPIRIT OF THAT CIVILISATION OF WHICH THEY ARE THE MERCENARY VINDICATORS."

KARL MARX

112

113

114

116

113. Captive Communards in the dungeon of Orangerie prison in Versailles

114. Wall of the Communards

115. "Poor France—the trunk is no more, but the roots are intact"

116. "The corpse is buried, the idea survives"

"THE PRINCIPLES OF THE COMMUNE WERE ETERNAL AND COULD NOT BE CRUSHED; THEY WOULD ASSERT THEMSELVES AGAIN AND AGAIN UNTIL THE WORKING CLASSES WERE EMANCIPATED."

KARL MARX

"THE CIVILISATION AND JUSTICE OF BOURGEOIS ORDER COMES OUT IN ITS LURID LIGHT WHENEVER THE SLAVES AND DRUDGES OF THAT ORDER RISE AGAINST THEIR MASTERS. THEN THIS CIVILISATION AND JUSTICE STAND FORTH AS UNDISGUISED SAVAGERY AND LAWLESS REVENGE. EACH NEW CRISIS IN THE CLASS STRUGGLE BETWEEN THE APPROPRIATOR AND THE PRODUCER BRINGS OUT THIS FACT MORE GLARINGLY."

KARL MARX

"THE LAST MOVEMENT WAS THE COMMUNE, THE GREATEST THAT HAD YET BEEN MADE, AND THERE COULD NOT BE TWO OPINIONS ABOUT IT—THE COMMUNE WAS THE CONQUEST OF THE POLITICAL POWER OF THE WORKING CLASSES."

KARL MARX

THE

CIVIL WAR IN FRANCE.

ADDRESS

OF

THE GENERAL COUNCIL

OF THE

INTERNATIONAL WORKING-MEN'S

ASSOCIATION

Printed and Published for the Council by

EDWARD TRUELOVE, 256, HIGH HOLBORN

1871.

ГРАЖДАНСКАЯ ВОЙНА

ВО ФРАНЦІИ.

(1870—71)

КАРЛЪ МАРКСЪ

ПЕРЕВОДЪ СЪ НѢМЕЦКАГО.

Der

Bürgerkrieg in Frankreich.

Adresse des Generalraths

der

Internationalen Arbeiter-Assoziation

an

alle Mitglieder in Europa und den Vereinigten Staaten.

Separatabdruck aus dem Volksstaat.

LA

GUERRE CIVILE

EN FRANCE.

ADRESSE

DU

CONSEIL GÉNÉRAL

DE

L'ASSOCIATION INTERNATIONALE

des Travailleurs.

TROISIÈME ÉDITION REVUE.

117

117. *Karl Marx*, The Civil War in France

The English, Russian, German, and French editions that appeared in 1871 and 1872.

The Civil War in France gained a wide readership all over the world in next to no time. In 1871 and the following year it appeared in English, French, German, Russian, Italian, Spanish, and Dutch, and was circulated in Europe and the United States. A later Russian translation was edited by Vladimir Lenin.

Lenin wrote that Marx's evaluation of the Commune was "profound, clear-cut, brilliant, *effective*". Looking back on the experience of the Paris Commune, Marx elaborated upon the theory of class struggle, revolution, and of the state in the period of transition from capitalism to communism.

L'Internationale.

C'est la lutte finale.
Groupons nous et demain.
L'internationale
Sera le genre humain.

Debout! l'âme du prolétaire!
Travailleurs, groupons nous enfin.
Debout! les damnés de la terre!
Debout! les forçats de la faim!
Pour vaincre la misère et l'ombre
Foule esclave, debout! debout!
C'est nous le droit, c'est nous le nombre:
Nous qui n'étions rien, soyons tout

C'est la lutte finale,
groupons-nous et demain.
L'Internationale
Sera le genre humain:

Il n'est pas de Sauveurs suprêmes:
Ni dieu, ni cesar, ni tribun.
Travailleurs Sauvons-nous nous-mêmes;
Travaillons au Salut Commun.
Pour que les voleurs rendent gorge,
Pour tirer l'esprit du cachot,
Allumons notre grande forge!
Battons le fer quand il est chaud!

E Pottier

119

"NO PUBLICATION IN THE HISTORY OF LONDON HAS CAUSED SUCH A STIR AS THE ADDRESS OF THE GENERAL COUNCIL OF THE INTERNATIONAL (*THE CIVIL WAR IN FRANCE—ED.*)... THE ENTIRE PRESS HAS HAD TO CONFESS UNANIMOUSLY THAT THE INTERNATIONAL IS A GREAT POWER IN EUROPE TO BE RECKONED WITH, WHICH CANNOT BE ELIMINATED BY REFUSING TO TALK ABOUT IT."

FREDERICK ENGELS

In the summer of 1871, fleeing from persecution, Eugène Pottier, a member of the Paris Commune and of the International, arrived in London. He brought with him verse he had written at the height of the Versailles reaction.

118. *Eugène Pottier's verse for the* Internationale
Manuscript

Years have passed, but Pottier's verse translated into several scores of languages, has become the anthem of the proletariat of all countries, a rallying cry for peoples rising against oppression.

119. *Eugène Pottier*

120

121

122

120. *Jenny Marx, Karl Marx's eldest daughter*

121. *Eleanor Marx, Karl Marx's youngest daughter*

122. *The pass issued to Jenny and Eleanor Marx by the French police for crossing into Spain, and giving their descriptions*

Worried about what had happened to the Lafargues, who were living in France, Marx's daughters Jenny and Eleanor left London for Bordeaux at the end of April 1871. From that city they observed the events in Paris. After the fall of the Commune, reprisals were loosened on participants in the revolution. The two sisters followed the Lafargues to the south of France, whence Lafargue, pursued by the French police, was forced to cross urgently into Spain. A few days later Laura, Jenny and Eleanor visited him, and thereupon the girls returned to France. On the border, they were detained by the French police, interrogated and searched, and their British passports were taken from them. The police wanted information from them about Lafargue and the International. The passports were returned to them ten days later, and they were able to return to London.

123

123. *Collection List of the Paris Communards' refugee fund*

124. *Engels' letter to Marx, dated August 23, 1871, on the inclusion of Léo Frankel and other Paris Commune members who had escaped to London in the General Council of the International*

A page of the manuscript

124

125. *Karl Marx, London, 1869*

126. *Frederick Engels, Manchester, 1868-69*

127

Marx and Engels attended the London Conference (1871) and the Hague Congress (1872), which held a special place in the history of the IWA. Their resolutions summed up the experience of the revolutionary movement and the Paris Commune, and charted the further course of the class struggle: constitution of independent proletarian parties and invigoration of the political struggle congruent with scientific revolutionary theory, which will thus merge with the workers' class struggle.

127. A view of London in the latter half of the 19th century

128. Minutes of the afternoon session of the London Conference on September 19, 1871

A page of the minutes

"REVOLUTION IS THE SUPREME ACT OF POLITICS; WHOEVER WANTS IT MUST ALSO WANT THE MEANS, POLITICAL ACTION, WHICH PREPARES FOR IT, WHICH TRAINS WORKERS FOR REVOLUTION AND WITHOUT WHICH WORKERS WILL ALWAYS BE DUPED BY THE FAVRES AND THE PYATS THE DAY AFTER THE STRUGGLE. BUT THE POLITICS WHICH ARE NEEDED ARE WORKING-CLASS POLITICS; THE WORKERS' PARTY MUST NOT BE CONSTITUTED AS THE TAIL OF SOME BOURGEOIS PARTY."

FREDERICK ENGELS

128

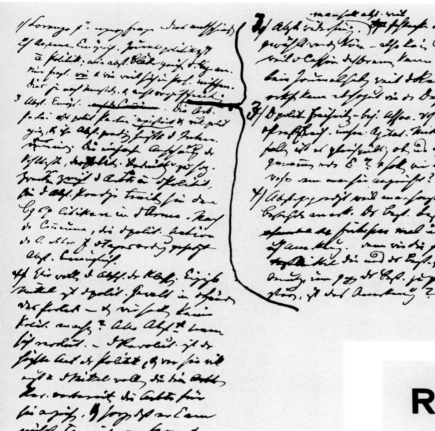

129. Notes for a speech on the political action of the working class drawn up by Engels for the meeting of September 21, 1871

130. Resolutions of the 1871 London Conference drawn up by Marx and Engels

RÉSOLUTIONS

DES DÉLÉGUÉS DE LA CONFÉRENCE

DE

L'ASSOCIATION INTERNATIONALE

DES

TRAVAILLEURS.

Réunie à Londres, du 17 au 23 Septembre 1871.

(Circulaire publiée par le Conseil Général de l'Association)

LONDRES

Imprimé pour l'Association, par l'Imprimerie Internationale.

1871.

"CONSTITUTION OF THE WORKING CLASS INTO A POLITICAL PARTY IS INDISPENSABLE IN ORDER TO INSURE THE TRIUMPH OF THE SOCIAL REVOLUTION AND ITS ULTIMATE END—THE ABOLITION OF CLASSES... THE COMBINATION OF FORCES WHICH THE WORKING CLASS HAS ALREADY EFFECTED BY ITS ECONOMICAL STRUGGLES OUGHT AT THE SAME TIME TO SERVE AS A LEVER FOR ITS STRUGGLES AGAINST THE POLITICAL POWER OF LANDLORDS AND CAPITALISTS."

KARL MARX
and FREDERICK ENGELS

130

131

131. *The Hague in the 1860s*

132. *Marx's mandate to the Hague Congress issued by the International's Federal Council of North America and signed by Friedrich Adolf Sorge*

133. *Engels's mandate to the Hague Congress issued by the 6th New York section of the International*

132

The last of the International's congresses gathered in The Hague on September 2 through 7, 1872, under the immediate direction of Marx and Engels.

Sixty-five delegates attended from 15 countries. Marx had a mandate from the German section of North America and the Leipzig section, and also from the Italian Workers' Society of Porto Maurizio.

The Congress was of the utmost importance for the international working-class movement, for it set the stage for the establishment of independent political parties in various countries on the basis of scientific revolutionary theory.

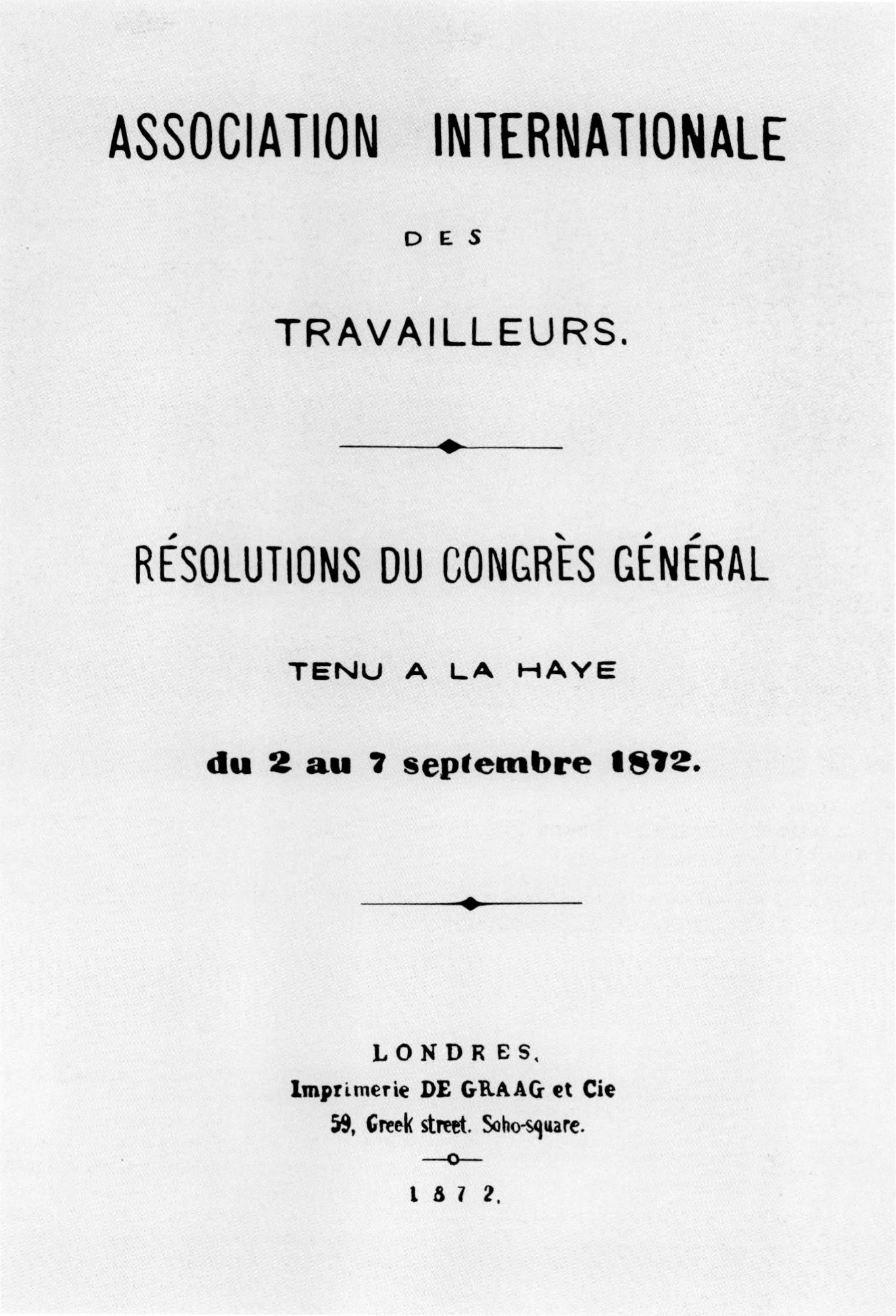

134. Resolutions of the Hague Congress of the International

The Congress incorporated in the IWA Rules the resolution of the London Conference on working-class political action and the constitution of proletarian parties.

ASSOCIATION INTERNATIONALE

D E S

TRAVAILLEURS.

—◆—

RÉSOLUTIONS DU CONGRÈS GÉNÉRAL

TENU A LA HAYE

du 2 au 7 septembre 1872.

—◆—

LONDRES,
Imprimerie DE GRAAG et Cie
59, Greek street. Soho-square.
—o—
1 8 7 2.

134

135

135. *Hague Congress delegates after a session*

136. *List of delegates to the Hague Congress*

Association Internationale des Travailleurs.

LISTE NOMINALE DES DÉLÉGUÉS

composant le 5ᵐᵉ Congrès universel, tenu à la Haye. (Hollande),
du 2 au 7 Septembre 1872.

1. Arnaud, (Antoine) Chimiste, délégué de la Section de Carouge, Genève. (Suisse.)
2. Alerini, délégué de la Fédération d'Espagne.
3. Becker, (Philippe) Brossier, délégué du comité Fédéral Romand de deux sections de Bale, section de Zudgen, section de Lucerne, section allemande de Genève, (Suisse.)
4. Barry, Cordonnier, délégué d'une section de Chicago, (Amérique du Nord).
5. Becker, (Bernard) Homme de Lettres, dél. sect. de Brunswick, (Prusse).
6. Brismée, (Désiré) Imprimeur, dél. section de Bruxelles (Belgique).
7. Cournet, (Frédéric) Professeur, dél. du Conseil-Général de Londres et dél. du comité central de Copenhague (Danemarck).
8. Cuno, dél. sect. de Dusseldorf, Prusse Rhénane et Sect. de Stuttgard, (Wurtemberg).
9. Coenen, Cordonnier, dél. sect. d'Anvers, (Belgique).
10. Cyrille, Employé de Commerce, dél. sect. française de Bruxelles, (Belgique).
11. Dumon, dél. sect. française de Paris et Rouen.
12. Dietgen, Tanneur, dél. sect. de Dresde, (Saxe).
13. Dupont, (Eugène) Facteur d'instruments de musique, dél. du Conseil Général de Londres.
14. Dave, (Victor) dél. sect. de la Haye, Hollande.
15. Duval, Menuisier, dél. du comité Fédéral Romand, Genève(Suisse).
16. Dereure, (Simon) Cordonnier, dél. du Congrès de New-York, Amérique du Nord.
17. Eberhard, Tailleur, dél. sections des Mégissiers, Cordonniers, Tailleurs, menuisiers, peintres, teinturiers en peaux et marbriers de Bruxelles, (Belgique).

30. Hepner, (Adolphe) Journaliste, dél. sect. 8 de New-York. (Amérique du Nord).
31. Hales, (John) dél. sect. de Hackney-road, Branche de Londres.
32. Heim, dél. sect. de Bohème, (Autriche).
33. Johannard, Feuillagiste, dél. sect. Française, (France).
34. Karl Marx, homme de Lettres, dél. du Conseil Général, sect. 1 de New-York, dél. sect. de Leipzig et sect. de Mayence, (Prusse).
35. Kugelmann, Docteur en médecine, dél. sect. de Celle, (Hanovre).
36. Lucain, dél. sect. Française, (France).
37. Lessner, Tailleur, dél. sect. Allemande de Londres.
38. Lafargue, (Paul) Docteur en Médecine, dél. de la Nouvelle Fédération de Madrid et de la Fédération de Lisbonne. (Portugal).

Bakuninism suffered a crushing defeat at the Hague Congress.

The Congress condemned the divisive activity within the IWA of a secret Bakuninist organisation called Alliance of Socialist Democracy. Mikhail Bakunin and his followers were expelled from the International. "Here we have a society," wrote Marx and Engels of the Alliance, "which, under the mask of the most extreme anarchism, directs its blows not against the existing governments but against the revolutionaries who accept neither its dogma nor its leadership... It infiltrates the ranks of the international organisation of the working class, at first attempts to dominate it and, when this plan fails, sets to work to disorganise it. It brazenly substitutes its sectarian programme and narrow ideas for the broad programme and great aspirations of our Association."

L'ALLIANCE

DE LA

DÉMOCRATIE SOCIALISTE

ET

L'ASSOCIATION INTERNATIONALE

DES TRAVAILLEURS.

RAPPORT ET DOCUMENTS PUBLIÉS PAR ORDRE DU
CONGRÈS INTERNATIONAL DE LA HAYE.

LONDRES:
A. DARSON, SUCCESSEUR DE FOUCAULT,
46B, RATHBONE PLACE, OXFORD ST.

HAMBOURG:
EN VENTE CHEZ OTTO MEISSNER.

1873.

LES

PRÉTENDUES SCISSIONS

DANS

L'INTERNATIONALE

CIRCULAIRE PRIVÉE

DU

CONSEIL GÉNÉRAL

DE

L'ASSOCIATION INTERNATIONALE DES TRAVAILLEURS

GENÈVE
IMPRIMERIE COOPÉRATIVE, RUE DU CONSEIL-GÉNÉRAL, 8
1872

138

---

137. *Karl Marx and Frederick Engels, The Alliance of Socialist Democracy and the International Working Men's Association, London-Hamburg, August 1873*
Report and documents, published by decision of the International's Hague Congress
The title page

138. *Karl Marx and Frederick Engels, Fictitious Splits in the International. Private Circular from the IWA General Council, Geneva, 1872*
The title page

"THE INTERNATIONAL DOMINATED ONE SIDE OF EUROPEAN HISTORY—THE SIDE ON WHICH THE FUTURE LIES—FOR TEN YEARS AND CAN LOOK BACK UPON ITS WORK WITH PRIDE."
FREDERICK ENGELS

"THE FIRST INTERNATIONAL HAD PLAYED ITS HISTORICAL PART, AND NOW MADE WAY FOR A PERIOD OF A FAR GREATER DEVELOPMENT OF THE LABOUR MOVEMENT IN ALL COUNTRIES IN THE WORLD, A PERIOD IN WHICH THE MOVEMENT GREW IN *SCOPE*, AND *MASS* SOCIALIST WORKING-CLASS PARTIES IN INDIVIDUAL NATIONAL STATES WERE FORMED."
V. I. LENIN

1873-1883

Karl Marx was one of the rare men who could be leaders in science and public life at the same time: these two aspects were so closely united in him that one can understand him only by taking into account both the scholar and the socialist fighter.

Paul Lafargue

1. Karl Marx, London, 1875

Following the defeat of the Paris Commune, a relatively tranquil period began for capitalism. "The West had finished with bourgeois revolutions," Lenin wrote of that period. "The East had not yet risen to them. The West entered a phase of 'peaceful' preparations for the changes to come."

For Marx the years 1873 to 1883 were a period of intense scientific and practical revolutionary activity.

He was mainly occupied with completing his *Capital*. In those last ten years of his life he was busy summing up and gathering new material for the second and third volumes of his major academic project.

Marx made an especially careful study of new developments in the capitalist economy that surfaced in the 1870s and early 80s—the unheard-of concentration and centralisation of capital, the gravitation towards monopoly, the grown role of the banks, and the mounting export of capital.

2. A page of the manuscript of Volume II of Marx's Capital

3. The first page of the manuscript of Volume III of Capital

4. Marx at work

Working on the manuscripts of volumes II and III of *Capital*, Marx concluded that he needed data on capitalism's development in Russia, especially in the period since the abolition of serfdom in that country.

In 1869, he began learning Russian on his own. As his wife wrote at that time, he began to study Russian "hammer and tongs".

5. A page of Marx's notebook with exercises in Russian grammar, 1870

5

6

The first text that Marx read in Russian with the aid of a dictionary was the chapter, "Prison and Exile", from Alexander Herzen's *My Past and Thoughts*, published in London in 1854. Notes in Marx's and Engels's hand are extant on the margins of the book.

6. *Alexander Ivanovich Herzen (1812-1870)*

7. *A. Herzen*, My Past and Thoughts. *The first page of the chapter, "Prison and Exile"*

With deep interest, Marx read N. Flerovsky's book, *The Condition of the Working Class in Russia*, in Russian. He observed: "This is the first book to tell the truth about Russian economic conditions."

8. *N. Flerovsky, pen-name of Vassily Vassilievich Bervi (1829-1918), Russian sociologist, journalist and economist*

9. *N. Flerovsky*, The Condition of the Working Class in Russia, *St. Petersburg, 1869*

10. *Building a railway in Russia*

ПОЛОЖЕНІЕ
РАБОЧАГО КЛАССА
ВЪ РОССІИ.

———

НАБЛЮДЕНІЯ И ИЗСЛѢДОВАНІЯ
Н. ФЛЕРОВСКАГО.

———

С.-ПЕТЕРВУРГЪ.
ИЗДАНІЕ Н. П. ПОЛЯКОВА.
1869.

8
9

10

11

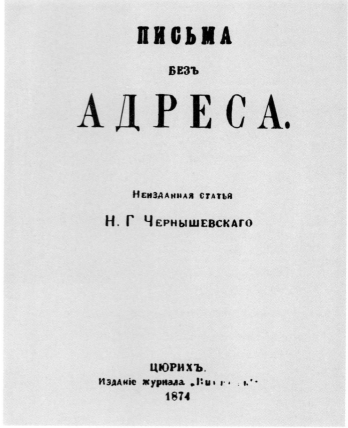

ПИСЬМА
БЕЗЪ
АДРЕСА.

НЕИЗДАННАЯ СТАТЬЯ
Н. Г. ЧЕРНЫШЕВСКАГО

ЦЮРИХЪ.
Изданіе журнала „Впередъ".
1874

12

13

Marx and Engels thought highly of Nikolai Chernyshevsky's activity as publicist, scholar, and revolutionary democrat. They commended his tenacity and civic courage in coming to grips with the tsarist autocracy. They admired his faith in the future socialist reconstruction, and his thorough knowledge of Russia. Engels referred to him as "that great thinker to whom Russia owes so much".

11. *Nikolai Gavrilovich Chernyshevsky (1828-1889)*

Marx read Chernyshevsky's *Unaddressed Letters* in a handwritten copy sent him by Danielson in 1881, and assisted in their being published. Later, on the basis of the *Unaddressed Letters*, Marx produced a manuscript which he called, "Apropos of the Abolition of Serfdom in Russia".

12. *Nikolai Chernyshevsky*, Unaddressed Letters, *Zurich, 1874*

13. *A page from the notebook containing Marx's "Apropos of the Abolition of Serfdom in Russia"*

Marx read countless books on the economy, politics, social relations and culture of Russia, and made a thorough study of Russia's history. "I know nobody who understood Russia as well and as thoroughly, inside-out, as he did," Engels wrote. Marx's deep knowledge of the internal processes in Russia led him to the following conclusion:

"THIS TIME THE REVOLUTION BEGINS IN THE EAST, HITHERTO THE UNTOUCHED CITADEL AND RESERVE ARMY OF COUNTER-REVOLUTION."

14. *The list of contents attached to Marx's notebook with entries for 1881. Written by Engels after Marx's death*

15. *Marx's notebook, with an entry made in 1881: "Russian on My Bookshelf"*

16. *"Off to town and apprenticeship in a factory"*

Studying political economy, Marx also kept abreast of the latest developments in natural science. Looking into the ground rent, for example, he also read up on agro-chemistry, chemistry, biology, geology, and so on. Often, he turned to Carl Schorlemmer, one of his close friends, for advice and explanations.

Some of Marx's economic studies called for complicated calculations. That was why he devoted much time to mathematics. He also studied the history of mathematics, commercial arithmetic, and algebra. All this back in the 1850s. And in 1878 to 1882 he compiled extensive material on the history of differential calculus, having preliminarily studied Descartes, Leibniz, Newton, Euler, Maclaurin, and others.

After his death, Engels intended to publish Marx's mathematical writings under separate cover. He considered them highly original. Marx's *Mathematical Manuscripts*, however, were not published until 1968 in the Soviet Union.

17. *"On the Concept of the Derived Function"—a page from Marx's notebook, "Algebra I"*

18. *Zénobe Théophile Gramme's industrial dynamo*

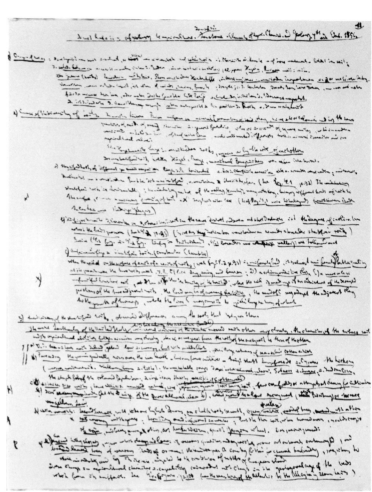

19. *Marx's exercises in chemistry*
   A page from an exercise-book

20. *The opening page of Marx's exercise-book for 1878 with a summary of Jones's Geology and Johnston's*

Catechism of Agricultural Chemistry and Geology

21. *Carl Schorlemmer (1834-1892), German scientist, specialised in organic chemistry; dialectical materialist,*

member of the German Social-Democratic Party, a friend of Marx's and Engels's

22. *Marx's exercises in geology. A drawing*

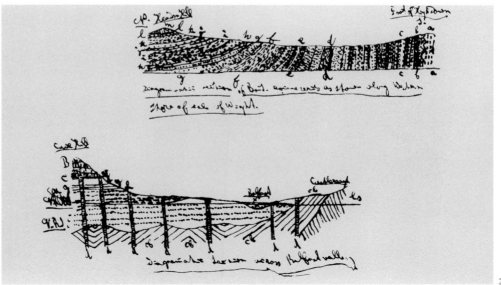

ANCIENT SOCIETY

OR

RESEARCHES IN THE LINES OF HUMAN PROGRESS
FROM SAVAGERY, THROUGH BARBARISM
TO CIVILIZATION

BY

LEWIS H. MORGAN, LL.D

Member of the National Academy of Science. Author of "The League of the Iroquois,"
"The American Beaver and his Works," "Systems of Consanguinity and
Affinity of the Human Family." Etc.

Nescit vox missa reverti.
HORACE.

London
MACMILLAN AND CO
1877

23

25

Studying agrarian relations and ground rent, Marx delved into the origin and development of landownership. In the 1870s he examined communal landownership in Asia, Europe, Africa, and America.

His studies helped him determine the specificities of the primitive communal system. He followed, too, the discoveries of the 1870s in archaeology, ethnography, anthropology, and paleontology.

Lewis Henry Morgan's book, *Ancient Society*, which Marx and Engels praised highly, appeared in 1877.

23. Lewis Henry Morgan, Ancient Society, *London, 1877*
The title page

24. Marx's précis of Lewis Henry Morgan's Ancient Society
A fragment of the manuscript

25. Lewis Henry Morgan (1818-1881), American historian and ethnographer, student of primitive society

The critical remarks concerning Morgan in Marx's précis were later used by Engels in his *Origin of the Family, Private Property and the State* (1884).

Paul Lafargue wrote of Marx's wide-ranging interest and the depth of his knowledge:

"YOU COULD QUESTION HIM AT ANY TIME ON ANY SUBJECT AND GET THE MOST DETAILED ANSWER YOU COULD WISH FOR... HIS BRAIN WAS LIKE A MAN-OF-WAR IN PORT UNDER STEAM, READY TO LAUNCH INTO ANY SPHERE OF THOUGHT."

L'INDIFFERENZA

in materia politica

« La classe operaja non deve costituirsi in partito politico; essa non deve, sotto alcun pretesto, avere azione politica, poichè combattere lo Stato è riconoscere lo Stato: ciò che è contrario ai principii eterni. Gli operai non devono fare degli scioperi; poichè fare degli sforzi per farsi crescere il salario o per impedirne l'abbassamento, è come riconoscere il *Salario*: ciò che è contrario ai principii eterni dell'emancipazione della classe operaja!

« Se nella lotta politica contro lo Stato borghese, gli operai non giungono che a strappare delle concessioni, essi fanno dei compromessi: ciò che è contrario ai principii eterni. Si deve quindi disprezzare ogni movimento pacifico, come gli operai inglesi ed americani hanno la cattiva abitudine di fare. Gli operai non devono fare sforzi per stabilire un limite legale della giornata di lavoro, perchè gli è come fare dei compromessi coi pa-

27
28

Though his scholarly research took up much of his time, Marx never failed his other duties—those of directing the working-class movement.

By the end of the 1870s revolutionary workers' parties were founded in a fairly large number of countries: in 1874 in Austria, two years later in Denmark, in 1879 in Belgium and Spain, and in Poland and Italy in 1882. All of them requested and expected assistance from Marx and Engels.

Assisting them, Marx and Engels did their best to consider the distinctive features and specificity of the country concerned, and the difficulties and obstacles facing the working-class movement there.

In countries with an as yet underdeveloped capitalism, such as Spain, Switzerland, and Italy, anarchist elements obstructed the founding and activity of mass proletarian parties.

Marx mounted an attack on anarchism in the Italian socialist press. At the request of Italian Socialist Enrico Bignami, Marx wrote an article, "Political Indifferentism", which appeared in the journal, *Almanacco Repubblicano per l'anno 1874*. Here Marx demonstrated the true implications of the anarchist postulate of abstaining from politics. The anarchists, Marx wrote, may pretend to be revolutionary, but in fact they doomed the working class to inaction and demoralisation. The anarchist call of abstaining from political action and class struggle, from setting up proletarian parties, was tantamount to perpetuating capitalism.

26. *Karl Marx, Summary of Mikhail Bakunin's* Statehood and Anarchy
A page from the summary

Marx took Bakunin to task, and set forth a number of important ideas concerning revolutionary theory: on the subjective factor, on the essence of the dictatorship of the proletariat, the relationship between the proletariat and the peasantry, and so on.

27. *Karl Marx, "Political Indifferentism"*
A page from the Almanacco Repubblicano per l'anno 1874

28. *Enrico Bignami (1846-1921)*

29

After the crushing defeat of the Paris Commune, the centre of the working-class movement shifted to Germany. The country's unification and the elimination of feudal fragmentation spurred swift industrial development. The number of the proletariat increased, and favourable conditions appeared for the development of the labour movement.

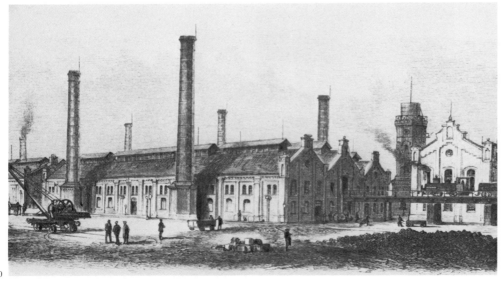

30

29. *An iron-and-steel works at Saar-brücken, 1876*

30. *A new gas factory in Cologne, 187*

31

When following the defeat of the Paris Commune, the government loosened reprisals against the German Social-Democrats, Marx countered by reissuing his pamphlet, *Revelations Concerning the Communist Trial in Cologne*. In an Epilogue, he demonstrated the fallacy and impotence of Bismarck's attempts "to drive the workers' party out of existence".

31. *Trial of the German Social-Democrats in Leipzig, 1872*

32. *Karl Marx*, Revelations Concerning the Communist Trial in Cologne
Der Volksstaat, *October 28, 1874*

32

33

33. The Gotha Congress

34-35. The house in Gotha and the premises where the unity congress (May 22-27, 1875) established the single Socialist Workers' Party of Germany

From 1869 on, two socialist parties were active in Germany—the Social-Democratic Workers' Party founded in 1869 at the congress in Eisenach, and the Lassallean General Association of German Workers founded in 1863. Marx maintained close contacts with the leaders of the Eisenach party, which followed some basic Marxist principles, though it did make concessions to Lassalleanism.

The existence of two proletarian political organisations tended to dissipate workers' activity in Germany, and, after long-drawn-out negotiations between the leaders of the two parties it was decided to hold a unity congress in Gotha in 1875.

34

The draft of the unity programme published in the party press on March 7, 1875, disappointed Marx and Engels. It contained a succession of erroneous approaches. To show his comrades in Germany the faults of their draft, Marx wrote marginal notes on the programme of the German Workers' Party. Subsequently, they were published under the title, *Critique of the Gotha Programme*, and sent by Marx to the leaders of the Eisenach party care of Wilhelm Bracke on May 5, 1875.

The *Critique of the Gotha Programme* contains important Marxist ideas concerning the period of the revolutionary conversion of capitalist into socialist society, on the dictatorship of the proletariat as the State of that period, on the two phases of communist society, production and distribution in the first phase of communism, and the basic features of the higher phase.

36. Marx's letter to Wilhelm Bracke, May 5, 1875

Pages of the manuscript

37. Wilhelm Bracke (1842-1880), organiser of the German Social-Democratic Workers' Party (Eisenachers)

Time and again Marx voiced his fears that the Gotha Programme, which contained considerable concessions to the Lassalleans, would fling open the party's doors to all sorts of opportunists. This came true within the next year, as the petty-bourgeois socialist ideas of Eugen Dühring, an assistant professor at Berlin University, gained currency in the Socialist Workers' Party of Germany. Marx urged Engels to take public issue with that gentleman. That was how Engels's *Herr Eugen Dühring's Revolution in Science*, more commonly known as *Anti-Dühring*, came into being. Marx took part in writing the book. He produced the chapter criticising Dühring's views on the history of political economy.

Engels did not confine himself to refuting Dühring's unscientific outlook. He produced an integral exposition of the three components of Marxist theory: dialectical and historical materialism, political economy, and the doctrine on socialism and communism. The book contributed to the spread of Marxist ideas and to the ideological advancement of the German Social-Democrats.

38. *Marx and Engels at work, 1870s*

39. *Frederick Engels*, Herr Eugen Dühring's Revolution in Philosophy

The book was first published in the form of articles, appearing in *Vorwärts*, the central organ of the German Social-Democrats, as from January 1877.

40. *Karl Marx*, Remarks on Dühring's book, "A Critical History of Political Economy"

A page of the manuscript

41

43

45

46

Marx and Engels helped the German Socialists to find the right forms of struggle and to get around the Anti-Socialist Law that operated in the country from 1878 to 1890. Right-wing opportunism had grown into the chief menace at that time. In a letter to Bebel, Liebknecht, Bracke, and others, Marx and Engels warned that concessions to opportunism, and any conciliatory approach, would jeopardise the revolutionary proletarian character of the party.

41. Deputies August Bebel and Friedrich Wilhelm Fritzsche during the debate of the Anti-Socialist Law in the Reichstag in October 1878

42. Karl Marx and Frederick Engels, Circular Letter to August Bebel, Wilhelm Liebknecht, Wilhelm Bracke, and others, September 17-19, 1879
A page of the manuscript

43. A cartoon ridiculing the Anti-Socialist Law

Marx and Engels sought to assist the French Socialists in founding and consolidating an independent revolutionary party of the French working class. At the request of Jules Guesde and Paul Lafargue, Marx took part in drafting a programme, which was eventually adopted at the party's congress in Le Havre in 1880. This was a big success for Marxism in France.

44. Karl Marx, Preamble to the Programme of the French Workers' Party L'Égalité, *June 30, 1880*

"IT WAS AN ENERGETIC STEP TOWARDS PULLING THE FRENCH WORKERS DOWN TO EARTH FROM THEIR FOG OF PHRASEOLOGY."

KARL MARX

45. Paul Lafargue (1842-1911)

46. Jules Guesde (1845-1922)

47

48

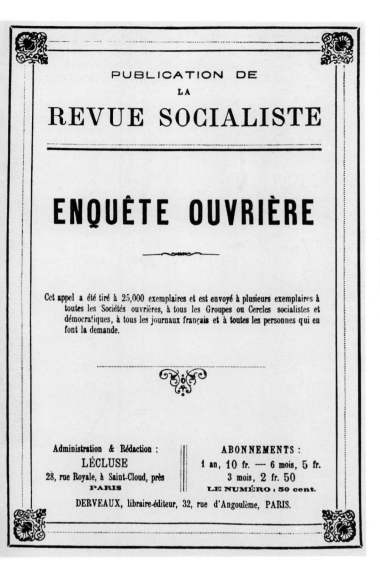

47. *Building workers' strike in Paris*

48. *Machinery on display at the World Exhibition in Paris in 1878*

49. *Karl Marx,* Workers' Questionnaire, *Paris, 1880*

At Paul Lafargue's request, Engels revised three chapters of *Anti-Dühring* for publication under separate cover, entitled *Socialism: Utopian and Scientific.* Marx wrote a special introduction to the French edition, with a biographical sketch of Frederick Engels, describing him as one of "the foremost representatives of contemporary socialism".

In April 1880, Marx composed a 100-question *Workers' Questionnaire* for *La Revue socialiste.* It helped pinpoint all the forms and methods of exploiting the working class, and was of great help to the proletarian party in directing the labour movement.

50. *Karl Marx, "Introduction to the French Edition of Frederick Engels's booklet* Socialism: Utopian and Scientific", *1881*

A page of the manuscript

In the last few years of his life, Marx followed the swift growth of capitalism in the United States. He saw the difficulties that hampered the development of the labour movement in the USA, where the bourgeoisie was cunningly creating what he called a "workers' aristocracy". The continuous influx of emigrants from Europe was a big reason why the US working class was of a gaudily heterogeneous nature.

In 1876, a Workingmen's Party of America was founded under the influence of the IWA, with some of the leaders, like Friedrich Sorge, Otto Weydemeyer (Joseph Weydemeyer's son), and Patrick MacDonnel, being well known to Marx. They maintained continuous contact with Marx and Engels.

51. The World Exhibition in Philadelphia, 1876

52. Approach tracks and granary in the New York port, 1877

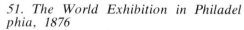

53. The New York police disperses a demonstration of émigré Communards

In 1877, labour-capital clashes proliferated in the United States. On July 25, 1877, Marx wrote to Engels:

"WHAT DO YOU THINK OF THE WORKERS IN THE UNITED STATES? THIS FIRST ERUPTION AGAINST THE OLIGARCHY OF ASSOCIATED CAPITAL WHICH HAS ARISEN SINCE THE CIVIL WAR WILL OF COURSE BE PUT DOWN, BUT IT COULD QUITE WELL FORM THE STARTING POINT FOR THE ESTABLISHMENT OF A SERIOUS LABOUR PARTY IN THE UNITED STATES."

54

55

54. *Railroad workers' strike in the USA, 1877*

55. *Karl Marx and Frederick Engels,* Manifesto of the Communist Party *Published in Chicago in German in 1883 by the Federation of the North American States*

The cover

56

In the last ten years of his life, Marx devoted much of his time to studying the revolutionary movement in Russia, and Russia's economic and political condition, history and culture. The letters Marx and Engels wrote to Russian revolutionaries are filled with deep hatred for tsarism and with hope for the success of the revolutionary movement.

56. The foundry at an iron-and-steel works in the Urals

57. A revolutionary being arrested by tsarist gendarmes

58. A demonstration outside the Kazan Cathedral in St. Petersburg on December 18, 1876

59. Georgi Valentinovich Plekhanov (1856-1918), an outstanding leader of the Russian and international social-democratic movement, the first propagandist of Marxism in Russia

60. Karl Marx and Frederick Engels, Manifesto of the Communist Party, translated into Russian by Plekhanov, with a special preface by the authors, Geneva, 1882

The cover

The preface to the Russian edition of the *Manifesto of the Communist Party* spoke of the bright outlook for revolutionary struggle in Russia and stressed the need for deposing the tsarist tyranny. It noted that revolution in Russia was inescapable. "Russia," the authors of the *Manifesto* said, "forms the vanguard of revolutionary action in Europe."

57

58

59

MANIFESTE DU PARTI COMMUNISTE
par Karl MARX et Fr. ENGELS

РУССКАЯ СОЦІАЛЬНО-РЕВОЛЮЦІОННАЯ БИБЛІОТЕКА
Книга Третья

МАНИФЕСТЪ

КОММУНИСТИЧЕСКОЙ ПАРТІИ

Карла Маркса и Фр. Энгельса

ПЕРЕВОДЪ СЪ НѢМЕЦКАГО ИЗДАНІЯ 1872.

СЪ ПРЕДИСЛОВІЕМЪ АВТОРОВЪ

Prix 1 Fr.

ЖЕНЕВА
Вольная Русская Типографія.

1882

61

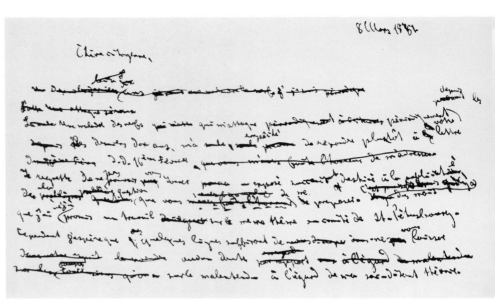

63
64

Seeing that a polemic had broken out among the Narodniks over the Russian peasant commune and the development of capitalism in Russia, Vera Zasulich requested Marx to elucidate the matter. In a letter to Zasulich of March 8, 1881, Marx warned against the Narodniks' infatuation with the peasant commune.

61. Vera Ivanovna Zasulich (1849-1919), prominent figure in the Narodnik and then social-democratic movement in Russia. In the 1880s and 90s she translated into Russian The Poverty of Philosophy *by Marx and* Socialism: Utopian and Scientific *by Engels*

62. Karl Marx, Draft of the letter to Vera Zasulich, March 8, 1881
                                    A fragment

65

Marx showed a deep interest in Maxim Kovalevsky's scholarly study, *Communal Landownership, and the Causes, Course and Consequences of Its Disintegration*, which he was given as a gift by its author, a Russian scholar.

63. Maxim Kovalevsky, Communal Landownership, and the Causes, Course and Consequences of Its Disintegration, *Moscow, 1879*

64. Maxim Maximovich Kovalevsky (1851-1916), historian, lawyer and sociologist

65. Engineering works in Kolomna, Russia

66

66. *Russian books in Karl Marx's library*

67. *Marx's letter to the Editorial Board of* Otechestvenniye Zapiski, *November 1877*

A page of the manuscript

In that letter, Marx wrote:

"IF RUSSIA WANTS TO BECOME A CAPITALIST NATION ... SHE WILL NOT SUCCEED WITHOUT HAVING FIRST TRANSFORMED A GOOD PART OF HER PEASANTS INTO PROLETARIANS..."

Members of the labour movement in all countries had boundless trust and deep respect for Marx.

"HIS POWER OF 'DRAWING OUT PEOPLE', OF MAKING THEM FEEL THAT HE WAS INTERESTED IN WHAT INTERESTED THEM WAS MARVELLOUS. I HAVE HEARD MEN OF THE MOST DIVERSE CALLINGS AND POSITIONS SPEAK OF HIS PECULIAR CAPACITY FOR UNDERSTANDING THEM AND THEIR AFFAIRS," Eleanor, Marx's youngest daughter recollected. "WHEN HE THOUGHT ANYONE REALLY IN EARNEST HIS PATIENCE WAS UNLIMITED. NO QUESTION WAS TOO TRIVIAL FOR HIM TO ANSWER, NO ARGUMENT TOO CHILDISH FOR SERIOUS DISCUSSION. HIS TIME AND HIS VAST LEARNING WERE ALWAYS AT THE SERVICE OF ANY MAN OR WOMAN WHO SEEMED ANXIOUS TO LEARN."

69

68. Karl Marx, London, August 1875

69. Jenny Marx, Marx's wife, the end of the 1870s

70. The house in London at 41 Maitland Park Road, where the Marxes lived from March 1875 to March 1883

The twenty years of émigré life in London saw many changes in the Marx family. By 1879, the elder daughters Jenny and Laura had grown up, and the youngest, Eleanor, was eighteen.

All three were exceedingly able, with highly fertile minds. All their lives they had compassion for the disinherited, and were always eager to help them in the fight for liberation. Marx's eldest daughter Jenny studied the history of the labour movement, and natural sciences. Laura was a gifted translator, and had translated many of her father's works into French, including the *Manifesto of the Communist Party*. In 1868, she married French Socialist Paul Lafargue, and was his faithful companion, helper and comrade in his revolutionary endeavours. In October 1872, Jenny left her father's home: she married Charles Longuet, a prominent personality in the IWA.

71. Laura, Marx's daughter, the mid-1880s

72. Paul Lafargue, Laura Marx's husband

73. Charles-Étienne Lafargue (1868-1872), Marx's grandson, son of Paul and Laura Lafargue

75

74. *Jenny Marx and her husband Charles Longuet*

75. *Eleanor Marx*

76. *Jean-Loran-Frederick (Jonney) Longuet (1876-1938), Marx's grandson, son of Jenny and Charles Longuet*

After Jenny, Marx's eldest daughter, married, Eleanor succeeded to her duties as her father's secretary. Like the elder sisters, she was happy to be of help to him: she copied manuscripts, and acted as his special ambassador. Like her sisters, she was on friendly terms with many leaders of the Paris Commune and the International.

77

Marx's powerful constitution had enabled him to bear superhuman physical and mental strains for several dozen years. But his hair turned gray at 40, and at 50 he looked far older. This was the effect of the hardships of émigré life, which had claimed the lives of four of his children.

In 1873, Marx's health deteriorated. On the insistence of his wife and Frederick Engels, he went for a rest cure to Karlsbad (Karlovy Vary).

Jenny, Marx's wife, died on December 2, 1881. This was a mortal blow for Marx. He had lost wife, friend, companion, and helper. Engels spoke with deep affection of this fine woman at her graveside: "What such a woman, with such a clear and critical intellect, with such political tact, with such passionate energy of character, with such capacity for self-sacrifice, has done in the revolutionary movement, that has not been pushed forward into publicity, that is not registered in the columns of the periodical press. That is only known to those who lived near her."

The doctors advised Marx to go to Algeria for a rest in February 1882, but he was forced to return soon owing to inclement weather. On the way home, he visited his daughter Jenny in Paris, and also saw Laura.

After his return to London, his health deteriorated again. On January 11, 1883, he suffered one more bereavement: his eldest daughter Jenny died after a short illness.

The efforts of his doctors and the devoted care lavished upon him by Helene Demuth, a loyal friend of the family, sustained the hope that Marx would recover. But that was not to be. He died on March 14, 1883.

77. Karlsbad (Karlovy Vary)
78. Germania Hotel in Karlsbad (Karlovy Vary) where Karl Marx stayed in 1874, 1875 and 1876
Eleanor twice accompanied him on these trips

79. Eleanor Marx

80. Karl Marx, Algiers, 1882. The last photograph

81. Engels's cable to Adolf Sorge, informing him of Marx's death

"MANKIND IS SHORTER BY A HEAD," Engels wrote, "AND THAT THE GREATEST HEAD OF OUR TIME. THE MOVEMENT OF THE PROLETARIAT GOES ON, BUT GONE IS THE CENTRAL POINT TO WHICH FRENCHMEN, RUSSIANS, AMERICANS, AND GERMANS SPONTANEOUSLY TURNED AT DECISIVE MOMENTS TO RECEIVE ALWAYS THAT CLEAR INDISPUTABLE COUNSEL WHICH ONLY GENIUS AND CONSUMMATE KNOWLEDGE OF THE SITUATION COULD GIVE... THE FINAL VICTORY REMAINS CERTAIN, BUT THE DETOURS, THE TEMPORARY AND LOCAL MISTAKES—WHICH ARE UNAVOIDABLE IN ANY CASE—WILL NOW OCCUR MUCH MORE OFTEN. WELL, WE MUST SEE IT THROUGH; WHAT ELSE ARE WE HERE FOR?"

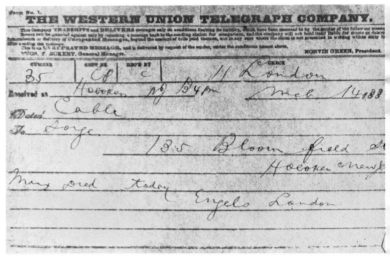

82. The Karl Marx memorial in Highgate Cemetery, London, by sculptor Lawrence Bradshow

The memorial was put up in 1956 on funds collected among workers of different countries.

After Marx's death, Engels carried on, elaborating upon the theories of scientific communism. He was adviser and leader of socialists in different countries.

Engels survived Marx by twelve years. During this time, he prepared for the printer the second and third volumes of *Capital*, which proved a gigantic undertaking. He also continued work on Marxist theory, and defended Marxist ideas against distortion by bourgeois ideologists and opportunists. His books of 1884 and 1886, *The Origin of the Family, Private Property and the State* and *Ludwig Feuerbach and the End of Classical German Philosophy*, have come down to us as brilliant contributions to Marxism's literary legacy.

While devoting much time to research and science, Engels had all those years also directed the international working-class and socialist movement.

"After his friend Karl Marx," Lenin wrote, "Engels was the finest scholar and teacher of the modern proletariat in the whole civilised world... Engels continued alone as the counsellor and leader of the European socialists... They all drew on the rich store of knowledge and experience of Engels in his old age."

The train of events after Marx and Engels has confirmed the correctness of their scientific theory and the great cause to which they had dedicated all their lives.

82

*83. Frederick Engels,
London, 1891*

THE BEGINNING
OF A NEW REVOLUTIONARY ERA

The great leader of the new generation of revolutionaries and of the world proletariat, and a brilliant successor to Marx and Engels, was Vladimir Lenin. Careful study of the works of Marx and Engels was for Lenin a rule he never failed to follow.

In the new historical environment, in the era of imperialism, when ever more intricate and complex tasks faced those who headed the proletarian struggle, Lenin safeguarded Marxism from distortion by opportunists and revisionists. In Lenin's works all aspects of the Marxist doctrine have been taken a step further.

In these and other works, Lenin took the Marxist science—philosophy, economic doctrine, and scientific socialism—a substantial step further. Having delved into the laws of capitalism in its monopoly stage, and drawing the profound conclusion that the revolution can initially win in one separate country, Lenin directed the Bolshevik Party and the working people during the victorious revolutionary overthrow of the autocracy in Russia. He created an integral doctrine on the party, and revealed its enormous powers as guide and organiser in building communist society. He shored up the party with his theory of the socialist state. And in doing all this, tilting the scales in favour of the Russian and international revolutionary movement, Lenin always acted on the theory of Marx and Engels.

84. *Vladimir Ilyich Lenin, 1897*

85. *Lenin's summary, "The Marx-Engels Correspondence", 1913*
A page of the manuscript

86. *V. I. Lenin*, Materialism and Empirio-Criticism, *Moscow, 1909*
The cover

87. *V. I. Lenin*, Imperialism, the Highest Stage of Capitalism, *Petrograd, 1917*
The cover

88. *V. I. Lenin*, The State and Revolution, *Petrograd, 1918*
The title page

89

89. *Storming the Winter Palace,
Petrograd, October 1917*

The Great October Socialist Revolution was an event of worldwide historic significance. It ushered in a new stage in the international working-class movement.

The ideas of Marxism-Leninism have become a guide in building communist society.

90. V. I. Lenin, 1918

91. Jubilee medal of Karl Marx issued in Petrograd in 1918

92. Lenin speaks at the unveiling of a monument to Marx and Engels in Moscow on November 7, 1918

93. Monument to Karl Marx in Moscow unveiled in 1962; by sculptor Lev Kerbel

The Life and Work of Karl Marx. Outstanding Dates

May 5, 1818	A son Karl is born to barrister Heinrich Marx and his wife, Henriette, in Trier
November 28, 1820	A son Frederick is born to textile manufacturer Friedrich Engels and his wife, Elisabeth, in Barmen
July 27-29, 1830	Revolution in France
September	Revolution in Belgium
1830-31	Uprisings in Poland
October 1830	Karl Marx is enrolled at the Trier Gymnasium
1831, 1834	Uprisings of Lyons weavers in France
May 27, 1832	The Hambach festivities, a mass political demonstration in the Palatinate demanding the unification of Germany and political freedoms
Late 1830s	Chartism, the first mass revolutionary workers' movement, emerges in England
August-September 24, 1835	Marx graduates from the Trier Gymnasium and receives his school-leaving certificate
October	Marx enrolls at Bonn University as a law student
Summer 1836	Marx is engaged to Jenny von Westphalen in Trier
Mid-October	Marx moves to Berlin. On October 22, he enrolls at Berlin University as a law student and soon becomes a member of the Young Hegelian Doctors' Club
Spring 1837	When on vacation in Stralow, a suburb of Berlin, Marx begins a serious study of Hegel's philosophy
May 10, 1838	Marx's father dies
1839-41	Marx studies the history of philosophy, mainly in Antiquity. *Difference Between the Democritean and Epicurean Philosophy of Nature* is the subject of his doctoral dissertation
March 30-early April 1841	Marx graduates from Berlin University and submits his dissertation to the University of Jena
April 15	The University of Jena confers on him the degree of Doctor of Philosophy
January-February 1842	Marx writes "Comments on the Latest Prussian Censorship Instruction", a critique of the Prussian feudal-absolutist system. That was Marx's first piece of journalism
May 1842	Marx begins to contribute to the *Rheinische Zeitung* founded in Cologne by the liberal bourgeoisie of the Rhine Province. His articles stress the need to protect the rights of the toiling masses
October 15, 1842-March 18, 1843	Marx becomes editor-in-chief of the *Rheinische Zeitung*. Under his direction the paper's line becomes increasingly more revolutionary and democratic. Marx's articles denoted a shift from idealism to materialism, and from revolutionary democracy to communist ideas
Latter half of November 1842	Marx first meets Engels, who visits the *Rheinische Zeitung* offices in Cologne on his way to England
January 19, 1843	The Prussian Government decides to ban the *Rheinische Zeitung* as of April 1, and introduces an especially stringent censorship for it in the interim
March 18	Police reprisals launched by Prussian authorities made further publication of the paper impossible. Marx is forced to resign
May-October	Marx stays at Kreuznach, a small resort town, where Jenny von Westphalen and her mother were staying at the time. There, Marx begins a critical revision of Hegel's doctrine of the state and law. The outcome of this work is an unfinished manuscript, published for the first time in 1927 in the Soviet Union under the title, *Contribution to the Critique of Hegel's Philosophy of Law.* Simultaneously, Marx studies world history, concentrating on analysis of socio-economic and socio-political processes. Seeing that political activity in Germany is impossible, Marx decides to move to France. He negotiates the publication in Paris of a magazine, *Deutsch-Französische Jahrbücher*
June 19, 1843	Marx marries Jenny von Westphalen
Late October	Marx and his bride move to Paris, where he takes up the history of the

French Revolution, studies the works of utopian socialists and English and French economists. In Paris, Marx attends workers' meetings, gets in touch with the leaders of the secret League of the Just, and meets members of clandestine French workers' societies

Late December	Marx meets Heinrich Heine
Late February 1844	The first and last, and double, issue of the *Deutsch-Französische Jahrbücher* comes out in Paris. Marx's articles in it show his final acceptance of materialism and communism
April-August	Marx works on economic and philosophic manuscripts, in which he criticises bourgeois political economy for the first time
May 1, 1844	A daughter, Jenny, is born to Karl and Jenny Marx
June 4-6	The uprising of the Silesian weavers
August 7 and 10	*Vorwärts!*, a German-language newspaper in Paris, publishes Marx's article, "Critical Marginal Notes on the Article 'The King of Prussia and Social Reform. By a Prussian'". It underscores the tremendous significance of the Silesian uprising as an intimation of the power of the working class
August 28	Marx and Engels meet in Paris; this is the beginning of a lifelong friendship and joint work. They embark on their first joint venture, *The Holy Family, or Critique of Critical Criticism. Against Bruno Bauer and Company*
Early September	After staying with Marx for ten days, Engels returns to Barmen, Germany, where he becomes involved in socialist propaganda, speaking at workers' meetings. He also works on the book, *The Condition of the Working-Class in England*
January 16, 1845	Under pressure of the Prussian government, Marx is ordered to leave France
Early February	Marx moves to Brussels, where his family joins him in mid-February
Late February	Marx's and Engels's book, *The Holy Family, or Critique of Critical Criticism. Against Bruno Bauer and Company*, appears in Frankfort on the Main. It expounds the foundations of the revolutionary materialist outlook
Spring, c. April	Marx writes *Theses on Feuerbach*, which Engels describes as "the first document in which is deposited the brilliant germ of the new world outlook"
Early April	Engels moves from Barmen to join Marx in Brussels
April-December	Marx and Engels establish contacts with Belgian democrats and socialists
Late May	Engels's *The Condition of the Working-Class in England*, which, as Lenin put it, "was a terrible indictment of capitalism and the bourgeoisie", is published in Leipzig
July 12-August 21	Marx and Engels visit England to study the latest English books on economics and also to gain insight into England's economic and political life and the English working-class movement. In London, Marx and Engels get in touch with Chartist leaders and heads of the London communities of the League of the Just
September 26	Marx's daughter Laura is born
September 1845-summer 1846	Marx and Engels work on *The German Ideology*, developing the principles of historical materialism and criticising Ludwig Feuerbach, Bruno Bauer and Max Stirner, as well as the theory of the "true socialists". The book's publication in Germany was made impossible due to the terms of the censorship. The book first appeared in the Soviet Union in 1932
December 1, 1845	Marx renounces his Prussian citizenship due to mounting persecution by the Prussian police
Early 1846	Marx and Engels set up the Communist Correspondence Committee in Brussels with a view to ideologically and organisationally uniting the socialists and the more politically aware workers of different countries, and paving the way for the establishment of an international proletarian organisation
May 5	The Brussels Communist Correspondence Committee adopts the "Circular against Kriege", criticising the sentimental preaching of the "true socialists"
Early 1847	Marx's son Edgar is born
Late January 1847	The London Committee of the League of the Just sends its representative, Joseph Moll, to Marx and Engels with a proposal that they join the League, take part in its reorganisation and draw up a new programme. Marx and Engels accept the proposal

January-June 15	Marx is working on *The Poverty of Philosophy. Answer to the "Philosophy of Poverty" by M. Proudhon*	February 22-24	Revolution in France
		Late February	Marx's and Engels's *Manifesto of the Communist Party*, the first programme document of scientific communism, is published in London
June 2-9	A congress of the League of the Just, in which Engels takes part, is held in London. The League of the Just is renamed the Communist League. The congress lays the foundation for an entirely new organisation with new ideological principles and structure. Engels participates in drawing up the new Rules subject to approval by the next congress. The congress also adopts the new motto of the League suggested by Marx and Engels, "Working Men of All Countries, Unite!"	February 28	On behalf of the Brussels Democratic Association, Marx signs a greeting to the Provisional Government of the French Republic
		March 1	Ferdinand Flocon, a member of the Provisional Government of the French Republic, invites Marx to France
Early July	Marx's *Poverty of Philosophy* is published in French in Brussels. Lenin regarded it as one of the first works of mature Marxism	March 3	The King of Belgium orders Marx out of the country within 24 hours. The Brussels Central Authority of the Communist League announces its dissolution and transfers its seat to Paris. Marx is authorised to form a new Central Authority there
August 5	On Marx's suggestion a community and district organisation of the Communist League are set up in Brussels		
August-September	The *Westphälische Dampfboot* journal prints one of the chapters of *The German Ideology* containing criticism of "true socialism"	March 4	Marx and his wife are kept under arrest for 18 hours by the Brussels police. They and the children leave Brussels and head for France
Late August	On Marx's and Engels's initiative, a German Workers' Society is established in Brussels; it unites mostly German working-class refugees	March 5	Marx arrives in Paris where, on the instruction received from the Central Authority, he forms a new central body of the Communist League
September 1847-February 1848	Marx and Engels contribute to the *Deutsche-Brüsseler-Zeitung* which, up to its last issue published on February 27, 1848, was, to all intents and purposes, the organ of the Communist League	Early March	On Marx's suggestion, a German Workers' Club is set up in Paris. At its meetings, Marx opposes the adventurist "export of revolution" planned by the petty-bourgeois leaders of the German émigrés in Paris
September-November 1847	Marx helps set up the Brussels Democratic Association which unites proletarian revolutionaries and bourgeois and petty-bourgeois democrats	March 13	Revolutionary events flare up in Vienna
		March 15	Revolution begins in Hungary
November 15	Marx is elected Vice-President of the Brussels Democratic Association	March 18	Barricade fighting in Berlin
November 29-December 8	London is the venue of the Second Congress of the Communist League, with Marx and Engels taking part in it. The congress supports their stand, and instructs them to draft the programme of the League in the form of a manifesto. The congress approves the Rules of the Communist League	March 21	Engels arrives in Paris
		Late March	In view of the revolution in Germany, Marx and Engels draw up the Communist League's political platform in the revolution: the *Demands of the Communist Party in Germany*
		Early April	Marx and Engels go to Germany to take part in the revolution
Latter half of December	Marx delivers lectures on political economy at the German Workers' Society. They come to be known as *Wage Labour and Capital*	April 11	On arrival in Cologne, Marx and Engels endeavour to start a daily paper
Early January 1848	Revolutionary events begin to brew in Italy. Revolution in Palermo	May 31	The first issue of the *Neue Rheinische Zeitung* dated June 1 is published in Cologne, its subtitle being *Organ der Demokratie*. Marx is its editor-in-chief, and Engels an editor.

	Marx and Engels use the paper to campaign for a unified democratic German state and support the peasants' and workers' struggle and the national liberation movement in Bohemia, Italy, Poland, and other countries
June 23-26	Rising of the Paris proletariat
June 29	The *Neue Rheinische Zeitung* carries Marx's article "The June Revolution" on the heroic effort of Paris workers
August 23-September	Marx goes to Vienna and Berlin to establish contacts with democratic and workers' organisations, and to collect money for the publication of the *Neue Rheinische Zeitung*
August 30	Marx speaks at the first Vienna Workers' Association on social relations in Europe and the place of the proletariat in the revolutionary struggle
September 2	Marx speaks at the first Vienna Workers' Association on wage labour and capital
September 13	On the initiative of the *Neue Rheinische Zeitung,* a mass public meeting is held in Cologne to rebuff counter-revolution. It elects a Committee of Public Safety, including Marx, Engels and other editors of the *Neue Rheinische Zeitung.* The Committee is to be the organising centre for the revolutionary struggle
September 25	Due to the defeat of the Frankfurt uprising and the declaration of a state of siege in Cologne, publication of the *Neue Rheinische Zeitung* is suspended
October 3	Publication of the *Neue Rheinische Zeitung* is resumed
October 6-31	Uprising in Vienna ending in victory for the counter-revolution
November 7	The *Neue Rheinische Zeitung* prints Marx's article, "The Victory of the Counter-Revolution in Vienna"
November 8	Counter-revolutionary coup in Prussia
November 11	In view of the Prussian counter-revolutionary coup, the *Neue Rheinische Zeitung* campaigned for refusal to pay taxes to undermine the finances of the counter-revolution and rally the masses
December	Marx publishes a series of articles, *The Bourgeoisie and the Counter-Revolution,* analysing specific aspects and the main stages of the revolution in Germany
February 7 and 8, 1849	Trials of the *Neue Rheinische Zeitung,* and Marx as its editor-in-chief, on charges of insulting the authorities. At the trials, Marx and Engels defend their newspaper and freedom of the press in Germany. The jury brings in a verdict of not guilty
April 5-8 and 11	The *Neue Rheinische Zeitung* prints Marx's *Wage Labour and Capital*
Early May	Armed uprisings flare up in Dresden, the Palatinate, Baden and Rhenish Prussia in defence of the Imperial Constitution adopted by the National Assembly on March 28, 1849. The *Neue Rheinische Zeitung* takes the side of the insurgents and urges them to close their ranks
May 10-15	Engels takes part in the Elberfeld uprising
May 16	The Prussian authorities hand Marx a government order to leave Prussia. Legal proceedings are instituted against Engels for participating in the Elberfeld uprising
May 19	The last, "red" issue of the *Neue Rheinische Zeitung* is published. Marx and Engels go to South-Western Germany, where the revolutionary events are still in progress. Engels is involved in the Baden-Palatinate uprising
Early June	Marx comes to Paris, where a major revolutionary outburst is expected. However, democratic petty-bourgeois leaders fail to direct the struggle of the people, and an attempted uprising fails
August 23	Marx is ordered by the French authorities to leave Paris within 24 hours
August 26	After being deported from Paris, Marx arrives in London, where his family joins him on September 17. In London, he helps organise the work of the Communist League's Central Authority, and sets up a Committee of Support for German Political Refugees
Early September	Marx joins the London German Workers' Educational Society closely associated with the Communist League
November 5	A fourth child, son Heinrich Guido, is born to the Marxes
c. November 10	Engels arrives in London
November 1849-autumn 1850	Marx lectures on political economy and the *Manifesto of the Communist Party* at the Educational Society
March 1850	Marx and Engels draw up the "Address of the Central Authority to the League,

March 1850", one of the first documents summing up the experience of the proletariat in the past revolution and outlining the action programme of Communists for the future

March 6-November 29
Marx and Engels publish six issues of the magazine, *Neue Rheinische Zeitung. Politisch-ökonomische Revue*, which prints Marx's *The Class Struggles in France, 1848 to 1850* and Engels's *The German Campaign for the Imperial Constitution* and *The Peasant War in Germany*, as well as a number of international and other jointly written reviews

Spring
Marx resumes his study of political economy

Early June
Marx and Engels write the second "Address of the Central Authority to the League, June 1850", with tactical and organisational advice and instructions to local branches

November 19
Heinrich Guido Marx dies

November
On the proposal of the London District of the Communist League, the Cologne Central Authority expels the Willich-Schapper faction for disruptive activities.
Engels moves to Manchester and joins the Ermen & Engels firm. This enables him to offer regular financial assistance to the Marx family

March 28, 1851
Marx's daughter Franziska is born

June 1851-1862
Marx and Engels contribute to the Chartist papers *Notes to the People* and *The People's Paper*, and generally assist the Chartist movement

August 1851-March 1862
Marx and Engels contribute articles to the *New-York Daily Tribune* on national liberation movements, international affairs, and the economics and politics of leading capitalist states

December 1851-March 1852
Marx writes *The Eighteenth Brumaire of Louis Bonaparte*, developing on the theory of revolution. In May 1852, it was printed in New York by the journal *Die Revolution;* publisher Joseph Weydemeyer

April 14, 1852
Marx's daughter Franziska dies

May-June
Marx and Engels write a pamphlet, *The Great Men of the Exile*, exposing the ambitions of petty-bourgeois refugee leaders, their pursuit of popularity and adventurist plans of revolution in a situation that was not yet ripe

October 4-November 12
The Cologne trial of Communist League members

October-December
Marx and Engels expose the Prussian government's frame-up in letters, articles and statements to the press.
Between late October and December, Marx writes a pamphlet, *Revelations Concerning the Communist Trial in Cologne*, in which he offers documentary evidence of fabrications by the Prussian police and judiciary.
In January 1853 the pamphlet was published in Switzerland and in April in the United States

November 17
As reaction gains ground on the European continent and many active members of the Communist League are arrested, a meeting of the League's London District assents to Marx's proposal to dissolve its branches and recommends the branches on the continent to close down as well

October 22-December 24, 1853
The Chartist *People's Paper* prints a series of Marx's articles, *Lord Palmerston*, a satirical portrayal of that prominent English politician. Also published in the *New-York Daily Tribune* and, later, as a separate pamphlet

March 1854
Marx covers the Labour Parliament for the *New-York Daily Tribune*.
In an open letter to the Labour Parliament in *The People's Paper* of March 18, 1854, Marx calls for the establishment of a mass working-class political party in England

August-December
The *New-York Daily Tribune* runs Marx's series of articles, "Revolutionary Spain", with an in-depth examination of the train of events in the light of the revolutionary history of the Spanish people

January 16, 1855
Marx's daughter Eleanor is born

January-December
Marx contributes to the democratic *Neue Oder-Zeitung*, which prints his articles on the Crimean War and the economic and political situation in Britain and France

April 6
Marx's eight-year-old son Edgar dies

1857
Worldwide economic crisis.
Marx's articles on the progress of the crisis in Europe and the USA appear in the American, British, and German press

July 1857-March 1859
Marx sums up his economic studies. He hastens to complete his study of political economy, wanting the proletariat to have a knowledge of the

	objective economic laws governing the life of society	March 19-April 8, 1865	Marx stays with his Dutch relatives in Zalt-Bommel
July 1857-November 1860	Marx contributes to *The New American Cyclopaedia*	June 20 and 27	Marx lectures on wages, price and profit at General Council meetings, expounding the fundamental ideas of the future Volume I of *Capital*
June 11, 1859	*A Contribution to the Critique of Political Economy,* Part One, is published in Berlin	September 25-29	The first conference of the International is held in London. Marx helps to prepare it, and takes part in it
June-August	Marx and Engels examine the proletariat's revolutionary theory and tactics in the columns of *Das Volk*	January 1866-April 1867	Marx works on the final version of Volume I of *Capital* and prepares it for the printer
Late January 1860	Slanderous attacks on the proletarian party prompt Marx to start collecting material for a pamphlet, *Herr Vogt*	March 15-April 13, 1866	Marx has a holiday in Margate
December 1	*Herr Vogt* appears in London, exposing Vogt as a typical underling of the bourgeoisie	July	Marx draws up instructions for delegates to the Geneva Congress of the International, stressing the need for working men's international unity
April 1861-April 1865	The US Civil War	September 3-8	The Geneva Congress of the First International gathers to approve the programme documents submitted by the General Council
August 1861-July 1863	Marx works on an economic manuscript containing all parts of the future *Capital,* including its historical and critical section, *Theories of Surplus Value*		
October 1861-December 1862	Marx contributes to the Viennese liberal newspaper *Die Presse,* on the US Civil War, economic conditions in Britain, and the foreign policy of Napoleon III	April 10, 1867	Marx takes the manuscript of Volume I of *Capital* to publisher Otto Meissner in Hamburg
		April 17-May 15	Marx stays with Ludwig Kugelmann in Hanover
May 23, 1863	The General Association of German Workers is founded in Leipzig	September 2-8	The Lausanne Congress of the First International, at which a fight flares up with Proudhonists over the agrarian question (socialisation of land) and the question of struggle for political freedoms
August 1863-December 1865	Marx writes a new version of *Capital,* with a special interest in the problems dealt with in the future volumes II and III		
November 30, 1863	Marx's mother dies in Trier	September 14	Volume I of *Capital,* Marx's principal economic study, comes off the presses
May 9, 1864	Wilhelm Wolff, Marx's close friend and staunch supporter, dies in Manchester. Marx dedicates *Capital* to him	October 12, 1867-late June 1868	Engels writes reviews of *Capital* with an eye to popularising it
September 28	At a meeting in St. Martin's Hall, London, the International Working Men's Association (the First International) is founded. Marx is elected member of its Provisional Committee, which later became known as the General Council	Spring 1868	Marx goes back to economic manuscripts written before 1865. He works on them until his last day
		April 2	Marx's daughter Laura marries Paul Lafargue, a French socialist
Late October	Marx drafts the Provisional Rules and Inaugural Address of the IWA	September 6-13	The Brussels Congress of the First International, where the conflict with the Proudhonists comes to a head. Proudhon's theory is torn to pieces. The Congress passes a resolution confirming the advantages of collective, socialist ownership of the means of production and of land.
Late 1864-February 1865	Marx and Engels contribute to *Der Social-Demokrat,* popularising the International and its ideas in Germany		

	It also passes a resolution recommending working men in all countries to study Marx's *Capital*
August 7-9, 1869	The Inaugural Congress of the Social-Democratic Workers' Party of Germany is held in Eisenach
September 6-11	The Basle Congress of the First International is held. It confirms the socialist platform of the International
c. September 10-October 11	Marx and his daughter Jenny visit the Kugelmanns in Hanover
October 2	The first issue of *Der Volksstaat*, the central newspaper of the Social-Democratic Workers' Party of Germany, comes out in Leipzig; Marx and Engels become its contributors
November	On Marx's proposal, the General Council of the First International discusses the Irish people's national liberation movement
Late November	Volume II of *Capital* is devoted to landownership. Marx sets out on a close study of Russian economic writings, and starts learning Russian. Six months later, he reads official Russian publications and other literature on the country's agrarian relations and socio-political development
February-April 1870	In collaboration with her father, Jenny, Marx's eldest daughter, writes eight articles for *La Marseillaise*, a Paris newspaper, exposing British policies in Ireland
March 24	Responding to the request of the Russian section of the First International, Marx becomes corresponding secretary of the General Council for Russia
July 19	France declares war on Germany. The Franco-Prussian War begins
July 19-23	On the instructions of the General Council, Marx writes the "First Address of the General Council of the International Working Men's Association on the Franco-Prussian War", exposing its true character and urging German workers to prevent the war against Bonapartist France from becoming a war against the French people
July 29, 1870-February 18, 1871	On Marx's proposal, Engels writes a series of articles on the Franco-Prussian War for the British *Pall Mall Gazette*
September 1-2, 1870	The Battle of Sedan culminates in the defeat of the French army
September 4	Following the French defeat at Sedan, a revolution breaks out in Paris, resulting in the downfall of the Second Empire and proclaiming the French Republic
September 9	The General Council approves Marx's "Second Address of the General Council of the International Working Men's Association on the Franco-Prussian War", in which Marx calls on the proletariat to prevent the Prussian militarists from carrying out their expansionist plans
c. September 20	Engels moves from Manchester to London
October 4	Engels is unanimously elected to the General Council of the First International. He is made corresponding secretary for Belgium, Italy, Spain, Portugal and Denmark
March 18, 1871	Proletarian revolution in Paris
March 18-May 28, 1871	As the proletarian revolution wins in Paris and the Commune is established, Marx and Engels organise workers' demonstrations in its support. The General Council discusses the Commune, and sends representatives to Paris. Marx and Engels keep in touch with the Commune, give recommendations to the Communards, and launch a large-scale campaign in defence of the Commune
March 28	Festive proclamation of the Paris Commune
March 29	The Commune passes a decree on the abolition of levies and substitution of the armed people for a standing army
March 30	The Commune passes a decree on the transfer of administrative powers in Paris arrondissements to the Commune
April 2	The Commune passes a decree separating the Church from the State
April 16	A decree on the transfer of inoperative workshops to workers' production associations
April 18-May 30	Marx works on an address of the General Council, *The Civil War in France*, which stresses the worldwide significance of the Paris Commune as the first attempt at establishing a proletarian dictatorship
May 30	The General Council unanimously approves the address, *The Civil War in France*
September 17-23	The London Conference of the First International. Drawing on the lessons

	of the Paris Commune, Marx and Engels substantiate the need for political struggle by the working class and for independent proletarian parties in each country; these ideas are incorporated in a resolution of the Conference
March 5, 1872	The General Council approves a private circular, *Fictitious Splits in the International*, written by Marx and Engels, which exposes Bakuninist intrigues and disruptive activity in the International
March 27	Publication of the Russian translation of Volume I of *Capital*, its first foreign edition
May	*Fictitious Splits in the International* is published in Geneva as a pamphlet
July 1872-June 1873	The second German edition of Volume I of *Capital* appears in nine instalments
September 2-7, 1872	Marx and Engels take part in the Hague Congress of the First International, which confirms the principal resolutions of the London Conference and takes to task the anarchists for their divisive activity. It expels their leaders Bakunin and Guillaume from the International, and resolves to move the seat of the General Council to New York
September 17	The first series of five instalments of the French edition of Volume I of *Capital* is published
October 10	Marx's daughter Jenny marries French socialist Charles Longuet
Early June 1873	The second German edition of Volume I of *Capital* appears in Hamburg
December	The Italian annual, *Almanacco Repubblicano*, carries Marx's article "Political Indifferentism" and Engels's "On Authority", which show the harm of anarchist theories
August 19-early October 1874	Marx accompanied by his daughter Eleanor takes a cure in Karlsbad. On his way to London, he stops over at Dresden, Leipzig, Berlin and Hamburg and meets Liebknecht and Blos to discuss the situation in the Party and the need to combat Lassalleanism
May 5, 1875	Marx despatches to Germany his marginal notes on the draft programme drawn up for the forthcoming unity congress of Eisenachers and Lassalleans in Gotha. Subsequently, it came to be known as the *Critique of the Gotha Programme* which was first published in 1891 on Engels's initiative
May 22-27	The unity congress in Gotha. The foundation of the Socialist Workers' Party of Germany
August 15-September 11	Marx takes a cure in Karlsbad. Meets Maxim Kovalevsky, a Russian ethnographer, historian and lawyer
August 16-September 15, 1876	Marx is accompanied by Eleanor on a cure in Karlsbad
1877	Marx works on Chapter X of Part II of Engels's *Anti-Dühring*. *Herr Eugen Dühring's Revolution in Science* originally published in instalments by *Vorwärts*
August 8-c. September 27	Marx, accompanied by his wife and daughter Eleanor, takes a cure in Neuenahr (Germany) and Scotland
1878-1882	Marx studies mathematics, and continues his research into mathematical analysis begun in the 1860s
Late May-June 1878	Marx studies agrochemistry and geology
October 19	The German Reichstag passes a law against "the harmful and dangerous aspirations" of social-democrats (the Anti-Socialist Law)
January-December 1879	Marx continues his political and economic research, drawing on Russian and American sources
Mid-September	Marx and Engels write a "Circular Letter" to August Bebel, Wilhelm Liebknecht, Wilhelm Bracke and other German social-democratic leaders, criticising opportunism
September 28, 1879	The first issue of *Der Sozialdemokrat*, central organ of the German social-democrats who continue their struggle underground, is published in Zurich. Marx and Engels contribute to it
c. October 1879-October 1880	Making a special study of the ground rent and agrarian relations, Marx reads up on the village commune (Maxim Kovalevsky's *Communal Landownership, and the Causes, Course and Consequences of Its Disintegration*)
January-December 1880	Marx works on volumes II and III of *Capital*
April	Marx draws up a *Workers' Questionnaire* for the monthly *La Revue socialiste*, elucidating the economic demands of the working class
May	Marx writes Engels's biography as a preface to a separate edition of three

chapters of *Anti-Dühring* prepared by Engels for French readers under the title, *Socialism: Utopian and Scientific*

January-June 1881 Marx studies material, monographs and other writings on Russia's social and economic development after the peasant reform of 1861

July 26- August 16 Marx and his wife visit their daughter Jenny in Argenteuil near Paris

December 2 Marx's wife Jenny dies in London after a long illness

January 21, 1882 Marx and Engels write a preface to the Russian edition of the *Manifesto of the Communist Party*, stating that "Russia forms the vanguard of revolutionary action in Europe"

February-October With his health deteriorating, Marx goes to Algeria, the south of France and Switzerland for a rest and cure, and visits his daughter Jenny in Argenteuil

June 1882- January 1883 Marx studies organic and inorganic chemistry

January 11, 1883 Marx's eldest daughter Jenny dies in Paris

March 14 Marx dies in London

March 17 Marx is buried at Highgate Cemetery, London

Index of Quoted Literature

Introduction

K. Marx, F. Engels, *Selected Works* (in three volumes), Vol. 3, Moscow, 1983, p. 163.—7.

V. I. Lenin, *Collected Works*, Vol. 28, Moscow, 1977, p. 165.—7.

K. Marx, F. Engels, *Collected Works*, Vol. 1, Moscow, 1975, pp. 17-18.—7.

Ibid., p. 17.—7.

V. I. Lenin, *Collected Works*, Vol. 21, Moscow, 1978, p. 80.—7.

K. Marx, F. Engels, *Collected Works*, Vol. 3, Moscow, 1975, p. 313.—7.

Ibid., p. 182.—8.

K. Marx, F. Engels, *Selected Works*, Vol. 1, p. 100.—8.

V. I. Lenin, *Collected Works*, Vol. 2, Moscow, 1977, p. 24.—8.

K. Marx, F. Engels, *Selected Works*, Vol. 3, p. 163.—8.

Reminiscences of Marx and Engels, Foreign Languages Publishing House, Moscow [1957], p. 250.—10.

V. I. Lenin, *Collected Works*, Vol. 19, Moscow, 1977, p. 554.—8.

K. Marx, F. Engels, *Collected Works*, Vol. 42, Moscow, 1987, p. 366.—10.

Reminiscences of Marx and Engels, p. 102.—10.

Frederick Engels, Paul and Laura Lafargue. *Correspondence*, Vol. 3, Foreign Languages Publishing House, Moscow, 1963, p. 342.—10.

Marx, Engels, *Werke*, Bd. 36, Dietz Verlag, Berlin, 1967, S. 18.—10.

K. Marx, F. Engels, *Collected Works*, Vol. 20, Moscow, 1985, p. 231.—10.

K. Marx, *Capital*, Vol. I, Moscow, 1978, p. 30.—10.

Reminiscences of Marx and Engels, p. 352.—10, 12.

Marx and Engels, *Selected Correspondence*, Moscow, 1982, p. 313.—12.

Ibid., p. 296.—12.

K. Marx, *Capital*, Vol. III, Moscow, 1978, p. 7.—12.

Ibid., p. 820.—12.

Marx, Engels, *Werke*, Bd. 36, S. 7.—12.

Ibid., Bd. 22, Dietz Verlag, Berlin, 1963, S. 341.—12.

V. I. Lenin, *Collected Works*, Vol. 21, p. 49.—12.

Reminiscences of Marx and Engels, p. 164.—12.

K. Marx, F. Engels, *Collected Works*, Vol. 21, Moscow, 1985, p. 9.—12.

V. I. Lenin, *Collected Works*, Vol. 12, Moscow, 1972, p. 110.—14.

Ibid., Vol. 25, Moscow, 1980, p. 430.—14.

Marx and Engels, *Selected Correspondence*, p. 247.—14.

K. Marx, F. Engels, *Collected Works*, Vol. 22, Moscow, 1986, p. 355.—14.

Marx and Engels, *Selected Correspondence*, p. 247.—14.

Karl Marx. A Biography, Moscow, 1984, p. 542.—14.

V. I. Lenin, *Collected Works*, Vol. 2, p. 26.—14.

K. Marx, F. Engels, *Collected Works*, Vol. 23, Moscow, 1988, p. 256.—16.

Mikhail Gorbachev, *Political Report of the CPSU Central Committee to the 27th Party Congress*, Novosti Press Agency Publishing House, Moscow, 1986, p. 5.—16.

1818-1841

K. Marx, F. Engels, *Collected Works*, Vol. 1, p. 8.—21.

Ibid., Vol. 10, Moscow, 1978, pp. 155, 156.—23.

Ibid., Vol. 1, p. 635.—23.

Ibid., pp. 8-9.—30-31.

Ibid., p. 643.—31.

Ibid., pp. 10, 11, 17, 18, 19, 21.—36.

Ibid., p. 19.—36.

K. Marx, F. Engels, *Selected Works*, Vol. 3, p. 339.—36.

Karl Marx. A Biography, p. 28.—39.

K. Marx, F. Engels, *Selected Works*, Vol. 3, p. 344.—41.

1842-1844

V. I. Lenin, *Collected Works*, Vol. 18, Moscow, 1973, p. 582.—45.

K. Marx, F. Engels, *Collected Works*, Vol. 29, Moscow, 1987, pp. 261-62.—48.

V. I. Lenin, *Collected Works*, Vol. 21, p. 80.—49.

K. Marx, F. Engels, *Collected Works*, Vol. 1, p. 376.—51.

Marx, Engels, *Werke*, Bd. 19, Berlin, 1974, S. 294.—54.

K. Marx, F. Engels, *Collected Works*, Vol. 1, p. 27.—56.

Ibid., pp. 525, 526-27.—57.

Ibid., Vol. 29, p. 262.—58.

Ibid., Vol. 1, p. 397.—59.

K. Marx, F. Engels, *Selected Works*, Vol. 1, p. 396.—60.

K. Marx, F. Engels, *Collected Works*, Vol. 10, p. 48.—61.

Heinrich Heine to Julius Campe, February 20, 1844.—64.

V. I. Lenin, *Collected Works*, Vol. 21, p. 47.—66.

K. Marx, F. Engels, *Collected Works*, Vol. 3, p. 355.—67.

Ibid., pp. 201, 205.—69.

Ibid., Vol. 2, Moscow, 1975, p. 577.—72.

Ibid., pp. 584, 585.—73.

Ibid., p. 422.—76.

Ibid., p. 10.—77.

Ibid., p. 443.—77.

Ibid., p. 336.—80.

K. Marx, F. Engels, *Selected Works*, Vol. 3, p. 178.—83.

V. I. Lenin, *Collected Works*, Vol. 2, p. 24.—85.

1844-1848

V. I. Lenin, *Collected Works*, Vol. 2, p. 26.—87.

K. Marx, F. Engels, *Selected Works*, Vol. 3, p. 178.—88.

K. Marx, F. Engels, *Collected Works*, Vol. 4, Moscow, 1976, p. 36.—88.

V. I. Lenin, *Collected Works*, Vol. 2, p. 22.—89.

K. Marx, F. Engels, *Selected Works*, Vol. 3, p. 336.—92.

K. Marx, F. Engels, *Collected Works*, Vol. 5, Moscow, 1976, p. 4.—92.

Ibid., p. 5.—92.

Ibid., Vol. 43, Moscow, 1988, p. 518.—94.

Ibid., Vol. 6, Moscow, 1984, p. 6.—95.

Ibid., Vol. 29, p. 264.—96.

Ibid., Vol. 5, pp. 36, 37.—97.

Ibid., p. 74.—97.

Ibid., Vol. 6, p. 35.—99.

Reminiscences of Marx and Engels, p. 271.—100.

Marx, Engels, *Werke*, Bd. 19, S. 229.—101.

The London Communist Correspondence Committee to the Brussels Communist Correspondence Committee, January 20, 1847.—102.

Marx and Engels, *Selected Correspondence*, p. 386.—102-03.

K. Marx, F. Engels, *Collected Works*, Vol. 6, p. 633.—103.

Reminiscences of Marx and Engels, p. 153.—104.

K. Marx, F. Engels, *Manifesto of the Communist Party*, Moscow, 1973, p. 19.—106.

V. I. Lenin, *Collected Works*, Vol. 2, p. 24.—107.

Ibid., Vol. 21, p. 48.—107.

K. Marx, F. Engels, *Collected Works*, Vol. 17, Moscow, 1981, pp. 78-79.—111.

1848-1849

V. I. Lenin, *Collected Works*, Vol. 13, Moscow, 1980, p. 37.—113.

K. Marx, F. Engels, *Collected Works*, Vol. 10, p. 122.—113.

Ibid., Vol. 6, p. 559.—117.

Reminiscences of Marx and Engels, p. 154.—117.

K. Marx, F. Engels, *Collected Works*, Vol. 17, p. 320.—120.

V. I. Lenin, *Collected Works*, Vol. 21, p. 81.—124.

K. Marx, F. Engels, *Selected Works*, Vol. 3, p. 167.—124.

K. Marx, F. Engels, *Collected Works*, Vol. 7, Moscow, 1977, p. 74.—126.

Ibid., Vol. 9, Moscow, 1977, p. 449.—126.

K. Marx, F. Engels, *Selected Works*, Vol. 3, p. 169.—128.

K. Marx, F. Engels, *Collected Works*, Vol. 7, p. 49.—128.

Ibid., p. 295.—129.

Ibid., p. 11.—130.

Ibid., p. 166.—132.

Ibid., p. 119.—133.

Ibid., Vol. 10, p. 67.—134.

Ibid., Vol. 7, p. 149.—136

Ibid., p. 164.—137.

Ibid., pp. 147-48.—138.

Ibid., p. 595.—141.

Ibid., p. 590.—145.

Reminiscences of Marx and Engels, p. 157.—148.

K. Marx, F. Engels, *Collected Works*, Vol. 7, p. 505.—148.

Ibid., Vol. 8, Moscow, 1977, p. 36.—151.

Ibid., p. 414.—152.

Ibid., p. 227.—153.

Reminiscences of Marx and Engels, p. 157.—154.

K. Marx, F. Engels, *Selected Works*, Vol. 3, p. 171.—156.

K. Marx, F. Engels, *Collected Works*, Vol. 9, p. 467.—156.

1849-1863

V. I. Lenin, *Collected Works*, Vol. 12, p. 108.—161.

Reminiscences of Marx and Engels, p. 225.—162.

Ibid., p. 226.—167.

K. Marx, F. Engels, *Collected Works*, Vol. 10, p. 281.—169.

Ibid., p. 5.—170.

Ibid.—170.

Ibid., Vol. 11, Moscow, 1979, p. 186.—174.

Reminiscences of Marx and Engels, p. 103.—174.

K. Marx, F. Engels, *Collected Works*, Vol. 39, Moscow, 1983, pp. 62-65.—176.

Ibid., Vol. 11, p. 457.—178.

Ibid., Vol. 39, p. 577.—179.

K. Marx, *The Class Struggles in France, 1848 to 1850*, Moscow, 1983, p. 14.—182.

K. Marx, F. Engels, *Collected Works*, Vol. 12, Moscow, 1979, p. 308.—184.

Ibid., Vol. 13, Moscow, 1980, p. 58.—186.

Reminiscences of Marx and Engels, p. 228.—188.

Marx, Engels, *Werke*, Bd. 22, S. 340.—193.

K. Marx, F. Engels, *Collected Works*, Vol. 39, p. 480.—194.

Ibid., Vol. 16, p. 153.—195.

K. Marx, F. Engels, *Selected Works*, Vol. 3, p. 385.—196.

P. Vinogradskaya, *Jenny Marx*, Mysl Publishers, Moscow, 1978, pp. 146-47 (in Russian).—197.

K. Marx, F. Engels, *Collected Works*, Vol. 40, Moscow, 1983, p. 54.—198.

Ibid., Vol. 41, Moscow, 1985, p. 571.—200-01.

Ibid., p. 572.—201.

Ibid., Vol. 19, Moscow, 1984, p. 250.—205.

Ibid., p. 50.—205.

Ibid., p. 297.—207.

Ibid., Vol. 15, Moscow, 1985, p. 568.—209.

Ibid., Vol. 40, p. 226.—210.

Ibid., Vol. 12, p. 308.—213.

Ibid., p. 221.—215.

Ibid., p. 93.—217.

Ibid., Vol. 18, Moscow, 1982, p. 67.—219.

Ibid., Vol. 41, p. 54.—220.

Ibid., Vol. 17, p. 159.—221.

Ibid., Vol. 41, p. 478.—222.

Capital

K. Marx, F. Engels, *Collected Works*, Vol. 20, p. 231.—225.

Ibid., Vol. 40, p. 217.—226.

V. I. Lenin, *Collected Works*, Vol. 19, p. 26.—226.

K. Marx, F. Engels, *Collected Works*, Vol. 29, p. 263.—227.

Ibid., pp. 264-65.—228.

Ibid., Vol. 42, p. 227.—228.

Ibid., pp. 578-79.—231.

Reminiscences of Marx and Engels, p. 274.—232.

K. Marx, *Capital*, Vol. I, pp. 19, 20.—233.

Ibid., p. 11.—236.

Charles Darwin to Karl Marx, October 1, 1873.—236.

K. Marx, F. Engels, *Selected Works*, Vol. 3, p. 162.—237.

K. Marx, F. Engels, *Collected Works*, Vol. 42, pp. 402, 405.—237.

Marx, Engels, *Werke*, Bd. 33, Berlin, 1966, S. 477.—241.

K. Marx, *Capital*, Vol. I, p. 30.—243.

V. I. Lenin, *Collected Works*, Vol. 2, pp. 25-26.—245.

Marx, Engels, *Werke*, Bd. 36, S. 99.—246.

K. Marx, *Capital*, Vol. II, Moscow, 1977, p. 20.—248.

K. Marx, *Capital*, Vol. I, p. 16.—248.

Ibid.—251.

The First International

K. Marx, F. Engels, *Collected Works*, Vol. 23, p. 256.—253.

Ibid., Vol. 20, p. 12.—253.

K. Marx, F. Engels, *Selected Works*, Vol. 3, pp. 82-83.—257.

K. Marx, F. Engels, *Collected Works*, Vol. 42, p. 16.—257.

Ibid., p. 20.—257.

Reminiscences of Marx and Engels, p. 171.—259.

Ibid., p. 164.—262.

K. Marx, F. Engels, *Collected Works*, Vol. 21, p. 14.—268.

Ibid., p. 12.—270.

Ibid., Vol. 20, p. 163.—272-73.

Ibid., Vol. 21, pp. 138-39.—273.

Ibid., Vol. 20, p. 186.—275.

Friedrich Lessner to Karl Marx, September 7, 1869, Central Party Archives of the Institute of Marxism-Leninism.—279.

K. Marx, F. Engels, *Collected Works*, Vol. 20, p. 78.—281.

Marx and Engels, *Selected Correspondence*, p. 272.—282.

K. Marx, F. Engels, *Collected Works*, Vol. 21, p. 127.—285.

Ibid., p. 54.—287.

The Russian section's letter to Marx of March 12, 1870. In: R. P. Konyushaya, *Marx and Revolutionary Russia*, Moscow, 1975, p. 169 (in Russian).—289.

K. Marx, F. Engels, *Collected Works*, Vol. 42, pp. 220-21.—291.

V. I. Lenin, *Collected Works*, Vol. 20, Moscow, 1964, pp. 441, 442.—293.

K. Marx, F. Engels, *Collected Works*, Vol. 20, p. 19.—294.

Ibid., Vol. 23, p. 56.—295.

The Paris Commune. 1871

K. Marx, F. Engels, *Collected Works*, Vol. 22, p. 355.—299.

Ibid., p. 7.—301.

Ibid., p. 5.—301.

Ibid., p. 459.—302.

Ibid., p. 263.—302.

Ibid., p. 311.—304.

Ibid., pp. 437, 438.—308.

Ibid., p. 266.—308.

Ibid., p. 322.—311.

Ibid., p. 499.—314.

Marx and Engels, *Selected Correspondence*, p. 247.—314.

Paul Lafargue to Marx, April 8, 1871. In: *The First International and the Paris Commune*, Moscow, 1972, p. 462 (in Russian).—317.

Elizaveta Dmitrieva to Hermann Jung, April 24, 1871, *ibid.*, p. 478.—318.

K. Marx, F. Engels, *Collected Works*, Vol. 22, p. 490.—328.

Ibid., p. 341.—329.

Paul Lafargue to Marx's daughter Jenny, April 23, 1871. In: *The First International and the Paris Commune*, p. 475.—332.

Ibid., p. 126.—334.

K. Marx, F. Engels, *Collected Works*, Vol. 22, p. 348.—337.

Ibid.—339.

Ibid., p. 595.—339.

Ibid., p. 634.—339.

V. I. Lenin, *Collected Works*, Vol. 21, p. 49.—340.

K. Marx, F. Engels, *Collected Works*, Vol. 22, p. 375.—341.

Ibid., p. 417.—346.

Ibid., p. 427.—347.

Ibid., Vol. 23, p. 458.—350.

Marx and Engels, *Selected Correspondence*, pp. 270-71.—351.

V. I. Lenin, *Collected Works*, Vol. 21, p. 49.—351.

1873-1883

Reminiscences of Marx and Engels, p. 72.—353.

V. I. Lenin, *Collected Works*, Vol. 18, p. 583.—354.

K. Marx, F. Engels, *Collected Works*, Vol. 43, p. 557.—356.

Ibid., p. 428.—357.

K. Marx, F. Engels, *Selected Works*, Vol. 2, Moscow, 1973, p. 399.—358.

Marx, Engels, *Werke*, Bd. 36, S. 527.—359.

Marx and Engels, *Selected Correspondence*, p. 289.—359.

Reminiscences of Marx and Engels, p. 77.—362.

Marx, Engels, *Werke*, Bd. 18, Berlin, 1973, S. 570.—365.

Marx and Engels, *Selected Correspondence*, p. 312.—371.

Marx, Engels, *Werke*, Bd. 19, S. 181.—373.

Marx and Engels, *On the United States*, Moscow, 1979, p. 272.—374.

K. Marx, F. Engels, *Selected Works*, Vol. 3, p. 100.—376.

Marx and Engels, *Selected Correspondence*, p. 293.—379.

Reminiscences of Marx and Engels, p. 250.—381.

Marx, Engels, *Werke*, Bd. 19, S. 294.—384.

Marx and Engels, *Selected Correspondence*, p. 340.—386.

V. I. Lenin, *Collected Works*, Vol. 2, pp. 19, 26.—386.

Index of Illustrations *

---

* This index includes engravings, lithographs, drawings and paintings. Photographs, documents, covers and title pages of the first editions of Marx's and Engels's works, pages of Marx's manuscripts and the remaining illustrations in the album are based on the material from the Karl Marx and Frederick Engels Museum (MEM), the Central Party Archives (CPA) and the Library of the Institute of Marxism-Leninism (IML) of the CC CPSU.

22. Engraving by I. Kolb from a drawing by H. Osterwald, 19th cent., MEM.

23. Lithograph from a drawing by L. Arntz, 19th cent.

32. Engraving, *Der Wahre Jacob*, 1898.

34. Lithograph, 19th cent.

35. Drawing by F. Engels, 1848.

36. Lithograph by A. Boddien, 19th cent., MEM.

38. Lithograph, mid-19th cent., MEM.

39. Engraving, *I.Z.*, 1848.

41. Engraving, *I.Z.*, 1848.

43. Lithograph, 19th cent.

47. Engraving, *I.Z.*, 1848.

49. Engraving, mid-19th cent., MEM.

50. Painting by an unknown artist, 1st half of the 19th cent.

52. Engraving, *I.Z.*, 1848.

53. Engraving, *L'Illustration*, Paris, 1848.

54. Engraving, 19th cent., MEM.

55. Engraving by Deschamp, mid-19th cent.

56. Lithograph by V. Adam and J. Arnout, mid-19th cent.

57. Engraving, *Journées illustrées de la Révolution 1848*, Paris, 1848.

58. Lithograph, 19th cent., MEM.

60. Engraving, *I.L.N.*, 1848.

61. Lithograph by M. de L'Aigle, 19th cent., MEM.

62. Painting by Ye. Sapiro, 1961, MEM.

64. Engraving by J. Poppel from a drawing by L. Lange, 19th cent., MEM.

66. Pen drawing by Kretschmer, *L'Illustration*, Paris, 1848.

67. Lithograph by Sandmann, 19th cent., MEM.

70. Lithograph, mid-19th cent., MEM.

72. Lithograph, 19th cent., MEM.

74. Engraving, *L'Illustration*, 1848.

78. Lithograph, 1848, MEM.

79. Engraving, 1848.

80. Lithograph, mid-19th cent., MEM.

81. Lithograph, mid-19th cent., MEM.

83. Engraving, *I.Z.*, 1848.

84. Engraving, *L'Illustration*, 1848.

85. Lithograph by Loeillot de Mars from a drawing by K. Steffek, mid-19th cent., MEM.

91. Lithograph from a drawing by J. Albrecht, mid-19th cent., MEM.

95. Engraving, *I.L.N.*, 1849.

96. Lithograph, 19th cent., MEM.

98. Engraving, *L'Illustration*, 1849.

99. Engraving, *L'Illustration*, 1849.

102. Engraving, 19th cent. In: *Karl Marx und Friedrich Engels. Ihr Leben und ihre Zeit*, Dietz Verlag, Berlin, 1978.

1849-1863

1. Engraving. In: *Meyer's Universum oder Abbildung und Beschreibung des Sehenswertesten und Merkwürdigsten der Natur und Kunst auf der ganzen Erde*, Bd. 2, Druck und Verlag vom Bibliographischen Institut, Hildburghausen, Amsterdam und Philadelphia, 1835.

2. Engraving, 1861, MEM.

3. Engraving, 19th cent. In: *Karl Marx und Friedrich Engels. Ihr Leben und ihre Zeit*, Dietz Verlag, Berlin, 1978.

4. Engraving, *I.L.N.*, 1872.

15. Drawing by N. Zhukov, 1930s, MEM.

22. Engraving, *I.L.N.*, 1872.

25. Engraving. In: T. Delord, *Histoire illustrée du Second Empire*, t. II, Paris, 1880-83.

26. Lithograph, mid-19th cent., MEM.

29. Engraving, *I.Z.*, 1859.

30. Engraving, 19th cent.

44. Engraving by E. Bourdelin, 19th cent.

45. Engraving, 19th cent.

46. Engraving, *I.L.N.*, 1851.

47. Engraving, *L'Illustration*, 1851.

48. Engraving. In: T. Delord, *Histoire illustrée du Second Empire*, t. IV, Paris, 1880-83.

49. Lithograph by Gavarni, 19th cent., MEM.

50. Engraving, *I.L.N.*, 1853.

54. Drawing by N. Zhukov, 1930s, MEM.

67. Engraving, *I.L.N.*, 1854.

69. Engraving, *I.L.N.*, 1860.

70. Engraving, *I.L.N.*, 1860.

78. Painting by an unknown artist, 1st half of the 19th cent. A copy of 1937-39, MEM.

81. A copy of Rafael's "Madonna in the Armchair" by Marx's daughter Jenny, 19th cent., MEM.

82. A plate painted by Marx's daughter Jenny, 19th cent., MEM.

83. A copy of Horace's portrait by Marx's daughter Jenny, 19th cent., MEM.

84. A locket which belonged to Marx's daughter Jenny, MEM.

85. Marx's wallet, MEM.

93. Engraving, 19th cent.

94. Engraving, 19th cent.

97. Engraving, 19th cent.

99. Engraving, *L'Univers illustré*, Paris, 1863.

102. Lithograph, *Russky khudozhestvenny listok Timma*, St. Petersburg, 1854.

103. Lithograph, *Russky khudozhestvenny listok Timma*, St. Petersburg, 1854.

105. Painting by V. Pukirev, 2nd half of the 19th cent.

106. Painting by S. V. Gerasimov.

107. Drawing by N. Zhukov, 1930s, MEM.

109. Lithograph by H. Daumier, 19th cent., MEM.

110. Engraving, *I.L.N.*, 1858.

113. Engraving, *I.L.N.*, 1860.

114. Engraving, *I.L.N.*, 1857.

115. Engraving, 19th cent.

116. Engraving, *I.L.N.*, 1857.

120. Engraving by L. Lebreton, 19th cent.

121. Engraving, 19th cent.

125. Engraving, 19th cent., MEM.

130. Lithograph, 19th cent., MEM.

131. Lithograph, *Russky khudozhestvenny listok Timma*, St. Petersburg, 1862.

132. Medal in commemoration of the Exhibition, 19th cent., MEM.

Capital

1. Lithograph by H. Gellert, 1933, MEM.

10. Engraving, *I.L.N.*, 1857.

16. Lithograph by H. Gellert, 1933, MEM.

18. Engraving, *I.Z.*, 1882.

22. Drawing by N. Zhukov, 1939, MEM.

27. A mock up of Marx's study, 1961, MEM.

28. Marx's desk chair, MEM.

The First International

1. Easel engraving by O. Vereisky, 1961, MEM.

4. Engraving, *I.L.N.*, 1850.

26. Engraving, *I.L.N.*, 1869.

28. Painting by M. Munkacsy, 1895.

32. Engraving, *L'Illustration*, 1868.

34. Engraving, *The Graphic*, London, 1870.

35. Engraving, 19th cent.

37. Engraving, *L'Illustration*, 1870.

38. Engraving, *I.L.N.*, 1870.

39. Engraving, 19th cent. In: *120 Jahre deutsche Arbeiterbewegung in Bildern und Documenten*, Dietz Verlag, Berlin, 1964.

40. Drawing. *I.Z.*, 1866.

44. Engraving, 19th cent., MEM.

46. Lemonnier's lithograph from a drawing by Lauters, 19th cent., MEM.

48. Lithograph by H. Gellert, 1933, MEM.

50. Engraving, 19th cent., MEM.

54. Standard, MEM.

63. G. Heisinger's engraving from a drawing by L. Rohbock, 19th cent. In: *Karl Marx und Friedrich Engels. Ihr Leben und ihre Zeit*, Dietz Verlag, Berlin, 1978.

69. Engraving, *L'Illustration*, 1870.

70. Engraving, 19th cent.

86. Engraving, *L'Illustration*, 1867.

90. Engraving, *I.L.N.*, 1866.

The Paris Commune. 1871

1. Drawing by I. Robertsen, *L'Illustration*, 1871.

3. Engraving. In: L. Rousset, *Histoire générale de la guerre franco-allemande 1870-1871*, Vol. I, Paris, 1912.

5. Engraving, *I.L.N.*, 1870.

6. Engraving, *I.Z.*, 1870.

7. Engraving, 19th cent.

8. Lithograph by A. Said, 19th cent.

9. Engraving, *I.Z.*, 1870.

10. Engraving, *I.L.N.*, 1870.

12. Lithograph by G. Pilotell, 19th cent., MEM.

13. Lithograph by G. Pilotell, 19th cent., MEM.

14. Lithograph by J. Corseaux, 1871, MEM.

15. Lithograph, 19th cent. In: *Karl Marx und Friedrich Engels. Ihr Leben und ihre Zeit*, Dietz Verlag, Berlin, 1978.

16. Engraving, *I.L.N.*, 1870.

17. Engraving, *Le Monde illustré*, Paris, 1870.

18. Photo. In: Georges Soria, *Grande histoire de la Commune*, t. 1, Robert Laffont, Paris, 1970.

19. Engraving, 19th cent. In: Georges Soria, *Grande histoire de la Commune*, t. 1, Robert Laffont, Paris, 1970.

20. Lithograph by Faustin, 1871, MEM.

21. Lithograph, 19th cent. In: Georges Soria, *Grande histoire de la Commune*, t. 1, Robert Laffont, Paris, 1970.

22. Lithograph by Juvenal, 1871, MEM.

23. Lithograph by G. Pilotell, 1871, MEM.

24. Photo. In: Georges Soria, *Grande histoire de la Commune*, t. 2, Robert Laffont, Paris, 1970.

25. Photo, *Paris sous la Commune*, No. 7, 1871.

26. Lithograph by G. Pilotell, 1871, MEM.

27. Engraving, *L'Illustration*, 1871.

28. Engraving, *L'Illustration*, 1871.

30. Lithograph by F. Fréville, 1871, MEM.

33. Engraving, *Le Monde illustré*, 1871.

34. Engraving, *The Graphic*, 1871.

36. Engraving, *Le Monde illustré*, 1871.

43. Engraving, *Le Monde illustré*, 1871.

44. Engraving, 19th cent.

79. Engraving, *Le Monde illustré*, 1871.

82. Lithograph by A. Démare, 19th cent., MEM.

83. Poster by Moloch, 1871, MEM.

85. Lithograph by A. Said, 1871, MEM.

90. Engraving, 19th cent.

91. Engraving, *I.L.N.*, 1871.

95. Photo, *Paris sous la Commune*, No. 25, 1871.

97. Photo, *Paris sous la Commune*, No. 25, 1871.

98. Engraving, 19th cent.

100. Lithograph by de la Tremblais, 1871, MEM.

101. Engraving, *The Graphic*, 1871.

103. Photo. In: Georges Soria, *Grande histoire de la Commune*, t. 4, Robert Laffont, Paris, 1971.

104. Engraving, *The Graphic*, 1871.

105. Lithograph by Moloch, 1871, MEM.

107. Engraving, *I.L.N.*, 1871.

108. Battle standard, 1871. MEM.

109. Painting, 19th cent.

110. Engraving from a drawing by Robid, *Le Monde illustré*, Paris, 1871.

111. Painting by Pichio, 1873, MEM.

112. Water-colour, MEM.

113. Engraving, *Le Monde illustré*, 1871.

115. Lithograph by H. Daumier, 19th cent., MEM.

116. Lithograph by G. Pilotell, 19th cent.

127. Engraving, 19th cent.

131. Engraving, 19th cent. MEM.

135. Engraving, *L'Illustration*, 1872.

1873-1883

4. Lithograph by V. Lapin, 1957, MEM.

10. Painting by K. Savitsky, 1879.

16. Painting by A. Fendrikh, 19th cent.

18. Engraving, *I.L.N.*, 1878.

29. Engraving, *I.Z.*, 1876.

30. Engraving, *I.Z.*, 1879.

31. Engraving, *I.Z.*, 1872.

33. Painting by Kohlmann.

38. Drawing by N. Zhukov, 1930s, MEM.

48. Engraving, *I.L.N.*, 1878.

51. Engraving, *I.Z.*, 1876.

52. Engraving, 19th cent. In: *Vsemirnaya istoria*, Vol. VII, Moscow, 1960.

53. Engraving, *L'Illustration*, 1874.

54. Engraving, *I.L.N.*, 1877.

56. Photo. In: *Vsemirnaya istoria*, Vol. VII, Moscow, 1960.

57. Painting by I. Repin, 19th cent.

58. Drawing by Broling, *I.Z.*, 1876.

77. Engraving from a drawing by J. Poppel, 19th cent., MEM.

89. A shot from S. Eisenstein's film *October*, 1927.

91. Medal, 1918, MEM.

92. Photo, Moscow, November 7, 1918.

REQUEST TO READERS

Progress Publishers would be glad to have your opinion of this book, its translation and design and any suggestions you may have for future publications.

Please send all your comments to 17, Zubovsky Boulevard, Moscow, USSR.

"The Marxist doctrine is omnipotent because it is true."

V. I. Lenin